The Wonders of prayer : a record of well authenticated and wonderful answers to prayer

George Müller, Daniel W. Whittle

FACTS STRANGER THAN FICTION.

The Wonders of Prayer:

A RECORD OF WELL AUTHENTICATED AND WONDERFUL
ANSWERS TO PRAYER.

AS NARRATED BY

GEORGE MULLER,	W. W. PATTEN, D. D.,
D. L. MOODY,	CHAS. CULLIS,
C. H. SPURGEON,	S. I. PRIME, D. D.,
BISHOP SIMPSON.	F. KRUMMACHER,
NEWMAN HALL, D. D.,	MARTIN LUTHER,
BISHOP T. BOWMAN,	JOHN KNOX,
CHAS. G. FINNEY,	ABRAHAM LINCOLN,

AND HOSTS OF OTHERS.

NEW EDITION.

REVISED BY D. W. WHITTLE.

FLEMING H. REVELL,

CHICAGO: | NEW YORK:
148 AND 150 MADISON ST. | 12 BIBLE HOUSE

Publisher of Evangelical Literature.

INTRODUCTION TO FIRST EDITION.

THE incidents which are published in this volume, are vouched for upon the strongest proofs of authenticity possible to obtain, and are either of circumstances known amid my own experience, or connected with the lives of my correspondents and their friends. They are the thankful record and tribute to the power of *persevering faith.*

Nothing has been published concerning which there is the least shadow of doubt. All have been carefully investigated.

Every case has been one of real prayer, and the results that have come, came only in answer to the prayer of faith, and were not possible to obtain without it.

They demonstrate to a wonderful degree, the immediate practical ways of the Lord with his children in this world, that He is far nearer and more intimate with their plans and pursuits than it is possible for them to realize.

Neither have we depended upon the relation of facts of a few, to convince the world of the real power of faith, but have added concurrent testimony of incidents actually known in the experience of such eminent clergymen as Charles Spurgeon, Newman Hall, Martin Luther, W Huntington, Dr. Waterbury, George Muller, Dr. Cullis, Dr. Patton, Dr. Adams, Dr Prime, Bishop Simpson, and many others.

Also we have added some incidents known and investigated and found absolutely true, by the editors of the following journals, who add their unquestioning belief in the power of prayer : *The Christian, The Evangelist, The Observer, The Congregationalist, The Advance, The Illustrated Christian Weekly, The American Messenger, The Witness.* Likewise we have been greatly assisted by some of our Home Missionaries, who, from their daily experiences with the poor and suffering, have been eye-witnesses to remarkable experiences and the wonderful help of the Lord in answering their prayers.

These testimonies here recorded must be accepted as true. They demonstrate that answers to prayer are not occasional, and therefore remarkable that they do occur, but are of constant occurrence.

There may be many minds who, having carried no trial to the Lord, have never been brought into intimate acquaintances of the ways in which the Lord tries the faith of his children, nor led to see and observe his wonderful control over human wills and circumstances. The power of the Lord is learned only by those who in deep trouble have faithfully sought Him and seen His ways of deliverance.

None can ever understand the full power of prayer until they have learned the lesson of trust. It is only when for the *first time* in the Christian's own life of faith, it realizes the hand of God in his personal dealings with him, how near He is, or how clearly he feels the presence of that tremendous over-ruling Spirit which

" *Turneth the heart whithersoever He will.*"

The actual existence of our God is therefore proved, not alone from *History*, nor from the Bible alone, nor from current natural or religious feeling and beliefs, nor from the testimony of old witnesses several thousand years old, *but from the actual incidents of present prayer*, and the *literal answer.* Daily faith and trust and prayer have made the Christian deeply acquainted with Him and His ways, and humbly dependent upon His care and love and help, in the events of life. *No one ever faithfully trusted the Lord in vain.*

Circumstances so clouded that it has been impossible for men to control, have, through believing prayer, been so made to change, that through them have been revealed *living evidences* of the presence of

The Ever Living God..

Discerning Prayer.

INTRODUCTORY.

BY D. W. WHITTLE.

To recognize God's existence is to necessitate prayer to Him, by all intelligent creatures, or, a consciously living in sin and under condemnation of conscience, because they do not pray to Him. It would be horrible to admit the existence of a Supreme Being, with power and wisdom to create, and believe that the creatures he thought of consequence and importance enough to bring into existence, are not of enough consequence for him to pay any attention to in the troubles and trials consequent upon that existence.

Surely such a statement is an impeachment of both the wisdom and goodness of God.

It were far more sensible for those who deny the fitness and necessity of prayer to take the ground of the atheist and say plainly " We do not pray, for there is no God to pray to," for to deny prayer, is practical atheism.

So in the very constitution of man's being there is the highest reasonableness in prayer. And, if the position of man in his relation to the earth he inhabits is recognized and understood, there is no unreasonableness in a God-fearing man looking to God for help and deliverance under any and all circumstances, in all the vicissitudes of life. The earth was *made* for man. One has said " there is nothing great in the world but man; and there is nothing great in man but his soul." With this in view, how absurd to talk about " fixed laws " and " unchangeable order," in a way to keep man in his trouble from God. It is all the twaddle of the conceit of man setting himself up to judge and limit his maker. " To whom then will ye liken Me, or shall I be equal? saith the Holy One." The Creator is greater than his creation; the law giver is supreme over all law. He created the earth that it might be inhabited by man, and He governs the earth in subordination to the interests, the eternal and spiritual welfare of the race of immortal beings that are here being prepared for glory and immortality.

Laws, indeed, are fixed in their operation and results as subserving the highest good in the training and the disciplining of the race, giving them hope in their labor and sure expectation of fruit from their toil. But as set in operation for *man's good*, so, in an exigency that may make necessary their suspension, to secure his deliverance from peril and bring man back to the recognition of the personal God, as above law, is it unreasonable to believe that God has power thus to suspend or over-rule his own arrangements? A wise father will govern his children by rules as securing their best good. But he will retain in his power the suspending of those rules when special occasions arise, when the object for which they exist can be better secured by their suspension. Shall not the living God have the same right?

So much as to the reflections suggested by the dogmas of natural religion. They sustain in reason our faith in prayer. The basis, however, of our faith rests upon the unchanging and unchangeable revelation of God, and not upon man's philosophy. Jesus taught his disciples to pray, saying, " Our Father which art in Heaven." As Christians, this is our authority for prayer. In the words, " OUR FATHER," our Blessed Lord has given us the substance of all that can be said, as to *the privilege of prayer, what to pray for,* and *how to pray.* There can be no loftier exercise of soul ever given to created intelligence than to come into conscious contact with the living God, and be able to say " *My* Father."

And surely, as my Father, with a loving father's heart, it must be his desire that I should tell him *all* my needs, *all* my sorrows, *all* my desires. And, so his word commands, " Be careful for nothing, but *in everything*, by prayer and supplication, with thanksgiving, let your requests be made known unto God." (Phil. iv., 6.) Under this verse there is positively no exception of any request that may not be made known unto God. So there is true faith and right Christian philosophy in the remark, " if a *pin* was needful to my happiness and I could not find one I would pray to God for it."

The mistake of Christians is in *not* praying over *little* things. " The hairs of your head are all numbered." Consult God about everything. Expect His counsel, His guidance, His care, His provision, His deliverance, His blessing, in everything. Does not the expression, " Our *daily* bread," mean just this? Can there be any true life of faith that does not include this? Whatever will serve to help God's children to a better understanding of the blessed privileges of prayer, and prove to them the reality of God's answering prayer in the cares, trials and troubles of *daily life*, will approve itself to all thoughtful minds as a blessing to them and an honor to God. It is the purpose of this volume to do this. We are more helped by testimony to *facts* than by theories and doctrines. When we have illustrations before our eyes of God's care for his children, and His response to their faith, even in the minutest things, we understand the meaning of His promises and the reality of His providences.

The writer had many thoughts in this line suggested to him by an incident, with which he was connected, in the life of George Muller. It was my happiness to cross the Atlantic in the company of this dear brother on the steamship Sardinian, from Quebec to Liverpool, in June, 1880.

I met Mr. Muller in the express office the morning of sailing, about half an hour before the tender was to take the passengers to the ship. He asked of the agent if a deck chair had arrived for him from New York. He was answered, No, and told that it could not possibly come in time for the steamer. I had with me a chair I had just purchased and told Mr. Muller of the place near by, where I had obtained it, and suggested that as but a few moments remained he had better buy one at once. His reply was, "No, my brother, Our Heavenly Father will send the chair from New York. It is one used by Mrs. Muller, as we came over, and left in New York when we landed. I wrote ten days ago to a brother who promised to see it forwarded here last week. He has not been prompt as I would have desired, but I am sure Our Heavenly Father will send the chair. Mrs. Muller is very sick upon the sea, and has particularly desired to have this same chair, and not finding it here yesterday when we arrived, as we expected, we have made special prayer that Our Heavenly Father would be pleased to provide it for us, and we will trust Him to do so." As this dear man of God went peacefully on board the tender, running the risk of Mrs. Muller making the voyage without a chair, when for a couple of dollars she could have been provided for, I confess I feared Mr. Muller was carrying his faith principles too far and not acting wisely.

I was kept at the express office ten minutes after Mr. Muller left. Just as I started to hurry to the wharf a team drove up the street, and on top of a load just arrived from New York, *was Mr. Muller's chair!* It was sent at once to the tender and placed in *my hands* to take to Mr. Muller (the Lord having a lesson for me) just as the boat was leaving the dock. I found Mr. and Mrs. Muller in a retired spot on one side of the tender and handed him the chair. He took it with the happy, pleased expression of a child who has just received a kindness deeply appreciated, and reverently removing his hat and folding his hands over it, he thanked his Heavenly Father for sending the chair. "In *everything* by prayer and supplication let your requests be made known unto God." "Casting *all* your care upon Him, for He careth for you."

So the word of God teaches us as His children (*inviting* us to pray, *commanding* us to pray, and *teaching us* how to pray), that there is a divine reality in prayer. Experience abundantly corroborates the teaching.

Every truly converted man knows from this experience that God answers prayer. He has verified the promise. "Call unto me, and I will answer thee, and shew thee great and mighty things, which thou knowest not" (Jer. xxxiii., 3.) His life is a life of prayer, and grows more and more to be a life of almost unconscious dependence upon God, as he becomes fixed in the habit of prayer. This, and it is the purpose of God, is the result secured by prayer. With this in view, it will not be so much what we expect to get by praying, as a consciousness of coming into closer relations to God, the giver of all, in our prayers, that will give us true joy.

Often God's children are driven to the throne of grace by some desperate need of help and definite supply of an absolute want, and, as they cry to God and plead their case with tears before him, he so manifests his presence to them and so fills them with a consciousness of his love and power, that the burden is gone and *without the want being supplied* that drove them to God, they rejoice in *God himself* and care not for the deprivation. This was Paul's experience when he went thus to God about the thorn, and came away without the specific relief he had prayed for, but with such a blessing as a result of his drawing near to God, that he little cared whether the thorn remained or not—or, rather, rejoiced that it was not removed; that it might be used to keep him near to God, whose love so filled his soul.

A widow once told the writer of the turning point in her Christian life, when God's love was so shed abroad in her heart that she had been enabled to go on through all her trials rejoicingly conscious of God's presence, and casting all her burdens upon Him. She was driven to seek God by great need. Her husband's death left her destitute, with little children to provide for, and few friends from whom to look for continuous aid. Winter drew on, and, one day, her little boy came in shivering with cold and asked if he could not have a fur cap, as his straw hat was very cold and none of the boys at school wore straw hats. She was without a cent in the world. She gave a

hopeful answer to the boy and sent him out to play, and then
went to her bedroom and knelt and wept in utter desolation of heart before God, praying most earnestly that God
would give her a token that He *was* her God and was caring
for her by sending her a cap for her boy.   While she prayed
the peace of God filled her soul.   She was made to feel the
presence of her Saviour in such a way that all doubts as to
his love for her and his fulfillment of all his promises to care
for her vanished away, and she went out of her room, rejoicing in the Lord and singing his praise.   She had no burden
about the cap, and was quite content for God to send it or not
as it pleased Him; and, in the afternoon, when a neighbor
called, occupied with the Lord and his wonderful love, the
thought of the cap had gone from her mind.   When the neighbor rose to depart, she said, " You know my little boy died
last fall.   Just before he died I bought him a fur cap: he only
wore it two or three times.   After his death I put away all
his things and thought I could never part with any of them.
But, this morning, as I went to the drawer to look them over,
I felt that I should give you this cap for your little boy.   Will
you take it of me?   As she took the cap and told her neighbor
of the morning trial, prayer and blessing, two souls were
filled with the sense of the reality of prayer and the love of
God for his children.   "My little boy," said the widow, "wore
that cap for three winters.   And often, when sorely tried by
my circumstances, has God lifted the burden from my heart,
by my just looking at it, and remembering the blessing that
came with it."

Experiences like this God gives to all his children, not for
the purpose of leading them to look to Him for supplying
their physical necessities, as an end, but to make Himself
known to them, and to secure their confidence and love, for
"this is life eternal, that they might know Thee, the only true
God and Jesus Christ, whom Thou hast sent." (Jno. xvii, 3.)

The use of prayer is to bring us into communion with God,
for the growth of the spiritual life, that is ours by faith in

Christ Jesus. To leave it upon any lower plane than this, is to rob it of its highest functions and to paralyze it of lasting power for good in any direction. The promises of God are conditioned upon our being in this state of heart toward God. "If ye abide in me and my words abide in you, ye shall ask what ye will, and it shall be done unto you. (Jno. xv., 7.) Abiding in Christ, our will will be His will, as to desiring that which will most advance the divine life and promote confidence in God, and all our desires for material blessings will be subordinated to this motive. Right here must come in a line of truth that will lead us from the spirit of dictation in our prayers to God in all matters pertaining to our worldly concerns. We cannot tell what is for our highest spiritual good. The saving of our property or the taking it away. The recovery from sickness or the continuance of it; the restoration of the health of our loved one, or his departing to be with Christ; the removing the thorn or the permitting it to remain. "*In everything*" it is indeed our blessed privilege to let *our requests* be make known unto God, but, praise his name, he has not passed over to us the awful responsibility of the assurance that *in everything* the requests we make known will be granted. He has reserved the decision, where we should rejoice to leave it, to his infinite wisdom and his infinite love.

There is a danger to be carefully guarded against in the reading of this book and in the consideration of the precious truth. The incidents it relates bring before the mind, of the unlimited resources and the unquenchable love of God, that are made available to believing prayer. That danger has been suggested by what has been said, that the highest use of prayer is to bring the soul nearer to God, and *not the making of it a mere matter of convenience to escape physical ills or supply physical necessities.*

"That which is born of the flesh is flesh" and continues flesh until the end. "Have no confidence in the flesh" is always a much needed exhortation. Now, unquestionably, the desires of the natural heart may and do deceive us, and often lead us to believe that our fervent earnest prayer for temporal blessing is led of the Spirit, when the mind of the Spirit is, that we will be made more humble, more Christ-like and more useful by being denied than by being granted. Again, we are in danger of disobeying the plain commands of *God's word* in allowing prayer ever to take the place of anything *in our power to do*, and *that we are commanded to do as a means to secure needed good*. He who has said " pray always," has also said, " Be ambitious to be quiet and to do your own business, and to work with your hands, even as we charged you; that ye may walk honestly toward them that are without, and may have need of nothing." (1 Thess., iv., 11, 12; R V.)

How often the *flesh* has led men to read (Phil. iv., 19): "My God shall supply all your need according to his riches in glory by Christ Jesus," in a spirit entirely opposed to this exhortation. They have ceased to labor with their hands, and, without warrant in the providences of God and the judgment of brethren, have turned from doing their own business, expecting the Lord to pay their debts and provide for their necessities. The quotations of Scripture made by our Lord to Satan, "Thou shalt not tempt the Lord, thy God," is surely applicable in all such cases. The spirit of a "sound mind" (see 2 Tim. i., 7) will surely recognize this.

So in *all* things, that which God has given me intelligence and power to do, in avoiding evil or securing good, I am under direct command from him to do, always depending upon His blessing to secure the needed result. A *true faith* in God will be made manifest by careful obedience to known commands. An *intelligent* faith can never allow dependence upon means used to take the place of dependence upon the living God, who alone makes them efficacious.

It must result in *presumptious* faith, if obedience is neglected, and the results only promised to obedience are expected. That God *can* give blessing, without the use of the ordinary means, on man's part, there is no question. That he *has* done so is a matter of record. Yet we should remember that there were but *two* miraculous draughts of fishes, and *only twice* did our Lord make bread without the use of seed-time, harvest, grinding and baking. The *rule* of Christ in his earthly ministry was, most certainly, to receive the supply of his physical wants from His Heavenly Father, in the use of means to secure the results offered in the ordinary operation of the laws of God. He went into the corn-field at autumn and visited the olive tree for sustenance as did other men. And the question for his disciples is not what God *can* do, and not what he *has* done (that he may be known as God over all creation, blessed for evermore) in the suspension of natural laws, but what has he revealed to us as his will during the time of the present dispensation of the church on this earth, as to his children using means for the avoidance of evil and securing of good, or depending entirely upon miraculous interference in answer to the prayer of faith for all need without reference to use of means.

Does the prayer, " Give us this day our daily bread," mean that we are to do nothing to secure our bread, lest we show no faith in God, and simply wait in idleness for God to repeat the the miracle of sending it by a raven? or, does it mean that with thankful hearts to God for the ability he has given us to work, that we go forth diligently fulfilling our task in the use of all appropriate means to secure that which his loving bounty has made possible for us in the fruitful seasons of the earth, and return with devout recognition that He is the Creator, Upholder and Giver of all, bringing our sheaves with us. When seed-time and harvest fail and death is on the land, when corn fails in Egypt and there is no bread, when *we have obeyed him* and sought to toil with our hands and no man has given unto us, then we will expect his interposition and will have faith that he who has fed us by use of means, will supply us without means, and that He alone is the living God.

It is noticeable that the prophet Elisha, whose prayers God heard in the multiplication of the twenty loaves during the dearth at Gilgal, was made Elijah's successor when following his twelve yoke of oxen at the plough in the field, diligently using means to obtain bread, and undoubtedly communing with God all the while and recognizing the evidences of his love and power in every upturned daisy as he ploughed the sod, and in every seed that he dropped into the fertile earth, and thought it grand to be a fellow worker with God in the husbandry of the earth and not one to be fed in idleness, neglecting the toil appointed to man, and losing the blessing that is promised in the word of God, in the discipline and the knowledge of God in the operations of His laws, that comes in a greater or less degree to all of earth's honest toilers.

It is the opinion of many of God's children that as the present dispensation draws to its close, there will be among the spiritually minded and consecrated ones of the church, a reproduction of the gifts of Pentecost for a last testimony to the world before Christ comes in glory. There is much Scripture that might be quoted to sustain this opinion. God grant in His grace and mercy that it may be so. But neither the church or the world have any *claim* upon God for it. The church has abused grace and the world has despised mercy. All the promises as to miracles wrought for a testimony as to the truth of Christ's resurrection, have been fulfilled. If Christ were to come to-day, the world would be without excuse in having rejected him, and could not plead that signs and wonders had been abundantly wrought in His name in the establishing of His church upon the earth

The question of our Lord in Luke xviii., 8, " When the son of man cometh shall he find faith on the earth?" suggests to many minds that there may not be vouchsafed during the time immediately preceding his manifestations, any marked interference by God in the way of miracles or signs among his children, but that their faith in Him as the unseen God, and their trust in the truth and verity of His word, will be brought forth to the praise and glory of God and their joy, by their being left to the *word alone* and the operations of the Holy

Ghost by and through the word for their comfort and stability in the faith.

Coupled with this thought let it ever be borne in mind by the believer that the testimony of God's word as to miracles, signs and wonders wrought by *Satanic agency* in the church, during the last day, is clear and unmistakable, and warnings abound as to our danger from them.

" The Spirit saith expressly that in later times some shall fall away from the faith, giving heed to seducing spirits and doctrines of devils." 1 Tim. iv., 1.

" But know this, that in the last days grievous times shall come." " Evil men and imposters shall wax worse and worse, deceiving and being deceived." 2 Tim. iii., 1 and 13.

" Satan himself is transformed into an angel of light. Therefore it is no great thing if his ministers be transformed as the ministers of righteousness. 2 Cor. xi., 14.

" And then shall that wicked be revealed. Even him whose coming is after the working of Satan, *with all power, and signs, and lying wonders ;* and with all deceivableness of unrighteousness in them that perish, because they received not the love of the truth that they might be saved." 2 Thess ii., 8 to 10.

By these passages it is plain that a sign or a wonder does not establish a doctrine or endorse a man as certainly being *from God.* The doctrine and the man must be judged by the written word of God.

If there is ought in the doctrine that denies that Jesus is the Son of God, that derogates in the slightest degree from the merit of His atonement on the cross for our sins, or that takes the eye off from Him as the risen and coming Lord, the alone object of our faith and hope, or that dishonors in any way God's holy word, taking from or adding to it, *then* the more signs and wonders and manifestations of mysterious power that there may be connected with it, then the more certainly we may know that it is of Satan and not of God.

And if, in the man who exhibits signs and wonders, there is a spirit contrary to the spirit of Christ, in his seeking honor from man, and using his power to establish a claim to such honor, " speaking of himself as some great one," and not walking in humility as a sinner saved from hell and kept day by day by the power of God through faith in Christ, And if the purpose of his signs be to establish revelations he is receiving in any form apart from the written word, then, though his signs be as marvellous as those of the magicians in Egypt, or Simon Magnus in Samaria, he is, like them, a minister of Satan and not a minister of Jesus Christ.

The age abounds in doctrines and men of this kind. The life of faith lays the soul open to assaults of the Devil by their agency.

" Beloved try the spirits whether they be of God."

Let us not waver in our faith in God's overruling providence, and in the reality of His interposition in answer to prayer for the deliverance and help of his people under any and all circumstances. " In *everything*, by prayer and supplication with thanksgiving, let our requests be made known unto God," but let our first request be that we be kept in a sound mind obedient to the word, and let *all of* our requests close with the utterance, from a sincere heart, of the words, " Thy will be done." If this be the attitude of our hearts our prayers shall be abundantly and graciously answered, and God shall guide us from the wiles of the Evil One for the sake of His dear Son Jesus Christ our Lord, through whose precious blood we have all grace and all blessing. Amen.

LAKE VIEW, July 24th, 1885.

A Man Can Receive

Nothing

Except it be Given Him

From

Heaven.

John 3: 27.

His Covenant.

"*Know, that the Lord, thy God he is God, the faithful God, which keepeth covenant and mercy with them that love him, and keep his commandments, to a thousand generations.*"

"*My Covenant will I not break, nor alter the thing that is gone out of my lips.*"

"*I will not suffer my faithfulness to fail.*"

"*I have spoken it, I will also bring it to pass; I have purposed it, I will also do it.*"

"*He is faithful that promised.*"

"*I will make an everlasting covenant with you, even the sure mercies of David.*"

"*Once have I sworn by my holiness that I will not lie unto David.*"

"*God is not a man, that he should lie; hath he said and shall he not do it? hath he spoken and shall he not make it good?*"

"*Forever, O Lord, thy word is settled in Heaven; thy faithfulness is unto all generations, thy word is true from the beginning.*"

"*Thy faithfulness is unto all generations.*"

"*The word of our God shall stand forever.*"

"*So shall my word be that goeth forth out of my mouth; it shall not return unto me void, but it shall accomplish that which I please, and it shall prosper in the things whereto I sent it.*"

Answers to Prayer.

A Wonderful Answer to Prayer and Proof of the Existence of the Holy Spirit.

A trustful Christian, whose heart had been deeply touched with thoughts of religion, was one day thinking and pondering and wishing that he might be more truly convinced of the actual existence of the Holy Spirit. "If," thought he, "there is a Holy Spirit, a Superior Mind and Will, I reverently and sincerely wish that I may be convinced of it beyond all doubt; that I may indeed know God is a living reality and daily guide and mighty among the plans and ways of men." Though having all the needed mental, historic and heart belief and trust in God—still there was desired that special satisfaction which can only come by *personal evidence.*

With reverent feeling one morning, he asked the Lord humbly, in Prayer, "*What can thy servant do for thee this day? Teach him, that he may gladly minister to any one in thy name.*" In the course of the day there came to him the thought of the revival services then proceeding in Brooklyn, and feeling a cordial sympathy, he sat down and wrote a letter to *Mr. Moody,* with these words: "*I know not how you are supported, or anything of your needs; but I feel like helping you in your good work. Enclosed find check for $25; take* *it and use it if you need it for yourself ; if not, then do some good with it."* The circumstance was almost forgotten, when the day after there came this wonderful reply from Mr. Moody :

" Your letter came to hand in the SAME MAIL, *at the* SAME INSTANT *of* TIME, *with a letter from a brother in distress* WANTING THE SAME AMOUNT. *And now you have made him happy, and my heart glad, and the Lord will bless you for it."*   D. L. MOODY.

Had there been a direct revelation from heaven, it could not have been more astounding than this, to the heart of that Christian.   His own prayer was answered, as to his search for the evidences of the Holy Spirit, but oh, how wonderfully !

None but a Superior, Higher, Overruling Spirit, could have known the thoughts and desires of each heart.   Nothing but an Omnipotent hand of Power and Wisdom could have brought these two letters together at that identical instant of time.   None but an All-knowing Father could have fixed the amount of money which the one was to give and the other was to pray for.

This was a wonderful conjuncture of time, desire and amount, and could never have happened by any chance operation of Nature or the natural heart and will.   Strangest of all, neither of the parties had ever met, known or corresponded with each other before.   Neither did Mr. Moody know of the desire of the one, nor the necessity of the other, until in the act of opening the two letters side by side.   In the one envelope was the prayer; in the other the answer.

That check, those letters, with all signatures and endorsements and those persons are this day living and can testify to the authenticity of the circumstance.

The Prayer of Faith.

The family of Mr. James R. Jordan has resided in Lake View, Chicago, since the spring of 1871. They are members of Lincoln Park Congregational Church. The father, Mr. James R. Jordan, died in October, 1882, aged eighty-four years. Through a long series of financial trials, sorrows, afflictions by death and pressing cares, this family learned to depend on God for their daily prosperity; and the cures wrought in them, according to God's Word, are only a small portion of the remarkable answers to prayer with which their history is filled.

It is an instructive fact for Christian meditation, that when the exercise of intelligent faith was necessary to their cures, the faith was there *ready for exercise.* They had not to begin, as, alas! so many do, at the very foundation, and find out first, what faith is, and next, how to exercise it. They had learned long before what faith is and what faith is not; that *faith is trustful obedience to the Word of God;* that it *is not* a determination to have one's own way, nor to expect the immediate gratification of a desire, simply because the desire has been made known to God. They knew that faith obediently accepts God's commands and promises, expects to comply with the conditions of those commands and promises, and, so complying, expects to receive the results of such obedience at such times and in such ways as God appoints; all of which truths they found, and all of which may be found in the Holy Scriptures.

Thus living in the hopes of the Gospel, realizing as much that their "home is in heaven" as that their "rest is not here," they have, through the years, performed the daily duties of their pilgrimage.

The writer has known them for thirteen years, and gratefully testifies that their faith has strengthened her's, and that their cheerful hope in the Lord has been a strong consolation to many who were in trouble.

After the sudden death of the youngest son of the family, in 1880, the care of the family devolved entirely upon the two daughters, Mrs. H. J. Furlong and Miss Addie S. Jordan.

In April, 1876, Mrs. Jordan fell and badly fractured her hip. She was then seventy-seven years old. On account of her age she could not well be etherized, nor endure the repeated necessary resetting of the bones, and consequently they grew together irregularly. Her hip-joint was stiff, so that she was never able to walk without the support of a cane or crutch. For eight years she could not leave her own little yard, nor climb into a carriage, nor walk without support.

Through this misfortune her afflictions grew worse. In January, 1884, she fell and broke one bone and dislocated another in the left wrist. Notwithstanding all that medical help could do, the shock brought on a severe sickness, and when, after eight weeks, she left her bed to move around feebly, she had almost lost her sight and hearing, her hand was useless, and her mind greatly impaired.

On her birthday, June 10, 1884, when she was eighty-five years old, she greatly mourned that she had outlived her usefulness; that she could no longer feed herself, nor read her Bible, nor remember the desirable subjects for her prayers, and she hoped that she should not linger here long in such a helpless and useless condition.

During the latter part of this time the two daughters were sick, Mrs. Furlong with paralysis and Miss Jordan with consumption.

In the latter part of 1882 Miss Jordan, then in feeble health, was needed at home to attend the father's last sickness, and Mrs. Furlong was left to conduct their business alone. The extraordinary exertion brought on paralysis. It began in her right arm, which became so insensible that the strongest ammonia produced no sensation or apparent effect. Gradually her whole right side lost power, her foot dragged, and though she did manage to move about, she was comparatively helpless. Physicians spoke not hopefully; and protracted rest was recommended as a *possible* relief. She planned to take electric treatment, though not very hopeful about the result. She failed once to meet her physician, and while planning the second time to take the treatment, and considering Christ's miracles of healing, and the Bible's promises to the sick, and having a feeling that possibly she might be doing wrong in not relying entirely on the Lord, who had hitherto so much helped them, she delayed a little, and failed again to meet the appointment. It was a Saturday evening in January, 1883.

She went home and sat down that evening alone, in the dining-room, depressed. The enfeebled family—the aged crippled mother, the sick sister and her own young son—had retired. As she thought the subject through, she became convinced that it was not good to spend time and money in the way proposed. Instantly the words THE SAVIOUR filled her soul with indescribable hope, and as she thought of His miracles, and how *the same Jesus*, on earth, healed paralyzed ones, the hope grew that He would heal her.

With the well hand she stretched out her paralyzed hand on the table and said: "Dear Lord, will you heal me?" Like an electric shock the life began to move in her arm, and the continued sensation was as though something that, previously, had not moved was set in motion. The feeling passed up to the head, and down the body to the foot. *She was healed! and she was grateful!* She did not speak of her experience to the family, but retired. She rose early the next morning, and awoke her son,—a prayerful, dutiful young man,—and said to him, "I'm going to church, to-day." He replied, "Then I'll get up and go with you," expecting that she must ride.

Her soul was solemnly full that day of the felt presence of the Holy Spirit, and she did not like to talk. Her son watched her movements, astonished.

She went to the church, took a class again in Sunday School, and, in going back and forth to church that day and evening, walked about sixty blocks without weariness.

We are not permitted, here, to draw aside the curtain, to dwell upon the surprises and the grateful joy of that ever-to-be-remembered, sacred day.

A few days after this healing, she, with a consciousness that she was running a risk, lifted a heavy weight, and a numbness returned. She confessed the sin to the Lord, and asked Him that, when she had been sufficiently chastened, He would take the trouble away. Gradually, within two days, it disappeared, and has never returned.

At the time when Mrs. Furlong was healed, in answer to prayer, Miss Jordan's case was considered hopeless. Her lungs had been diseased since 1876. In November, 1879, her physician had decided that tubercles had formed in the left lung, and that the right lung was much congested and hardened.

In 1882 she had many hemorrhages, and gradually grew worse, so that she could not use her left arm or shoulder without producing hemorrhage.

Mrs. Furlong, soon after her own healing, received a comforting assurance from the Lord that her sister would be healed; but Miss Jordan, herself, had not that assurance. At this time she took little or no medicines, the physicians and the family having no confidence in their curative effect; but, on the 1st of January, 1884, she had so many chills and hemorrhages, that they sent for the family physician to aid in checking, if possible, the severe attack.

During this apparently rapid descent deathward, Mrs. Furlong continued to repeat to the family and to the physicians that the Lord would heal her sister.

Miss Jordan was one day so low that she could just be aroused to take her medicine. As Mrs. Furlong went to give it, Miss Jordan said to her, "Do you want to throw that medicine away?" Mrs. Furlong said "Yes," and threw it away. Six hours of united waiting upon the Lord followed. They were hours of pain. From nine in the morning till three in the afternoon she suffered indescribable pain. A few minutes after three, the pain left her, and with a bright look she said, "I believe I'm better." She wanted to rise and dress, but Mrs. Furlong advised her to rest through the night. She said she had not, in five years, been so free from weariness and pain.

The aged mother was sick in bed with that broken wrist, and Mrs. Furlong feared that her sister's improved condition would shock and perplex her.

Miss Jordan lay on the lounge the most of the time for two days. One of her expressions was, "It's perfect bliss to lie here free from pain." Her breathing became perfectly natural, and very soon the great hollow place in the upper part of the chest, over the left lung, filled out. Shortly before her healing she only weighed eighty pounds; but a few months after her weight had increased to one hundred and twenty pounds.

She progressed in health rapidly, and on the second Sunday after the healing came she attended church. The feeble mother was most sensitively anxious lest her daughter should pursue some unwarrantable course which should lead to relapse.

Miss Jordan's health steadily improved, but it was several months before a cough entirely left her. You may be sure that doubters made the most of that cough! *But it left her!* At one time she brought on a slight relapse by giving lessons in crayon drawing. She came to the conclusion that the Lord had other work for her to do: and at this writing, September, 1885, having prayerfully and watchfully followed the leadings of the Lord, is a missionary among the freedmen of the South, and is strong in health and in faith, "giving glory to God."

One of the aged mother's perplexities was that the Lord should want her to live on in such a helpless and useless condition, while her daughters, who might be so useful, must die; but oh, how successful she had by precept and example taught those daughters that "He hath done all things well!" How patiently she suffered whatever she thought was the Lord's will! How sweet was her constant thanksgiving! Said a pious Christian neighbor, whose poor health restricted her attendance at church, "When I'm hungry for a blessing I go down to see old lady Jordan."

After eight painful weeks, she so far recovered from the sickness consequent on the broken and dislocated wrist as to move around feebly, but sight and hearing were almost gone. Her leg was stiff, her hand stiff, her wrist deformed, and her mind greatly impaired.

Miss Jordan became very hopeful, and received strong assurance, in answer to prayer, that her mother might be healed. Mrs. Furlong received no assurance whatever in her mother's case. There was a great deal of talking and praying about it, in the family, and finally Mrs. Jordan humbly claimed the Lord's help, beseeching Him that since He had recorded that He would make the blind to see, the lame to walk, and the deaf to hear, if it was His will He would heal her. This was the night of June 16th, 1884.

In the morning Miss Jordan was so hopeful that she rose early, and attentively listened to the movements in her mother's room. She called the little family's attention to them, saying, "Just listen to her;" and as, holding on by the banister, the aged mother came with her accustomed slow movements down to the dining room, Miss Jordan said to them, "Now, watch her."

According to the long habit of eight years, she began to reach out for her cane, unconscious that she had been walking around her room with new freedom. Miss Jordan went toward her and said, "Mother, do you want your cane?" and, wondering, the old lady walked freely into the dining room. They gathered around her, and said, "Are you not healed, mother?" and she began to think *she was*, and sat down in her chair by the table. Could she move her hand? The doubled-up thumb, and straight, stiff finger, were *perfectly free* and as *limber as ever*, and the stiff wrist joint *moved with perfect free-*

dom! She *heard as well as anybody!* Could she see? She went up-stairs to her Bible, whose blurred, dim pages she had thought closed to her forever, and *she could read as well as ever,* and without glasses! She could thread the finest needle. Could she kneel and thank the Lord? She had not knelt for eight years. Yes, she could kneel as well as when she served the Lord in her youth!

Christian reader, stop here and think what a joyful family that was that June morning. That aged saint, of a little more than 85 years, was in good health again! And her two daughters had been snatched from the jaws of death! What a triumph of blessed memories to leave in legacy to that young, hopeful, Christian son, who, in childhood, had himself repeatedly proved that the Lord hears and answers prayer!

Mrs. Jordan has never used cane or crutch since that morning. She has frequently walked five blocks, to go to her church; and, a few weeks after her healing, she one day walked the distance of about fifteen blocks. She has walked for hours in Lincoln Park, among the plants and flowers, and she goes up and down stairs, and wherever she likes, as well as anyone.

She has the use of her faculties, and an altogether comfortable use of her sight, though that is not so acute as at first. Her earliest joy was that she was permitted to see that the Lord had some purpose in sparing her so long.

Dear Christian reader, shall the wonderful manifestation of that "purpose" strengthen your faith? It helps me.

"Is anything too hard for the Lord?" "No good thing will He withhold from them that walk uprightly." "If ye then, being evil, know how to give good gifts unto your children, how much more shall your Father which is in heaven give good things to them that ask Him." "If we live by the Spirit, let us also walk by the Spirit."

In the hopes of the Gospel,

MISS E. DRYER.

150 Madison St., Chicago.

Almost a Bankrupt.

A prominent Christian had just entered a merchant's counting-room, when the head man of the place said to him, "Let us kneel and ask God to help me through, for without his help, I shall be a bankrupt before the setting of the sun." So they knelt and prayed. That man went through the press. ure, and did not become a bankrupt.

"He Could Not Flee from the Power of the Holy Spirit."

A clergyman of distinction gives this instance of the worth lessness of all attempts to flee from the Power of the Spirit.

"I looked out of my window one morning, while it was yet dark, and saw a lady standing at my gate, leaning against a post, and evidently weeping bitterly. I knew her. She was a member of the church, and was an earnest, consistent Christian. She was married to one of the most bitter Universalists I ever knew. I stepped down the steps to her, and asked, 'What is the matter?' She replied, 'Oh, my poor husband! I had so hoped and prayed that he might be converted in this revival! and now he has rode away, and says that *he will not come back till this religious flurry is over.* What shall I do to bear up under this?'

"I said, 'It is near the time for prayer. We will go and lay his case before the Lord, and make *special request* that God will bring him back again under the power of the Spirit. The Lord can bring him home, and I believe He will do it. We must pray for him.'

"She dried her tears in a moment, and seemed to seize hold of this 'strong hope,' as we walked to the place of prayer We found the room crowded. It fell to my lot to lead the meeting.

"At the opening, I stated the case of this Universalist husband, who had undertaken to run away from the influence of the Spirit, by fleeing into the country. I said that we must all pray *that the Holy Spirit may follow him, overtake him, and bring him back again*, show him his sins, and lead him to Jesus.

"The meeting took up the case with great earnestness, and I could not but feel that prayer would in some way be answered.

"*But can you imagine our surprise when, at our evening prayer meeting, this same Universalist came in?*

"After standing a few minutes, till the opportunity offered, he said:

"'I went away on horseback this morning, and told my wife I was going into the country to stay till this flurry was over. I rode right over the hills, back from the river, into the country, till I had got eighteen miles away. *There, on the top of a hill, I was stopped as Paul was, and just as suddenly*, and made to feel what a horrible sinner I am. I am one of the worst sinners that ever lived *I have lost my Universalism*, and I know I must be born again, or I can never see the kingdom of Heaven. Oh, pray for me that I may be converted; nothing else will do for me'

"He took his seat amid the tears and sobs of the whole assembly. The hour was full of prayer for that man's conversion.

"This strong and intelligent man, once one of the bitterest Universalists I ever knew, is now an elder in a Presbyterian church, and one of the most joyous, happy, energetic men of God you will meet in many a day. He believes he was 'converted on the spot in that prayer meeting.'"

Life Brought Back Again in the Midst of Death.

The following instance, when *death itself was made to give back the life it claimed*, is personally known to us to be true: A mother, in this city, sent a request for prayer to the Fulton street prayer-meeting, asking the Lord for the recovery of her daughter, who was sinking rapidly, and who she felt was almost dying.

Her husband, an eminent physician, and others, also, the most skilled physicians of the city, gave up the case as hopeless. The mother felt that now none but God could or would help; that in the Fulton street prayer-meeting were sympathizing friends, and to it sent her request. She came to the meeting herself, to join in their prayers and testify her faith. The moments of the meeting passed on. One request after another was read, but hers was not touched. She was sadly disappointed. Her child was so weak and almost dying, it could not live the day through, perhaps. The time was within a few minutes, less than three, of the close of the meeting. She, at last, with faltering steps and palpitating heart, pressed her way to the desk and asked if her request was there. Upon search, it was found that it had been overlooked *Too late*, said the leader, to *read it to-day.* See, the clock is at its last moment; but it shall be read first thing at 12 o'clock, tomorrow, and special prayer shall be offered immediately.

With what heavy heart the mother went away, back to the chamber of the dying one, none can ever know. All night the waiting ones watched, with their ceaseless attentions and silent prayers.

A few minutes before 12 o'clock the body sank, the eyes closed, pallor came over the features, the spirit seemed gone, and all was still; not a breath, not a motion—death had come.

The mother had taken her watch, hung it on the pillow of the bed, and with streaming eyes, yet ceaseless prayer, they watched the slow finger move to 12 o'clock. At precisely twelve, all joined in prayer, lifting their hearts to God. *At fifteen minutes past twelve, the daughter opened her eyes,* saying, "Mother, *I feel better,*" then sank into sleep, *breathing steadily;* after three hours awoke to consciousness and sat up in bed, and before night was able to walk the floor of her chamber.   Prayer brought that life back, even when death had taken it.   *At the very moment when that precious prayer was offered in the meeting, the Lord came and touched the dying one, and gave it new life.*   The mother's faith and prayer was honored, and the Lord remembered his promise, " *If ye believe, ye shall see the glory of God.*"   The same Lord who raised Lazarus and bade him come forth, also came and bade this precious life come back again to earth.

Saved from the Hands of a Desperado.

The following circumstance is communicated to us by a United States Surgeon:

"After the close of the Mexican war, and in the year 1849, a train was sent out from San Antonio to establish military posts on the upper Rio Grande, particularly at El Paso.   I was surgeon of the quartermaster's department, numbering about four hundred men.   While the train was making up, the cholera prevailed in camp, for about six weeks, at first with terrible severity.   On the 1st of June it had so far subsided that we took up the line of march   After about four days out from San Antonio, the health of the men became very good, and continued so through the whole route, with the exception of occasional cases of prostration from heat, and slight fevers, the Summer being unusually hot.   One evening in July, after coming into camp, I received a call to see a man who had been taken sick on the march.   I found him lying under his wagon.   The wagon was loaded with bacon, in bulk about two tons.   The heat with the pressure had caused it to drip freely.   I asked him to come from under the wagon, that I might examine his case and prescribe for him   This he refused to do; but demanded that I should crawl under the wagon to him, which I, of course, would not consent to do.   No persuasion could induce him to change his position in the least.   Becoming satisfied that he was not much, if at all sick, I left him.   His profanity, threats and

imprecations were fearful.   Perhaps it would be well to give
a short sketch of his life for the three years previous, as I
learned it from men who knew him, and had been with him
for considerable portion of that period.   He went to Mexico,
at the beginning of the war, a soldier in the regular army.
When his term of service expired, he was discharged, and
sought employment in the quartermaster's department, as a
teamster.   He had the reputation of being a thief, a robber
and an assassin.   In a few months he was ignominiously discharged from the service, and, at the close of the war, he came
to Texas, and sought and obtained employment as teamster in
the train then organizing for El Paso.   But, to return to my
narrative.   On the morning after the occurrence at the wagon,
a teamster came to me and said, in a hasty and abrupt manner,
'Doctor, Mc will kill you to-day or to-night.   He is full of
rage, and muttering terrible threats.   He was out very early
this morning and emptied his six-shooter, and came in and
reloaded it and put it in first-rate order.'   I said, 'Mc, what's
up now?'   He replied, 'I will kill that d—d old doctor to-day
or to-night;' and he will do it.   I have known him make
threats before, and have never known him fail to execute
them.   But I must go; he must not know that I have seen
you.'   Knowing the man, I realized the danger, and felt that
I was powerless, either to resist or avoid it.   I retired within
my tent and closed it up.   I prostrated myself before Him
who is able to save.   I prayed for deliverance from the hands
of the cruel and blood-thirsty man, and that I might not be
left in the power of him who was my enemy without cause.
I submitted my cause into the hands of Him who doeth all
things well, and prayed for entire submission to his will.
My anxiety subsided; my fear was removed, and I commenced the duties of the day with usual cheerfulness.

"Soon after this, the camp broke and we were on the march.
I fell back with the officers of the rear guard, and the excitement of the morning was soon forgotten.   About 10 o'clock,
a courier came back in haste, for me to see a man who had

been thrown from his mule and crushed under the wheels of his wagon. He did not know who the man was—he was about half or three-quarters of a mile ahead. The thought then occurred to me, I shall probably have to pass Mc's team. I will ride square up with the courier, and keep him between myself and the train. When we came to the spot I inquired who the man was, for he was so mutilated I could not recognize him. *It was Mc. God was there.* Awe and terror took hold upon me. I was dumb with amazement.

"Mc had dismounted and walked some fifty rods by the side of his team. Attempting to remount, his mule whirled and pitched, and he was thrown upon his back, and his team with fourteen others instantly stampeded. Both the fore and hind wheels on the near side of his wagon, passed directly over his face, and crushed every bone in his head. It was a fearful sight; not a feature of the human face could be discerned.

"The stampeded teams were flying wildly over the prairie, in spite of every effort of the teamsters to control them.

"I directed the head of the corpse to be inserted in some new, thick sacks, in such a way as to prevent the oozing of blood, and that it be wrapped in his blanket and taken to the next camp for burial. When the stampeded teams came in, it was found that no other person was injured, nor any damage done.

"The philosopher may tell us of the reign of law; of the coincidence of circumstances; of the action of natural causes; but, to the Christian, the fact still remains—prayer was answered. God heareth his people when they cry unto Him."

The Prayer of a Missionary in Mexico Answered.—Saved from Banditti.

"In the Spring of 1872, I was, with my wife and child, in the city of Cadereita, Mexico, where we had been laboring as missionaries, but felt it was our duty to return to the States for a little season, and had been asking God to open up the

3

way for us. At length, about the middle of March, the opportunity appeared to be given, the means being provided; but the country was in a state of revolution (a no uncommon thing there), and, consequently, there were no stages running out of the country, so we had to take conveyance in Mexican carts. Therefore, we engaged two men, with their carts; one in which we might ride and carry a mattress, which should serve as a bed at night, and the other, to carry the baggage and provisions for ourselves and the horses, as our way was mostly through an uncultivated country.

"We knew that General Cortinas, with his troops, was somewhere between us and Texas, as the State we were in was one of those in rebellion. The blood-thirsty character of General Cortinas is well known on the frontier, there being no less than seventeen indictments against him for murder in the State of Texas. He is regarded as having a special hatred against Americans, and the Mexicans, themselves, stand in terror of him

"Our friends and brethren in Cadereita tried hard to deter us from going, as most likely we would fall into the hands of General Cortinas; in which event, they said, the very utmost we could expect would be to escape with our lives, being left destitute of everything, in a wilderness road; but, as God had seemed to open up the way, providing the means, we determined to go forward, trusting that He also would protect us in the way. Therefore, having completed our arrangements, we started for Matamoras, some three hundred miles distant. on the 19th of March, the wives of the two men accompanying their husbands, making our party six adults and one child; the brethren in Cadereita promising to pray daily for our safety. The third morning, after commending ourselves, as usual, into the care of our covenant-keeping God, we started on our journey. Some two hours later, we espied the troops of General Cortinas, about two miles distant, marching toward us. We again all looked to God for protection, and prayed that, as he shut the mouths of the lions, that they should not hurt his servant Daniel, so He would now restrain the evil passions of men, that they might not hurt nor injure us—then we went on till we met the advance guard, who commanded us to halt and wait till the General came up. After nearly half an hour, General Cortinas, with his escort, rode up to where we were waiting for him. After the ordinary salutation, he asked: (¿de adonde vienen y adonde van?) 'From whence have you come, and where are you going?'—to which we replied properly; then he asked: 'What is the news from Nueva Leon?' (the State we left)—to which we replied as faithfully as we could. Then I asked him, 'Is the road safe between us and Matamoras?' He replied. 'Perfectly; you can go on without any fear, and as safely as you would in your own country.' Then, bidding us 'good morning,' he rode on, not even inquiring about or examining any of our baggage.

"When we arrived in Brownsville, Texas, and told of how gentlemanly General Cortinas had treated us, all pronounced it wonderful, and said, 'We could not have believed General Cortinas capable of such kindness to Americans so in his power. It was truly a miracle' We believed that it was God who restrained the naturally vicious passions of the man, in direct answer to prayer"

An Infidel's Life Spared a Few Days.

"During the Summer of 1862, I became acquainted with a Mr. A——, who professed infidelity, and who was, I think, as near an atheist as any I ever met. I held several conversations with him on the subject of religion, but could not seem to make any impression on his mind, and, when a point was pressed strongly, he would become angry.

"In the Fall, he was taken ill, and seemed to go into a rapid decline. I, with others, sought kindly and prayerfully to turn his mind to his need of a Saviour, but only met with rebuffs. As I saw that his end was drawing near, one day I pressed the

importance of preparing to meet God, when he became angry
and said I need not trouble myself any more about his soul,
as there was no God, the Bible was a fable, and when we die
that is the last of us, and was unwilling that I should pray
with him.   I left him, feeling very sad.

"Some four weeks after, on New Year's morning, I awoke
with the impression that I should go and see Mr. A——, and
I could not get rid of that impression ; so, about nine o'clock,
I went to see him, and, as I approached the house, I saw the
two doctors, who had been holding a consultation, leaving.
When I rang the bell, his sister-in-law opened the door for me,
and exclaimed, 'Oh! I am so glad you have come, John is
dying The doctors say he cannot possibly live above two
hours, and probably not one.'   When I went up to his room,
he sat bolstered up in a chair, and appeared to have fallen into
a doze.   I sat down, about five feet from him, and when, in
about two minutes, he opened his eyes and saw me, he started
up, with agony pictured on his face and in the tones of his
voice, exclaimed, 'O! Mr. P——, I am not prepared to die;
there is a God; the Bible is true! O, pray for me! pray
God to spare me a few days, till I shall know I am saved.'

."These words were uttered with the intensest emotion, while
his whole physical frame quivered through the intense agony
of his soul.   I replied in effect, that Jesus was a great Saviour, able and willing to save all who would come unto Him,
even at the eleventh hour, as He did the thief on the cross.

"When I was about to pray with him, he again entreated me
to pray especially that God would spare him a few days, till
he might have the evidences of his salvation.   In prayer, I
seemed to have great assurance of his salvation, and asked
God to give us the evidence of his salvation, by granting him
a few days more in this world   Several others joined in praying God to spare him a few days, till he should give evidence
of being saved.

"I called again in the evening; he seemed even stronger
than in the morning, and his mind was seeking the truth.

The next day, as I entered ιis face expressed the fact that peace and joy had taken the place of fear and anxiety. He was spared some five days, giving very clear evidence that he had passed from death to life. His case was a great mystery to the doctors. They could not understand how he lived so long; but his friends, who had been praying for him, all believed it was in direct answer to prayer."

Remarkable Preservation from Brain Difficulties.

"A few weeks ago, a man who had once been a member of my church, but had fallen from his steadfastness through strong drink, fell from a ladder, striking his head on the corner of a stone, which made a dent in the skull of over two and one-half inches in length, and three-fourths of an inch in width, and half an inch in depth. This happened on Friday afternoon. At our prayer-meeting, in the evening, most earnest prayers were offered in his behalf; the brethren prayed that God would restore him his senses and spare him a few days, that he might repent of his back-sliding and be saved.

"The surgeons raised the skull, and his senses were restored; his mind seemed clear. This continued over a week, when it was evident that there was still some pressure on the brain. The surgeons removed the skull, and found three pieces driven down into the brain. They expressed, from the first, no hope of his recovery; but wondered much at the clearness of his mind, which continued for over two weeks. We believed that it was in answer to the prayers of the church that he might have time and opportunity to repent and prepare to meet God, which we trust he did."

Little George's Prayer.

A clergyman writes us these incidents:

"I knew a poor family whose son George, four or five years old, was accustomed to pray. They lived five or six miles from neighbors, and, at times, were quite destitute. One day, as little George observed his mother weeping over their destitution, he said, "Why, mother, don't cry any; we shall not starve; God will send us something to eat, I know He will. I've just been praying, and asked Him to" The little fellow just as much believed God would send them food, as if he had asked a reliable neighbor and obtained his promise to supply their wants. In a day or two after this, some friends living at a distance and knowing they were poor, took them the welcome surprise of a wagon-load of substantial material for food and other comforts. The little boy grew up to be a Christian minister, and, about a year ago, on inquiry, his uncle told me he had been at the head of an institution of learning in the South-west."

A Prayer for a Horse.

"My horse died, and, after traveling through the snow-drifts to my appointments, till I was lame, half sick, and unfit for service—as I had not means to purchase a horse, I thought of quitting the work and going to teaching, and laid the matter before God, in prayer; soon after which, some person at a distance, who heard that I had lost my horse, without my saying a word about it, raised the means by which I procured another."

A Prayer for a Wife.

"When I believed it would be well for me to seek a companion for life, I asked of God direction in making a wise choice, and that, in a matter of so much importance to me and others, I might meet with success or *hindrance*, as my heavenly Father knew best. He led me to a choice and marriage, which I have not since regretted."

Church Troubles Quelled.

"I might mention a dozen instances in which church troubles were gathering, and trials between members appeared certain,

when all my tactics failed, and the wisdom of brethren was of
no avail; my last resort was to ask God to send help and deliver
from the threatened evil—and in ways that no one could fore-
see, complete deliverance came."

A Minister's Supplies Fall Short.

"When very much in need of funds to procure supplies for
a coming Winter, all expedients failed; then I asked God for
assistance, when, unexpectedly, a friend in California sent me
a little package of gold dust, which I sold, at once, for $130.
This came when it was needed, and it did us good."

A Prayer for a Servant.

"Some time after, we failed to find anything like suitable
help in the house, which we greatly needed. Before starting
out one morning, in secret I prayed to God to direct me as I
went on my uncertain business, and prayed as I called at different places, and soon found a colored girl sixteen years old
wanting a place, who came and proved to be the best help we
ever had, before or since. For seven years and a half she
lived in the family, taught two of our children to read; was
glad, from choice, to move with us to different places, till she
left to be married, fell sick and passed away. A dozen other
times when driven in straits, *in answer to prayer* God has
enabled us to procure necessary help, which was difficult to
obtain.

"In 1874, while on my way to see my mother in Pennsylvania—who had just been paralyzed, and died the next week—
I was suddenly paralyzed in my left arm, by which, I have
since been helpless and useless. After coming here to live,
being in want of a man to lift me in and out of bed, dress
me, etc, for which we inquired of people, and prayed to God
to send us the needed help. We had not means to hire and
pay any person to do such work, even if he could be found.

Soon the right one came, in the person of a young German, who was tramping through the country in search of employment and food; was ready and glad to do any work for a living For pay that satisfied him and us, he staid in the family over a year, working out doors and in; could be trusted to do business with money, and return every cent correctly. After being with us over a year, when we needed him no longer, he obtained a situation in a good family, where he is now living. In many instances, I have prayed to be healed of special sickness, always using what remedies I thought best, yet asking the divine blessing on their use."

Healing.

"For over three years, I was troubled with frequent raising of blood from my right lung, which physicians failed to cure. Of this I prayed to be relieved; after which, the soreness healed, and for several years it has ceased to trouble me."

That $18.75.

A man who had led a very wicked life, was converted and hopefully saved. Previous to this time, a debt of $18 75 had not given him the slightest thought. After receiving a new heart, he distinctly heard God's command, "Pay what thou owest;" so called on his creditor, and urged him to send to his house and get a bureau, table and looking-glass, which he desired him to sell and pay himself the sum due him; but, not wishing to deprive his debtor of such necessary articles, refused, saying he would wait till he could pay. The 18th of November was set, and, as the day approached, the prospect was no brighter; and when the night of the 17th came around, he spent it in prayer that God would deliver him, and rose from his knees at daybreak, with the full assurance that "He knoweth how to deliver."

On passing down a street the next morning, on his way to

business, a man who kept a large store was standing in the door-way, and called to him to stop a minute. Wondering what could be the nature of the call, he retraced his steps, to hear this astonishing news *"For three days I have been impressed with the idea that I must give you $18 75, and for three days have been trying to ascertain why I must give you this amount, for I do not owe any man a penny.* I cannot get rid of the thought, and if you value my peace of mind, I beg you take the money!" Seeing, instantly, the hand of God in it, he told the story to the astonished storekeeper, then left to pay his debt with the money so strangely given. His creditor, surprised to see him so promptly on time, questioned him as to the manner of obtaining it, thinking, perhaps, he had made a great sacrifice to do so. On being told just how it was given him, said, *"I won't take it; keep it. If God is as near to people as that, I don't want it; it seems as if it had come directly from his Almighty hand."* The result was the conversion of both the storekeeper and creditor, to whom the incident came as the undoubted evidence of God's presence among them.

God Sent the Bag of Flour.

In about the year 1830, in Central New York, there was a time of great scarcity of provisions Grain was very high, and difficult to be obtained at any price; and, of course, families of limited means were very much straitened. In one family, the wife and mother of six children, a Godly woman, worked at her trade (tailoress) to the extent of her ability, and prayed earnestly that God would deliver them from pressing want. Husband and children all knew of their need, and of the fervent prayers of the wife and mother for their supply; but no one knew by what means the supply was to come. Every day, as their scanty means were being consumed, the prospect grew darker. On the farm was a large quantity of pine timber. Four miles from there, in the next town, lived a man who needed some shingles; and, casting about him to see where he should obtain a supply, thought he would go and purchase a pine tree, and himself and man go into the woods and work it up into shingles. As he was about starting, the thought occurred to him, "Perhaps they may be in want of wheat flour—a bag cannot come amiss in this time of scarcity." So, putting two bushels in a bag, he proceeded to the next town, entered the house, and made known his errand, saying, "I have brought along two bushels of flour towards paying for the tree, thinking you might be in want of it in this time of scarcity, and I knew you live six or seven miles from the mill, and have no horse." "That is in answer to prayer," said the noble woman; and the husband believed it, though not a praying man. When, at night, the oldest son came in, the mother said to him, "God has answered our prayers, and sent a bag of flour." It is believed that, while this was not miraculous, it was as directly the interposition of God, as feeding Elijah by the ravens; and it was in direct answer to prayer for that special blessing."

Incidents from the Experience of a City Missionary.—A Prayer for Supper Answered.

An educated, accomplished lady, reduced to the very lowest round of poverty's ladder, whom we shall call Mrs. X——. bears unfailing testimony to God's hearing and answering the prayer of faith. The daughter came up-stairs one day to announce the utter emptiness of the larder. There was not even a piece of dry bread, nor a drawing of tea; not a potato, nor a bean; and "Charles, poor fellow, will come home from his work at six, tired and so hungry; what *shall* we do, mother?"

"The Lord will send us something, before he comes," said Mrs. X——. So, for three hours more the daughter waited. "Mother, it is five o'clock, and the Lord has not sent us anything." "He will, my dear, before half-past six ; " and the widow went in an adjoining room, to ask that her daughter might not feel it vain to call upon God. In fifteen minutes, the door-bell rang violently, and a gentleman, valise in hand, said, "Mrs. X——, I left the room which I hired of you one year ago, in a great hurry, you will remember; and I owed you five dollars. I have not been in the city since, and am rushing out of it again—jumped off the car just to give you this money. Good-bye."

Relief from a Creditor's Demands.

" At another time, being sorely pressed by a heartless cred-itor, and almost beside herself, she concluded to walk out and get free from the insupportable burden, by change of air and scene for two or three hours   Passing the house of a friend, just returned from Europe, she called for a few moments, and was presented with a small and peculiar plant, brought from Wales   All the way home she was asking the Lord to release her from this relentless creditor, and all the way home a man, without her knowledge, was following her. Arrived at her own stoop, he suddenly confronted her, bowed, apologized for the liberty, but said he had not had a sight of that dear old plant since he left home ; and if she would sell it to him, he would gladly give her ten dollars for it. As that was half the sum for which she was persecuted, and would probably relieve her from annoyance until she could raise the balance, she accepted the offer."

Two Hundred Dollars Needed and Given at the Last Moment.

"At the time of her husband's death, there were *two hun-dred dollars* due an institute, for board and tuition of their two little boys. His death was the flood-gate opened, which let in a successive torrent of perplexities, losses, dilemmas,

delays, law-suits, etc.   She had not been able to pay that bill;
the principal was importunate, persevering, bitter, and, at last,
abusive.   She cried to the Lord for a week, day and night,
almost without ceasing.   Then, a gentleman whom she had
taken to her own house and carefully nursed through a dangerous illness, three years before, called to say good-bye.   He
was on his way to a Bremen steamer, and all other adieus were
said, all his baggage on board, except the valise in his hand.
Might her boy ride down to the wharf and see him off?   Of
course she was glad to consent.   When her son returned he
brought back a letter, which opened, she found to contain *two
hundred dollars* and the words, 'Not that money can ever
express my gratitude, but the enclosed may be useful for gas-
bills or some other little household matter.'"

How the Lord Repaid a Generous Gift.

"Some gentlemen, urged to contribute to a most worthy
cause, said, 'Go first to Mr. Z.—whatever he gives, we will.'
Mr. Z., upon application, concluded to make his neighbors do
something worth while, and, as he was expecting a thousand
dollars in a very few days, subscribed the whole of that.   Upon
the arrival of the vessel which was to pay his subscription, he
found the difference in exchange between certain countries,
had swelled his thousand dollars to *twenty-two hundred*."

The Astonished Giver.

"A gentleman, not marching in the ranks of 'cheerful giv-
ers,' was urged to bestow five dollars toward the 'Fresh Air
Fund.'   'He could not; business wretched; poor enough himself,' and all the well known line of excuses.   The friend
assured him, if the Lord did not more than make it up to
him, before the end of the week, he himself would return the
money.   To those terms he agreed, quite sure he should call
on Saturday and get back the $5.   But, the very next morn-

ing, he ran to the office of his friend to say that an old debt, given up long ago, and for which he would have taken one hundred dollars any moment, was paid him about an hour after the friend left his store. So astonished was he, that he even doubted the check, which was for *five thousand dollars*, and sent it to the bank to test its genuineness before he would give a receipt for it!"

All Saved.

In a dismal basement, A. found a very interesting American family. The father, in the last stage of consumption; a little girl of ten years, an invalid from infancy. The mother and two daughters, both under fifteen, were out all day at work, trying to keep even such a wretched shelter, and a little coarse food, as daily supplies. The three together could not make over four dollars a week. The only person to wait on the two sick ones during the day, was a little boy four years of age, who, when the missionary entered, was reclining upon the bed. But he started up, put more coal on the fire, and brought a drink of water, first to his sister, then his father; without any bidding, and with the consideration of a grown person.

On A.'s next visit, a few days after, he found the mother at home, grief-stricken. Her eldest daughter had been taken ill the day previous. He gave her all the money he had, prayed with them, and sent at once a kind, assiduous physician. In a few weeks the daughter died, but not without a good hope in Christ; and was buried at the expense of the few kind friends whom A. had sent to see the family. The dying daughter exhorted her dying father to seek his soul's eternal welfare, and not boast, as heretofore, of his life-long morality. Her conversations led him to see his danger out of Christ, and, in a little while after his daughter's departure, he followed. The mother had not before had a sure Christian hope; but, amidst such influences, her heart was soon opened to admit the truth. Not long after her bereavement she began having a "cottage prayer-meeting" in her room, and united with an evangelical church. She immediately became anxious for the conversion of her two boys, who were away, and urged the missionary to write them. He did so, frequently, and his heaven-directed appeals led one of the boys very soon to Christ. Soon after, he died; the brother returned home with consumption. He took great pleasure in the little prayer-meetings, and in three months cheerfully and exultantly exchanged this world of suffering for the one where father, brother and sister awaited him. Worn out with anxiety, care, hard work and poor health, the mother followed; leaving the invalid girl and youngest boy; who are watched over, not only by their Friend in heaven, but friends on earth. The eldest surviving daughter is an esteemed and consistent member of a church of Christ.

"The Lord Woke Me Up in Time to Save My Clothes."

In the very top of a four-story building, used only for various manufacturing purposes, lived an old man and daughter. They lived literally by *faith in Christ*, from *day* to *day;* one hour at a time. At his voice, followed Him, whether into darkness or light. Neither took a step but as they held his hand A lady calling one day, said, " Oh ! Jennie, I thought of your large wash hanging on the roof, last night, when the drenching rain came ; and I was so sorry to think you would have your hard work all over again !" *"Oh! no mo'am. The Lord woke me up out of a sound sleep, just as the first few drops fell!* I hastened up and brought them all down nice and dry, and had only got to the foot of the stairs with the last armful, when it poured down. Now that was the Lord, ma'am, for there was not a single noise of any kind to waken me, and I was sound asleep !"

The Lord Takes Away the Custom of a Liquor Saloon.

At one time, the landlord rented the ground floor to a liquor seller. The loafers going in and out, especially on Sunday, were a great grief to Jennie and her saintly old father. They concluded to take it to the Lord together, and, said the old man, "He will be sure to attend to it; I have been young, and now am old, and I have never known Him fail me—He *never* does." *In three weeks after, the dram-seller closed his place for want of patronage.*

Help in Time of Need.

A poor, humble Christian woman had a claim on some property in a neighboring State. It was in law, and she was summoned to attend court at a certain time. Having scarcely money enough for her daily bread, she was obliged to borrow the means to take her there, and pay some cheap board while awaiting the conclusion of the trial. She was positively assured by the lawyers, that she would receive several hundred dollars. She was detained five weeks, instead of one, as she expected, and then the suit was postponed till Fall. She was in agony of mind; in a strange place—owing for board and washing, and no money to take her to her home. Having spent a whole night pacing the floor and calling on the Lord to redeem his promises, she felt the fresh air would do her good, and sadly took her way down a side street. She had gone but three blocks when she found a diamond ring. Being accustomed to the ownership of diamonds in her younger days, she knew very nearly its value; took it home, watched the principal papers, and the same evening saw a reward of seventy-five dollars offered for it. We can imagine that joy lent wings to her feet, and thanksgiving filled her whole heart. The sum was sufficient to pay her bills, bring her back and return a portion of the borrowed money.

Cast Out Into the Street, Yet Not Forsaken.

A piteous wail was heard on the street one day, and a poor Scotchman crossed over to see the trouble. A widow and three children sat on their few articles of household furniture. Put in the street, when they could no longer find five dollars for the rent of the kennel in which, for six months, they had not lived, but existed. He had just received five dollars for a piece of work, and was hurrying home with it to his sick wife, crippled mother and two children. He thought of the piece of meat—a long untasted luxury—he meant to buy; of the tea his mother so much craved, and hesitated. Could he give these up? But the streaming eyes of the children, and the mute despair on the face of the mother, took down the scale. He ran several blocks and found an empty basement; hired it for four dollars; enlisted the sympathy and help of a colored boy to carry the furniture; put up the stove, bought a bundle of wood, pail of coal, and some provisions with the other dollar; held a little prayer-meeting on the spot, and left with the benedictions of the distressed ones filling his ears. The recital of his adventure obliterated for the time all sense of their own desires, and they thanked God together that their loss had been the widow's gain. The next morning, while taking their frugal meal, a tea dealer, for whom this man had frequently put up shelves, came to say he was short-handed, and if the Scotchman was not very busy, he would give him a regular position in his establishment, at a better salary than he could hope to earn. Meanwhile, hearing his wife was sick, he had brought her a couple pounds prime tea, and it occurred to him that venison steaks were a little out of the ordinary run of meat, and, as he had a quantity at home, he brought a couple. Thus the Lord answered the prayer of the poor, and repaid the generous giver who sacrificed his money for the Lord.

A Persecutor Punished by the Lord.

A most devout, hard-working and poorly paid man, was the object of constant persecution by a cross-grained, ugly, infidel neighbor. For three years the thing went on, till the Christian thought he must remove from the place. He could not do it without breaking up his humble home, for which he had worked night and day. He and his wife were in deep distress, told their plans to the Lord; asked Him to direct them to another home, and then went to a newspaper office to advertise their little place for sale. The editor was out, and they preferred to see him—would return home and call again to-morrow The next morning the infidel was found dead in his bed, from a stroke of apoplexy.

How God Answered My Prayer for $90.

"Suffice it, then, I was in debt. I was owing the large sum (large for a poor home missionary) of $90.00. Expecting soon to be called upon for the payment of it, and not seeing any way to meet it, *I went to the Lord with it.* Early in life I had made this resolution : that no man whom I was *owing* should ever ask me for money, and I not pay him ; but now, I could see no way out ; and if, as I expected, it should be demanded, I was not in a condition to meet it. Such was my condition when, on a certain day, the demand came. I took the letter from the office at noon. What now was to be done ? Again I took the case to the Lord, and asked Him to help me pay it, so that my word need not fail, *or his cause suffer reproach.* I first determined to pay a part ; 'but, as no letter could be sent out that day, I awaited the results of the day following From the northern mail, which first arrived, I took a letter containing an unexpected draft of $50 to my wife, from parties whom we did not know, and had never seen, nor they us. Within twenty minutes more I was presented with a *surprise* of $40, from a people where I had

4

preached for the six months past.   Here was my $90, and,
before the mail went out, I had my letter written and in the
mail.   Both were as unexpected as if they had come from
heaven direct"

From Wealth to Poverty.

A lady of superior culture and refinement, fell from opu-
lence to extreme poverty, within four years.   No less ready
when at the bottom of fortune's ladder, than at the top, to do
good as she had opportunity, she paid another poor woman's
way to a neighboring State, where employment awaited her,
and did it literally with her *lost* dollar-and-a-half!   Supposing herself the possessor of a ten cent note, over and above
the twelve shillings, she went with her somewhat feeble pro-
tege over Jersey city ferry, and saw her safely in the cars
Starting back, she was dismayed to find no ten cents in her
pocket-book, and, all too late, remembered having paid it for
a quart of milk that morning; the sole breakfast of herself
and daughter.   Night was approaching—what to do she did
not know.   She had a plain, worn, old gold ring on her finger;
she took it off, offered it to the ferry-master, who would not
take it, though she told him she found her money gone and
would redeem it next day   She went back in the ladies' room
and told it to the Lord, beseeching his assistance.   Just then,
a girl passing, jostled against her and knocked down her par-
asol   She picked it up, happened to turn it upside down, and
out rolled a *five-cent nickel!*   The Lord, then, hears prayer
for even *five cents* to provide for the comfort and need of those
whom He loves.

A Prayer for Fifty Dollars.

A clergyman writes *The Christian* as follows.
"The Winter of 1872 I spent in missionary work, carrying
the glad tidings of the kingdom of God into new fields in the

'regions beyond.' With my devoted wife, I labored ardently for the salvation of men 'from the wrath to come.' We were full of comfort to be thus engaged, though without pledge from man for support, or promised salary for preaching.

"In spite of our rigid economy, I had contracted some debts for the necessaries of life. I have since learned to go without what the Lord does not provide means to pay for at once. I needed the money to pay the debts, and felt impressed to pray for fifty dollars. I said to my wife: '*I am going to pray for fifty dollars.*' 'Well,' said she, 'I will join you;' and we bowed before God and told Him our needs, and unitedly asked Him for fifty dollars; so that we might not bring ourselves or the truth we preached, into reproach, by being unable to pay debts. We were agreed in asking, and thus claiming the promise: 'If two of you shall agree as touching anything that they shall ask, it shall be done for them of my Father which is in heaven.' (Matt. xviii 19). We had the assurance that money would come; but from whence we did not know, nor care, for we knew the 'silver and gold' are the Lord's, as well as the 'cattle upon a thousand hills,' and he could easily cause some one to give or send us the money.

"We felt full of peace; for we knew it was for God's glory to answer that prayer. No one outside of the family knew we were praying for money. We did not go around among our friends and tell them we were praying for fifty dollars, in hopes that they would take it upon themselves to answer the prayer. We told none but the God whom we serve.

"Some little time passed, and no money came, but we did not lose our faith or assurance. One morning, at family prayer, I was led out to pray that we might see the Lord's working in our behalf that day, and I rose from my knees with perfect confidence that our hearts would be made to rejoice in God that day. When I came in to my dinner I asked my wife if any one had brought our mail from the post-office. She said, 'Yes, there are some papers on your table.' 'What!' said I, with surprise, 'no letters?' I saw a peculiar expression on her countenance, and I asked no more questions, but sat down to the dinner table and turned over my plate, and there saw a letter she had put beneath it; and as soon as I saw the hand-writing I felt, there is money in this, though, of all sources, this was from the one least expected. I opened the letter, and there was a draft for *fifty dollars,* '*a gift to aid in preaching the Gospel.*' If I ever recognized the hand of God in anything, I did in this; and if there was ever a time of devout thanksgiving to God, and a humbling of self before Him in my house, it was that day. Since then, it has been easier to trust in Him than before. He has said, 'I will never leave thee nor forsake thee.' He has also said, through his apostles, 'Be careful for nothing; but in everything, by prayer and supplication with thanksgiving, let your requests be made known unto God.' "

Concurrent Testimony of the Value of Prayer.

A request was published by the *Illustrated Christian Weekly,* asking that all who could report positive facts as direct results of prayer, and thus tend to show that "*God does answer prayer,*" should communicate them. Very many were communicated, regarding all trials and troubles of the heart, and daily temporal or spiritual life. No one can question they are authentic to the highest degree; they should silence the skeptic, and convince the worldly of the presence of the mysterious power and wonderful Spirit of God, which tempers the hearts and lives of men and controls them as He wills.

A Worldly Man Surrenders.

A clergyman says, "I was very anxious for the building of a mission chapel to accommodate a flourishing mission-school that had been organized under my pastorate. Knowing that a certain physician of the city was possessed of abundant means and had a praying Christian mother, though he had long since given up going to church, I resolved to call upon him. Before starting from my study I knelt down and asked God to prosper me in my appeal. Upon going out of my parsonage the physician was in the act of passing in his carriage. I hailed him, explained to him my desire, and the result was not only a contribution of money as large as the largest, but a gift of a lot for the chapel worth several hundred dollars."

A Servant's Prayer for a Good Home.

"I was brought up religiously as a servant in a family in Connecticut, and from twelve years of age until twenty-three, knew no other home. The old couple died, and I lived with their children, but they were so different that I became very unhappy and hardly knew what to do or which way to turn I had no relatives and knew nothing of any world save the little one in which I had all my life moved, and I was terribly afraid to try any other. I could only offer my constant prayer for help, and it was answered so much beyond my highest hope, and so kind were God's dealings with me that I was taken, almost without an effort of my own, into a warm, loving heart, and such a happy home, and all so easily and smoothly that to me it seems like a miracle; and never can I forget while I live, nor cease to believe that truly 'He is the hearer and answerer of prayer.'"

"Before They Call I Will Answer."—A Pastor Prays for Decision as to Good Choices.

"The writer was once in great trouble to know what was duty. Urged by ministers and laymen in high standing to undertake a work not exactly in the line of the ministry, he hesitated. God's displeasure was feared, lest in doing what was desired 'sin might lie at his door.' To refuse the wish

of good and wise men might be resisting God's call. In this
trial of conscience he sought in fasting and special prayer the
guidance of his Heavenly Father. While so doing the above
promise came very distinctly to his mind. He brought it to
God as his own promise, and pleaded, if it could be graciously
done, that He would literally fulfill it to the suppliant. In
the very act of thus pleading, he heard a rap on the door.
Opening it, there stood his mother-in-law. She said, 'Two
gentlemen are in the parlor waiting for you.' I went down,
and the interview revealed the exact fulfillment both of the
promise and the prophecy. The Lord answered my prayer
two days before I called on Him. One of the two came from
New York to my home in a Western city to inquire about *the
very thing which was troubling me.* *He was to me an entire
stranger,* never having heard of him until I saw him. Having consulted his friend, the Rev. M. W. Jacobus, D. D, they
together came to call on me about the matter at the very
moment I was pleading with God that He would mercifully,
'while yet speaking, hear me.' Now could Tyndall and his
followers desire a more literal, a more exact fulfillment of this
prophecy and promise as proof of its inspiration, and of prayer
as God's ordinance than that prayer for such fulfillment of
these words actually before the prayer was made, and while
the petitioner was 'yet speaking?'"

It will be noticed that the best judgment of good men advise one course, but trust in God for superior wisdom brought
the case to answer in a totally different manner, by means of
an unknown person, a total stranger, who neither knew him
nor his desire. The circumstance should convince the world.

A Family Pray for a Good Servant.

"About three years since my family comfort was very
much disturbed by failure to obtain a good housemaid. And,
having been accustomed to wait upon God for right direction
in my *temporal* as well as spiritual affairs, in simple faith I

asked Him to direct me on reaching New York City to where
I would find a girl of good character that would appreciate a
Christian home. My steps were led to a boarding-house on
Greenwich street, and on inquiring for a German or Swede
girl I was told they had a nice Swede just landed. I talked
to her through an interpreter and was satisfied from what she
said, as well as from her countenance, that she was the one I
was searching for. She came to my home and proved, in two
years' service, almost faultless. In conversation one day, a
short time after she came to our home, she said she had had
several places offered her that morning before I came, but she
did not like them; but as soon as she saw me, felt that she
could go with me—she was a Christian, member of the Lu-
theran church and wanted a Christian home. Her desire
was granted and my prayer was answered.'

A Recovery from a Death-Bed.

"Some forty years ago, in a rural parish in New England,
a young man lay apparently on his death-bed with a putrid
fever. His aunt, in whose family he was staying, was a
woman who had long lived in habitual intercourse with the
unseen world through prayer. One afternoon, when it
seemed to those around him that the sick one must die,
she went away alone to speak with God. With intense earn
estness she pleaded for the young man's life. And, being
deeply interested in the portion of our country then beginning to be settled, she asked also that he might become a
home missionary at the West. There were various circumstances which made this latter request, as well as the other,
seem very unlikely to be fulfilled. And yet it was. The
young man recovered, pursued a collegiate and theological
course, and still lives and labors as a most devoted and
useful Christian pioneer. More than once he has been a
member of the General Assembly of the Presbyterian
Church, and his name is familiar to many."

A Poor Student Prays for Money.

" I was a poor student in a Manual Labor Institute at the West. The month of February was our regular Winter vacation. We were privileged to keep our rooms and have board at one dollar a week. But I had absolutely no money. I was six hundred miles from my friends, and they were unable to furnish me with funds. I had no books for the new term, though these were a necessity if I went on with my class, and there was no work about the Institution, nor that I know of in the neighborhood at that season. My case seemed an exceedingly bad one ; and I had no idea from where any help could come. So I went to my room in the third story, locked my door and carried my case to the Lord. It was a long, earnest, tearful cry for help from Him who alone seemed able to give it. My prayer was answered. When I had been there I do not know how long, I heard footsteps in the empty hall, and in a moment a knock at my door. I wiped my eyes, and put myself into presentable shape as soon as I could, and opened the door. A lad stood there who said : 'A man wants to see you at the front door.' Down the stairs I went, wondering who could want me and what he could want me for. In the front yard was a man on a restless horse, who at once said : ' We want you to teach our school for a month. The boys have driven out the female teacher. We want you to take them in hand, and we'll give you fifteen dollars and your board.' I said, ' All right, I'll be down there to-morrow morning.' And then I went back to my room to thank God for hearing my prayer."

" I Can't Stop to Pray."

" A deacon living in a Berkshire town was requested to give his prayers in behalf of a poor man with a large family who had broken his leg. 'I can't stop now to pray,' said the deacon (who was picking and barreling his early apples for the city market), 'but you can go down into the cellar and get some corned beef, salt pork, potatoes, and butter—that's the best I can do.'"

Remarkable Healing of a Child.

A clergyman writes that during the ministration of his labors at Battle Creek, Mich., there were several remarkable manifestations of divine power—especially in the case of a little girl, the daughter of a Mr Smith, a child of about six years.

"In September last, she was taken very sick with spinal fever. She became much reduced, extremely nervous and helpless, excepting to move her hands. Physicians gave up the case as a hopeless one, deciding that should she live, her condition would be that of helplessness, a burden to herself and to her parents.

"But our gracious God had better things in store for that afflicted family. It was on a Sabbath afternoon, at the very hour when the crowded congregation in our house of worship were in prayer for the influences of the divine Spirit, that a holy, solemn influence came into the dwelling of Brother Smith, as if an angel had come to touch the child with healing power. The mother could not leave the bedside of her suffering child to attend the meeting, and she says that a sudden change came over her feelings, and it appeared to her that an angel had come into the house, and had shed a holy influence in every part of it. It was at that moment that the hitherto helpless child drew herself up in a sitting posture, and next rose upon her feet. She rapidly recovered to her usual habits of taking food and sleeping, and now takes the exercise of the most robust children of her age."

God Paid the Rent.—Answer to Prayer.

A poor Christian family were in distress. The husband, during a long and painful sickness, had borne his trials for months with cheerful Christian resignation; "but, on this day," said a City Missionary, "I found them, for the first time, in tears. The cause I soon learned was the want of means to pay the rent of their little home, which would come due on the following Monday, and must be paid then, or they would have to leave and go they knew not where. The amount needed, *fifteen dollars*, and the amount in hand but *fifty cents;* the future all dark, and no hope of recovery from sickness, and no hope of being able to meet their expenses—it might be of a long sickness and want—what could I do for them? If theirs had been the only case of like wants that day, I no doubt could have gone to a few friends and have collected the amount. But that would not do them the good I felt they needed But I felt sure of a better way to get it, and lead them to trust in the Lord, and glorify God and not man.

"On the wall, at the foot of the sick man's bed, I had hung, but a short time previous, one of those precious silent comforters, a scroll of Scripture texts, printed in large type, and a different prayer for every day in the month. On the page before us for *that day*, after calling their attention to it, I read the following words : '*And all things whatsoever ye shall ask in prayer believing, ye shall receive.*' Matt. 21.22. 'Again I say unto you, *that if two of you shall agree on earth as touching anything that they shall ask, it shall be done for them.*' Matt. 18.9; remarking, 'Are not those precious promises? Your fears, dear brother and sister, are that you will not be able to pay the rent on Monday, and may be turned out into the street, unless you get the means to pay the rent; are they not?' 'That is so,' said they. 'There are two ways: one, to try to get some one to lend you the amount until you can pay, if the landlord will not wait; another, to go and beg for it.' I have learned a better way, and wish I could lead you to do the same. Do as David did. Have you ever gone to the Lord as directed above, and found in Him, as David did, a very present help in time of trouble? Would not your faith and confidence in God's word and in his kind, overruling providence be more strengthened, if, in going to Him now and making known your present troubles and wants, He should in a way, without your making known your wants to any other person, on Monday enable you to pay all ? ' The answer was, ' We should '

"After prayer and encouragement to do so, I left them, with the promise to call the following Tuesday. Doing so, I was met at the door by the wife with a countenance full of joy. *Oh, brother, we could not wait until you came, to tell you the wonderful answer to our prayer.* On Monday, *the very day* that we had to pay the rent, one gentleman came and handed my husband *five dollars,* and early in the morning Mrs. F——— called and handed me *ten dollars,* making in all *just fifteen dollars,* the amount we needed; was it not wonderful? Oh, how good the Lord is !' The same week another called and gave them an order for fifty dollars more, so that they were able to pay up all their debts, and the sudden joy soon led to a speedy restoration to health, and the husband is now one of the most active Christian workers and teachers in a mission school, and the wife and daughter are also trying to do all they can to lead others to trust in Jesus "

He Forgetteth Not the Cry of the Humble.

A City home missionary has told us of the case of a poor colored family, the husband nearly one hundred years old, totally incapacitated for work, and confined to his room by sickness nearly twelve years.

Although very often in straitened circumstances, the Lord has never left them to want for any good they needed, having, in a truly wonderful manner supplied their wants, in answer to prayer. The wife, having for a long time been kept from the enjoyment of church privileges by close confinement, she had been sorely tempted to doubt her acceptance in Christ, and was in great darkness for days; but one day, in reading the following words, found in the fifteenth chapter of John,

"*If ye abide in me, and my words abide in you, ye shall ask what ye will and it shall be done unto you,*" she was led to go to God in prayer, and to ask, if not wrong in his sight, to grant her a request, that she might know that her prayer was answered, and that she was abiding in Him. The request was that, as they were in trouble for the rent coming due the next day, and still in need of *three dollars*, that the Lord would send them a friend in a stranger, some one that they had never seen before, and that he would put it into the heart of that stranger to give them three dollars, and then they would not be tempted to believe, as they had sometimes before, that it would have been sent by a friend even if they had not prayed.

"But," said she, "I knows if a stranger comes, none but the Lord could send, then I would know the Lord heard my prayer, and I was truly the Lord's. So I watch for the answer for you knows, brother, when we prays, the Lord says we must believe we shall receive what we ask of Him, and then He will give it. So I watch and listen for the knock at the door, and do you believe me, brother, about three o'clock in the afternoon, I hears a knock and opens the door, and a strange lady was there, one I never saw before, and asked me if Mrs. H—— lived here; and said she had been looking for us before, but could not find us; 'when, to-day I felt I must try again, and' I am so glad I have found you. I heard of you through a friend who has known you a long time.' She spoke many kind words, and when she took my hand to say good-by, she left a little roll of notes, and when she is gone I count it, and *it was just three dollars.* I is been so happy ever since. I loves to tell how good the Lord has been to us; every time I does so I feels so happy."

Incidents in the Life of an Invalid.—How God cares and comforts in small things.

The following incidents are from the life of an invalid, personally known to the editor of this book, and can be depended upon as authentic in every particular. They illustrate most beautifully the blessed way in which the Savior's everlasting arms are around, strengthening, and His presence comforting His weak and helpless ones, in all their little as well as great trials of life. The ways in which he sent relief, and the many hundred promises which he has given, will encourage other Christian hearts to trust the same *Omnipotent, ever Helping Friend.*

Giving her Last Money to the Lord.

" 'The first money the Lord gives me I will send to you,' were the last words I said to my old father, as I stood waiting for the train to bear me to distant friends. So the weeks passed on, but I remembered my promise and waited patiently for the Lord to enable me to fulfill that promise. I had two dollars, but thought I must not give it away until more came. But this feeling did not last long; something seemed to tell me the Lord would not send me any until that was gone. One day I received a letter from a friend containing this sentence: 'I have not had three cents in five weeks.' My whole nature responded in a moment. I put part of my money into a letter for him, the rest into a letter for my father. Now I felt clear. Then I told the Lord all about it. A week passed, and $5 came to me from my mother to pay my return fare. A few days longer, and another $5 came from a lady friend, so I was provided for. I needed a certain article of clothing, and one night made all arrangements to get it next day. Morning came, and I went to the Bible for my orders for the day; my eyes rested on these words: 'Be content with what ye have.' This seemed so strange, because the Lord knew I needed the dress; I was obliged to stay out of society on this account. 'But the Lord knows best,' I thought, and gave up all idea of getting it. Nor did it trouble me further. I gave it all into his hands, feeling He knew best. And afterwards it was made clear to my own heart I had not trusted in vain. '*Commit all thy ways untc the Lord, for He careth for thee.*'"

Money Wanted to Pay Railroad Fare.

"Once, on a visit, I left the company below, and went up stairs for an hour's quiet and prayer. I was to return the coming week and I had only just enough to pay my fare. For several days I had been anxious how I was to get some money. This afternoon I had to pray very earnestly, because the need was great. An hour passed; I felt weary and unrefreshed, when a voice clear and near said unto me: 'Trust in the Lord and do good, and verily thou shalt be fed.' It was not a human voice, for no one was near me, but I started and looked around, *almost* expecting to see an angel visitant. I saw nothing, but the sun shone brighter outside, and the room seemed brighter than before. And why should it not? The Lord had been there with words of cheer and comfort for his little child. I arose and went below, where I found other company had called, and I was introduced to the lady and her husband, whom I had met five years before. A pleasant chat and they left, after giving me an invitation to visit them. At the door, as I learned from my friend who attended them, Mrs. N—— said 'I should like to give Miss B—— something,' and handed my friend *a five dollar bill for me.* I was more than surprised. I cannot tell you the emotions of my heart. While I was yet asking, even, the messenger had brought my answer. I could yet hear the soft sound of the voice up-stairs, and the soothing influence of the unseen presence still lingered round me. How quickly our needs flow on the wings of prayer into the very presence of our Friend and Master."

Prayer Saves the Life of a Little Child

"A year ago this Summer, my sister's little baby, only five months old, was taken very ill with that distressing complaint

which often proves so fatal, and takes so many sweet little ones out of loving hearts and homes. I loved baby
Ernest, but never so well as when he lay so sick he could not
know it. We all loved him, and everything was done that
could be thought of to ease the little sufferer all those
long, close, hot days. Day after day, for four long weeks, we
tenderly cared for him. Sometimes his mother would watch
his every breath, fearing each would be the last. One Sunday he lay just where we put him, so quiet and still, with
the sweet baby face so white and calm, we thought we should
lose him soon, the little hands and feet were so cold. All
through his illness, I kept asking the Lord to let his parents
keep the tender bud he had sent them. We could not let
him die, and to-day I prayed very earnestly all the time—
even when we could not warm the little body at all—we could
not let him go. Well, Ernnie passed over the fearful day
and became a happy, well boy. He was saved. No physician
saved him. Our tender care did not save him. Prayer saved
our Ernnie. Precious baby! He is such a jolly, happy boy
now, filling every heart and the whole house with his sunshine. How I love the little fellow. When I am here at his
home, he always comes to Auntie for love and tenderness.
When I am resting on the lounge, he comes every few moments to kiss me, giving and receiving real heart-love. We
know God only lends these little treasures to their human
friends. But oh, they bring so much love with them, it
is hard to give them up."

The Lost Thimble.

"One day I lost my silver thimble, a gift from my mother
when I was a young girl. I prized it *very highly*. I looked
everywhere, long and faithfully. The tears would come, at
the best, it had been so long a constant companion. I gave
up the search after a while, thinking some one had taken it,
or a child had lost it—any way, it was gone. Feeling sad over

it, I sat down to console myself, and the thought came—pray about it; so I did, and while I knelt there something whispered, 'Look on the bed,' so plainly that I arose and went into my sister's sleeping-room where I had turned the spread aside, and there nestled, in a fold of the quilt, *my thimble.* I involuntarily said, 'Thank God!' out of the depths of my glad heart. I had lain down a moment on this bed with baby Ernest, early in the morning, and the thimble had fallen out of my pocket."

A Prayer for $25.

" God moves in a mysterious way
His wonders to perform "

" I had a present of twenty-five dollars once, which was a direct answer to earnest, pleading prayer. I was entirely out of money for months—I could not earn a dollar. I had those who might have assisted me, but they did not. I could have borrowed, but I might never be able to return it; I knew not what to do. One evening, thinking it all over, scanning the dark cloud with anxious eyes, I said, 'If the Lord cannot help me, no one else can; I will ask Him.' And so I did, bringing all the previous promises before Him, pleading my unworthiness, but my great need; asking first for *ten dollars;* then, as I grew more earnest, I asked for *twenty-five,* feeling almost frightened as the words came from my lips. Sometimes the thought would intrude, ' How can you ask for any given sum—how do you expect it will come ? ' so I said, one day, to the Lord, ' Any sum you choose; you know best; I will be content.' Several weeks passed, and a sweet feeling of rest and assurance came, that, whatever came of it, would be all for the best But, by-and-by, when the anxious pleading feeling was all gone, one morning came a letter from one I had never seen, with $25—just what I had asked for. I cannot tell you just how I felt; I only know I held the check long in my hand, scarcely realizing it could be for me."

Praying for Others.

"My sister's husband wished to raise a certain sum of interest money by a given time, but could see no way; was very much troubled about it; said he knew no one to whom he could apply. I told him to pray for it. He answered, 'God won't hear the prayer of the wicked; suppose you ask him yourself.' I did ask Him, earnestly and faithfully, and it was even given me the idea who my brother could ask to loan it him. I spoke of the man to him—said I thought he might get it; so he called on him one evening, and the way was made plain for my brother to introduce the subject; and when he came home that night, he brought with him the three hundred dollars."

A Visit to Friends.

"I will hold thee by thy right hand, saying unto thee, fear not, I will help thee"

"Once I held in my hand an open letter, containing an invitation to visit friends I had never seen. My heart bounded with pleasure at thought of the journey, and the pleasant visit to follow; but, on second thought, it almost stood still—where could I get money and proper clothing? Several weeks passed in thought. I could see no way, and so I wrote my friends I could not come at present; but, in my heart, I could not give it up. My parents were visiting in the far West, and I had no one to advise me; so, up in my little room, night after night, I made it a point to tell the Lord about it, and soon it seemed as easy and right as though I were talking to a friend. One day, my brother-in-law said he would pay my expenses to and fro. I thanked him, and took fresh courage, and still kept on praying. Then the same good brother gave me money for a dress; then a friend furnished other articles, and soon, I was en route for the quaint old city by the sea. Every step was accomplished by the simple way of prayer; and, when I slept, late that night, in a cosy room

5

at the Methodist parsonage in N. B., I could look back over the last few weeks, and thank God for the *power of prayer.* But the best of it all was the lesson I had learned—one which I shall never forget, while memory holds her magic power—to carry *everything* to God in prayer; to trust him in every matter, however small; and this is the whole secret of the power that lies in prayer."

"I found another lady visitor at my friend's and we were to share the same bed This was a little trial, I had to ask the Lord to give me patience—and He did. One night, I was very restless and nervous; I could not sleep. I knew I was disturbing my friend—soon she said, 'Annie, I am going to ask the Lord to come and put you to sleep Now, lay still, and in five minutes you will be all right' I did so, also breathing the words, 'Give me sleep, dear Saviour.' The room seemed to be full of a soft, soothing influence, and I fell asleep. Once only in the night I awoke, but soon went asleep. When I awoke in the morning, rested and refreshed, Tillie, who was dressing near me, looked up with her pleasant smile and said, 'Annie, how wonderful it was. You were asleep in less than five minutes It seemed as though Jesus stood close by your side; I could *almost see* Him, I felt so clearly His presence. He is here now, Annie; can't you feel Him near? He was very good to you last night' Yes, indeed, I felt the influence of His presence, and, all day, whenever I entered the room, I felt it, and it seemed as though I must tread softly, it was so like holy ground. This feeling lasted through my stay, and, last Winter, while again visiting the home of my friends, it all came back to me again This beautiful influence has ever kept with me, and I never close my eyes in sleep until I say, 'Oh, Lord, breathe upon me the sweet spirit of sleep.' However weary, sick or nervous I may be, I feel that the soothing power will come; and, with my hand in His, I rest peacefully, at last."

Praying for a New Hat.

"Whatsoever thing ye ask in *My* name"——

"For a long while I had been without money, and my need was very great. I wanted a new hat so much, and the question arose in my mind, 'What am I going to do about it?' As I had no human arm to depend on for anything, of course there was only one way for me to do—ask the Lord for money to get me a hat. With me, to think is to act, and so I told the Lord all about it, asking, if it was His will, to send me, in His own way, money for the article I needed. Day after day passed, and I felt almost discouraged. One day, a letter came from a lady friend I had never seen, enclosing one dollar. I bought my hat—neither could I have used that dollar for another purpose. Soon after this, my physician ordered something for me. I had no money to get it, but said I would get it soon as I could. Three weeks passed, and no money came. Then I asked the Lord for enough to get my medicine. Another letter came from an old nurse, with a gift of one dollar. I had my medicine. Time after time, I have not had wherewith to send my letters, and, as I have a large correspondence, it often is a real trouble The only way I have to do is to *pray for it*, and always, in some way, it comes ; not in *my way*—not just as soon as I ask for it—but in His own way, He always provides. I have learned to trust and not be afraid, even though the clouds hang heavy, and I see no ray of light, the promise is there, and for me, 'I will *never* leave thee, or forsake thee.' I am so entirely dependent on Him for everything that sometimes, in little matters, my faith will, for a brief season, droop Sometimes I have to plead and plead over again some particular promises ; but these times of waiting on Him only strengthen me for future conflicts 'Wait on the Lord, and he shall renew thy strength,' comes in beautifully on such occasions. No human being to help me ; no one but God. Sometimes, when I sit alone, such a flood of feelings come over me, I well nigh sink. Loneliness,

homesickness, and the great want in every human heart of sym·
pathy and love, leave me, for a moment, without hope or faith ;
but, when the heart is weakest, and the need greatest, the loving Saviour is nearest. 'Like as a mother comforteth her child,
so does He comfort me ; ' and then, soothed by his power and
love, how the aching heart rests 'by the still waters, and in
the green pastures.'   There is nothing but prayer for the
helpless sinner , nothing else will bring us into loving companionship with the Lord.   We may go to Him always, with
every trial, need or sorrow.   He is ever waiting—ever ready
to hear and answer."

Praying for a Sewing Machine.

"One day a lady friend said to me : 'Would you like some
nice sewing, easy to do ? '   I answered, 'Yes.' 'Have you a
sewing machine ? ' 'I have not, but am praying for one.'
'That is right; so you believe you will have it by praying for
it ? ' I replied : 'If the Lord thinks I need it, He will send
it.' I had learned to use my sister's, but I wanted one of my
own, to use just when I felt like it. So the thought kept
in my heart, 'Why can't I pray for one ? ' And yet it
seemed foolish to go in prayer to God for such a simple thing,
but I had not then learned that *all things*, with Him, meant
every wish and want of the human heart.   But there was no
other way.   He must send my machine, or I could have none.
I prayed very earnestly.   After a few weeks of waiting,
one golden winter morning it came—my beautiful machine—
just what I wanted.   This seemed so wonderful to me, that it
seemed to bring me into nearer companionship with the Lord,
and ever after, whatever I needed, I went directly to Him
for.   A ministerial friend once asked me what it was I had
covered up on the stand   I told him it was my piano, taking
the cover aside and showing him at once how my beautiful sewing machine worked.   '*What tune do you play
oftenest?*' he asked.   '*Rock of Ages* is its favorite one, and
I never sew without singing it.'"

Money for Postage.

"One day I opened my port-monnaie to get change for some little needful, when I found I had but ten cents. I used five of it. As visions of six or seven letters and many little things I needed came up before me, I said aloud: 'The Lord will have to send me some money pretty soon.' I think once through the day I prayed for some money, but felt no uneasiness about it. That evening a lady friend called to say good-by for the winter, and as she left gave me *fifty cents for postage*. While I was calling He answered me. About a week before this, I thought I would ask the Lord for $5 for my physician. He had come so faithfully, day after day, without ever expecting one dollar, because I had told him freely my circumstances. But I felt I must give him something for a gift at least. So I asked for five dollars. Day after day passed away, and I thought perhaps the Lord did not want me to have it. But still I prayed, asking it for His will, not mine. One morning a letter came from a very dear friend, containing a check for the amount for which I had prayed, and a little beside. It seemed such a signal answer to my prayer, that I could scarcely speak, and in my heart a glad prayer of thanksgiving went up to Him, who had told me *to ask and I should receive*. A friend, to whom I told this, said: 'Now you need this money yourself; I would not give it to the doctor now—wait awhile.' 'But,' I replied, 'I dare not do it. I need it, I know, but I asked God for it for my doctor, and I must give it.' And here let me say, when we ask God for money, it is sacred, and must be spent only to please Him."

Praying for a Bible.

"For a long while it has been my habit to be entirely guided for the day by the first verse in the Bible on which my eyes rested. While dressing for the day, I glance at the open page, or sometimes turning over the leaves. But my old Bible was poor print and small, and it troubled me for a long while. So I thought I would ask the Lord to send me a new one. I told Him all about it. One day, this Summer, the postman brought me a package of magazines and a letter. I began to undo the package, eager to scan their welcome pages. My sister laughingly said she would read my letter, and suiting the action to the word, opened the envelope. I really did not mind what she was doing, until she said: 'Why there is some money here, but no letter.' So she handed me the half sheet of paper, with the money folded inside. I looked it over, and there were only these words in pencil: 'For a Bible, and three dollars.' We looked at each other; I could not say a word, until she said, 'What does it all mean?' I answered, 'The Lord sent it, I know; where could it come from?' It was wonderful—wonderful because I could not remember as I ever told any one that I was praying for a Bible."

A Spring Mattress.

"Last Summer, when I bought my bedstead, I did not have money to get either springs or a mattress, so I fixed up a clean, straw bed, and covered it nicely with a thick comfortable. It was pretty hard—I did not rest well. So, one sleepless night, I said aloud, 'I will just ask the Lord to send me a set of springs' I kept on day by day. When I felt the severe pain which denoted illness, I thought of my hard bed and prayed more earnest. One day my physician spoke of my hard bed. I told him I was going to have a better one; I was praying for some springs. And so I kept on. One day, a lady friend said something about my bed. I did not say much. Somehow I felt I must not; I wanted to have it all the Lord's doings, if I ever had any. One day my sister said a man was at the door, who wanted to fit a set of springs to my bed. Why, I can't tell how I felt; even after God had answered my simple prayers, and honored my faith so many times, I was astonished at this. But she helped me up, and the bed was fitted with nice, new springs. And they were mine. The man could not tell anything about them. My sister says, 'Annie, did you order them?' I said, 'No.' 'Don't you know who sent them?' I said, 'No.' 'Did you ask Mrs. W—— to order them?' I said, 'I did not; I would lay here six years before I would do it. No, somebody had a hand in it, but the Lord sent them, because I prayed for them all the time.' A friend was present when my physician called. I told him about the new springs. His kind face lit up grandly at this new evidence that God did answer humble, faithful prayer, and he turned to my friend with the words: 'I am glad they were just what she has been praying for.' I do not think he had anything to do about them But these springs are only another proof of his love and power, in touching the hearts of his children to help others And they have their reward. Soon after this, a lady sent me a white spread for my bed. Surely, God is good to his little ones."

The Healing of Mary Theobald.

The following incident is related by her pastor, at Woburn, Mass., who, for three and a half years, was well acquainted with her physical condition, and who testified, in *The Congregationalist*, that no medicine, or physician's aid or advice, was of any avail:

"From the first of my acquaintance to the last, she had an unswerving confidence in her recovery. Many times has she said to me: 'I believe that I shall be well. Jesus will raise me up I shall hear you preach some day.'

"But, in common with the friends who were watching her case, and with the physicians who had exhausted their skill upon her in vain, I had little or no hope for her. It seemed to me that her life was to be one of suffering; that God was keeping her with us that we might have a heroic example of what His grace could enable one to bear and to become.

"A few days ago, I received from her lips the following statement of the origin and progress of her sickness: 'My first sickness occurred when I was about sixteen years old. This illness lasted for a year. Indeed, I was never well again. That sickness left me with a bad humor, which, for two years, kept me covered with boils. When the boils disappeared, the trouble was internal. Physicians feared a cancer. For ten years, I was sick, more or less—sometimes able to work, sometimes utterly prostrate.

"'My second severe illness began in the Autumn of 1871. I had been failing for two years. Then I was obliged to give up. I was on the bed five months. From this illness I never recovered so as to labor or walk abroad. When not confined to my bed, I have been on the lounge, as you have known me. No one can ever know the suffering which these years have brought me.'

"My acquaintance with her began in the Spring of 1873. Several times since I have known her, she has been carried so low that we have thought her release near at hand; and, indeed, the general tendency has been downwards. I recently asked an intelligent physician, who had attended her for a year or more, to give me the facts in her case. He replied: 'She is diseased throughout. Her system is thoroughly soured. It responds to nothing. Almost every function is abnormal. There is no help for her in medicine.' Other physicians had tried their skill with the same result. It was generally admitted by doctors, friends and family, that nothing more could be done for her. While all saw only suffering and an early death in store for her, yet she confidently expected to be well, and her faith never waned.

"It was her custom to spend a few weeks each year in the family of one of the sisters in the church. At her last visit, it was evident to this lady that Mary was not so well as in former years. One day, when conversation turned upon this topic, she felt constrained to express her fears. But Mary was hopeful. A proposition was made, and arrangements were perfected to visit Doctor Cullis, to secure the benefit of his prayers. But her feebleness was so great that the plan was abandoned. 'If,' said Mrs. F., 'faith is to cure you, why go to Doctor Cullis, or to any one? Let us go to God ourselves; and, Mary, if you have faith that God can and will cure you sometime, why not believe that He will *cure you now?*'

"She felt herself cast on God alone. All hope of human help was at an end. She had thought it, hitherto, enough patiently to wait His time. She saw that, after all, she must not dishonor God by limiting His power. Again her Bible opened to the familiar passages, '*the prayer of faith shall save the sick;*' '*according to your faith be it unto you.*' She felt that the time for testing her faith had come. She would dishonor the Lord no longer. Requesting the prayers of the family that God would now grant healing and restoration, she tottered to her couch, and, asking that in the morning she might be well, calmly closed her eyes in the assurance that it would be so. *And according to her faith, so it was. She came forth in the morning without a remnant of the pain which had filled a decade of years with agony.* That Sabbath was to her, indeed, 'a high day.' A week later the frequent prophecy that she should hear me preach was fulfilled.

"*Not a vestige of suffering remained.* So far as that is concerned, there was not a hint left that she had been an invalid for almost a score of years.

"*She immediately took her place in the family as a well person.* Two days after, I saw her. She came to meet me with a step light and strong, and with a face written all over with thankfulness and joy. Since that time all the abandoned duties of active life have been resumed. When last I saw her, she was in bounding health and spirits, declaring that she could not remember when she had felt so happy and well. That night—one of the coldest of the winter, the roads at their iciest—she walked more than half a mile to and from the prayer-meeting.

It is difficult for those who are not conversant with the case to believe it, yet there is no illusion in it. *That she went to sleep a suffering, feeble, shattered woman, and awoke free from pain, and that she has been gaining in strength ever since, are facts that cannot be doubted."*

How Prayer Helped him to Keep the Pledge.

In a rural district, in the North of England, lived a shoemaker who had signed the temperance pledge often, but never had strength to keep it. After a while, he was able to keep it, and reformed entirely. A friend was curious to learn how he had been able, at last, to win the victory, and went to see him.

"Well, William, how are you?"

"Oh, pretty well. I had only eighteen pence and an old hen when I signed, and a few old scores; but now I have about ten pounds in the bank, and my wife and I have lived through the summer without getting into debt. But as I am only thirty weeks old yet (so he styled himself), I cannot be so strong yet, my friend."

"How is it you never signed before?"

"I did sign; but I keep it different now to what I did before, friend."

"How is this?"

"Why, I *gae doon* on my knees and pray."

Here was the *real strength of prayer.* His own resolves were of no value; but when he called on God to help, then came new strength, and he was kept by restraining grace. The bitter experience of those who pledge and pledge over and over again, and never gain the victory, at last must come to either of two ends—their utter destruction, or else to call on God in prayer, to help them keep the pledge manfully, and make them steadfast in their resolutions.

One who Refused the Holy Spirit.

The following incident is related by D. L. Moody, the Evangelist, which contains a warning, how the Holy Spirit avenges itself to those who refuse its admonitions. It is a remarkable instance of the control of an over-ruling God, who alone knew that man's mind, and which alone could bring that text so often to his memory:

"There was a young man in my native village—he was not a young man when I was talking to him—we were working on the farm together one day and he was weeping; I asked him what he was weeping about, and he told me a very strange story. When he left home his mother gave him the text: '*Seek ye first the Kingdom of God and His righteousness, and all these things will be added unto you.*' He was ambitious to get rich, and thought when he had got comfortable, that was the time to give his attention to religion. He went from village to village, and got nothing to do. Sunday came, and he went into the village church. *What was his great surprise to hear the minister preach from that text.* It went down into his heart—he thought that it was his mother's prayers that were following him—he thought the whole sermon was for himself, and thought he would like to get out. For days he could not get that text and sermon out of his mind. He went on still, from village to village, and at last he went into another church after weeks had rolled away. He went for some Sundays to the church, and it wasn't a great while before the minister *gave out this very text.* He thought surely it was God calling him then, and he said, coolly and deliberately, *he would not seek the Kingdom of God.* He went on in this way, and in the course of a few months, to his great surprise, he heard the *third sermon from the third minister on the same text.* He tried to stifle it, but it followed him. At last he made up his mind he would not go to church any more. When he came back to Northfield, after years, his mother had died, but the text kept coming to him over and over, and he said, 'I will not become a Christian;' and said he to me, 'Moody, my heart is as hard as that stone.' It was all Greek to me, because I was not a Christian myself at the time. After my conversion, in Boston, he was about the first man I thought of. When I got back and asked my mother about him, she told me he was gone out of his mind, and to every one who went to the asylum to see him he pointed his finger and said: '*Seek ye first the Kingdom of God and His Righteousness.*' When I went back to my native village, after that, I was told he was still out of his mind, but at home. I went to see him, and asked him did he know me. He was rocking backwards and forwards in his rocking chair, and he gave me that vacant stare and pointed to me as he said, '*Young man, seek first the Kingdom of God and His Righteousness.*' When, last month, I laid down my younger brother in his grave, I could not help but think of that man lying but a few yards away. May every man and woman here be wise for eternity and seek now the Kingdom of God and His Righteousness, is my prayer."

The Praying Shoe-maker.

A correspondent of *The American Messenger* relates this instance of a poor man in the village where he lived, who, with a family of young children and a wife in very feeble health, found it extremely difficult to obtain a livelihood. He was at length compelled to work by the week for a shoe-dealer in the city, four miles from the village, returning to his family every Saturday evening, and leaving home early on Monday morning.

He usually brought home the avails of his week's labor in provisions for the use of his family during the following week; but on one cold and stormy night, in the depth of winter, he went towards his humble dwelling with empty hands, but a full heart. His employer had declared himself unable to pay him a penny that night, and the shoemaker, too honest to incur a debt without knowing that he should be able to cancel it, bent his weary steps homeward, trusting that He who hears the ravens when they cry, would fill the mouths of his little family. He knew that he should find a warm house and loving hearts to receive him, but he knew, too, that a disappointment awaited them which would make at least *one* heart ache.

When he entered his cottage, cold and wet with the rain, he saw a bright fire, brighter faces, and a table neatly spread for the anticipated repast. The tea-kettle was sending forth its cloud of steam, all ready for "the cup which cheers, but not inebriates," and a pitcher of milk, which had been sent in by a kind neighbor, was waiting for the bread so anxiously expected by the children. The sad father confessed his poverty, and his wife in tears begged him to make *some* effort to procure food for them before the Sabbath. He replied, "Let us ask God to give us our daily bread Prayer avails with God when we ask for temporal good, as well as when we implore spiritual blessings." The sorrowing group knelt around the family altar, and while the father was entreating fervently for the mercies they so much needed, a gentle knocking at the door was heard. When the prayer was ended the door was opened, and there stood a woman in the "peltings of the storm," who had never been at that door before, though she lived only a short distance from it. She had a napkin in her hand, which contained a large loaf of bread; and half apologizing for offering it, said she had unintentionally made "a larger batch of bread" than usual that day, and though she hardly knew why, she thought it might be acceptable there.

After expressing their sincere gratitude to the woman, the devout shoe-maker and his wife gave thanks to God with overflowing hearts. While the little flock were appeasing their hunger with the nice new bread and milk, the father repaired to the house where I was an inmate, and told his artless tale with streaming eyes, and it is unnecessary to say, that he returned to his home that night with a basket heavily laden, and a heart full of gratitude to a prayer-answering God.

How the Lord Controls even the Locomotive and the Railroad Train.

A remarkable instance of how the Lord controlled circumstances for the detention of one train, and speeded the arrival of the other, in answer to the prayer of a poor widow, who was in anxiety and distress, is thus known to the editor of *The Watchman and Reflector:*

"Not long ago an engineer brought his train to a stand at a little Massachusetts village, where the passengers have five minutes for lunch. A lady came along the platform and said: 'The conductor tells me the train at the junction in P—— leaves fifteen minutes before our arrival. It is Saturday night, that is the last train. I have a very sick child in the car, and no money for a hotel, and none for a private conveyance for the long, long journey into the country. What shall I do?' 'Well,' said the engineer, 'I wish I could tell you.' 'Would it be possible for you to hurry a little?' said the anxious, tearful mother. 'No, madam, I have the time-table, and the rules say I must run by it.'

She turned sorrowfully away, leaving the bronzed face of the engineer wet with tears. Presently she returned and said. 'Are you a Christian?' 'I trust I am,' was the reply. 'Will you pray with me that the Lord may, in some way, delay the train at the junction?' 'Why, yes, I will pray with you, but I have not much faith.' Just then, the conductor cried, 'All aboard' The poor woman hurried back to her deformed and sick child, and away went the train, climbing the grade. 'Somehow,' says the engineer, 'everything worked to a charm. *As I prayed, I couldn't help letting my engine out just a little.* We hardly stopped at the first station, people got on and off with wonderful alacrity, the conductor's lantern was in the air in half a minute, and then away again. Once over the summit, it was dreadful easy to give her a little more, and then a little more, as I prayed, till she seemed to shoot through the air like an arrow. Somehow I couldn't hold her, knowing I had the road, and so we dashed up to the junction six minutes ahead of time.' There stood the train, and the conductor with his lantern on his arm. 'Well,' said he, '*will you tell me what I am waiting here for? Somehow I felt I must wait your coming to-night, but I don't know why.*' 'I guess,' said the brother conductor, 'it is for this woman, with her sick and deformed child, dreadfully anxious to get home this Saturday night' But the man on the engine and the grateful mother think they can tell why the train waited. God held it to answer their prayers."

Think of this wonderful improbability according to natural circumstances. These trains never connected with each other, nor were intended to. There was no message sent ahead to stop. There was not the slightest business reason for waiting, yet the second conductor, on arrival of the first, asks this question, "*What am I waiting for,*" and the answer of the first is more singular, "I don't know."

Another Instance of Superhuman Control of the Locomotive, in Answer to Prayer.

An exact parallel instance to the foregoing is given in the experience of a correspondent of *The Christian*, which occurred in the latter part of November, 1864, while traveling with her aged father and two small girls:

"We started from New Hampshire on Thursday morning, expecting to have ample time to get through to Indiana

before Saturday night; but, after we crossed the St. Law-
rence River, the next day, I think, there was a smash-up on
a freight train, which hindered our train about two hours.   I
began to feel anxious, as I knew our limited means would not
permit us to stop long on the way.   After the cars had started
again, I inquired of the conductor what time we should get
to Toledo, fearing we should not reach there in time for the
down train.   *He said it would be impossible to gain the time.*
Soon they changed conductors, and I made a similar inquiry,
getting about the same answer.   Still I hoped, till we reached
the Detroit River   Here I found that, though they had put
on all the steam they dared to, they were *almost an hour
behind time,* so I should have to stay over till Sunday
night.

"After getting seated in the cars on the other side, I ventured to ask the conductor if we should get to Toledo in time
for the down train.   He readily said, '*No, madam, impossible!   If we put on all the steam we dare to, we shall be more
than half an hour behind time.*   If we were on some trains
we might hope they would wait; but on this, *never!   He is
the most exact conductor you ever saw.   He was never known
to wait a second, say nothing about a minute, beyond the time.*'
I then inquired if we could not stay at the depot   He said,
No; we should all freeze to death, for the fire is out till Sunday evening

"A gentleman sitting in front of us said he would show us
a good hotel near by, as he was acquainted there.   I thanked
him, but sunk back on my seat.   Covering my eyes with my
hand, and raising my heart to God, I said, 'O, God, if thou
art my Father, and I am thy child, put it into the heart of
that conductor to wait till we get there.'

"Soon I became calm, and fell asleep, not realizing that
God would answer my poor prayer; but, when we reached
Toledo, to the astonishment of us all, there stood the conduct-
or, *wanting to know the reason why he had to wait,* when
our conductor told him there was a lady with her crippled

father and two little daughters, who were going down on that train.

"Soon as all were out of the car, both conductors came with their lanterns and gave their aid in helping my father to the other train, where they had reserved seats by keeping the door locked All was hurry and confusion to me, as I had my eye on father, fearing he might fall, it being very slippery, when the baggage-master said, 'Your checks, madam!' I handed them to him, and rushed into the car; but, before I got seated, the car started, and I had no checks for my baggage. Again my heart cried out, 'O, Thou that hearest prayer, take care of my baggage!' believing He could do that as well as make the conductor wait. In a few moments the conductor came to me with a face radiant with smiles, saying, *'Madam, I waited a whole half hour for you,—a thing I never did before since I was a conductor, so much as to wait one minute after my time.'* He said, 'I know it was your father that I was waiting for, because there was nothing else on the train for which I could have waited.' I exclaimed, in a half suppressed tone, 'Praise the Lord!' I could not help it; it gushed out. Then he said, *'At the very moment all were on board, and I was ready to start, such a feeling came over me as I never had in my life before. I could not start.* Something kept saying to me, *you must wait,* for there is something pending on that train you must wait for. I waited, and here you are, all safe.' Again my heart said, Praise the Lord! and he started to leave me, when I said, 'But there is one thing.' 'What is it?' was his quick reply. 'I gave the baggage-master my checks, and have none in return.' 'What were the numbers?' I told him. 'I have them,' he said, handing them to me, 'but your baggage will not be there till Monday morning. We had no time to put it on, we had waited so long.'"

6

Another Wonderful Record of $25.

A Christian minister, living in Northern Indiana, was in want, and knelt in prayer again and again before his Father in heaven. His quarterly allowance had been withheld, and want stared him in the face. Constrained by urgent need, and shut up to God for help, he pleaded repeatedly for a supply of his temporal wants. Now see how extraordinary was the plan of the Lord to send relief.

"In one of the lovely homes of Massachusetts, while the snow was falling and the winds were howling without, a lady sat on one side of the cheerful fire, knitting a little stocking for her oldest grandson, and her husband, opposite to her, was reading aloud a missionary paper, when the following passage arrested the attention of the lady and fastened itself in her memory

"'In consequence of failure to obtain my salary when due, I have been so oppressed with care and want, as to make it painfully difficult to perform my duties as a minister There is very little prospect, seemingly, of improvement in this respect for some time to come. What I say of my own painfully inadequate support, is substantially true of nearly all your missionaries in this State. You, of course, cannot be blamed for this. You are but the almoners of the churches, and can be expected to appropriate only what they furnish. *This, however, the Master will charge to somebody as a grievous fault;* for it is not His will that his ministers should labor unrequited.'

"This extract was without name or date. It was simply headed 'from a missionary in Northern Indiana.' Scores of readers probably gave it only a passing glance. Not so the lady who sat knitting by the fire and heard her husband read it. The words sank into her mind, and dwelt in her thoughts. The clause, '*This, however, the Master will charge to somebody as a grievous fault,*' especially seemed to follow her wherever she went. The case, she said, haunted her. She seemed to be herself that very '*somebody*' who was to answer at the bar of God for the curtailed supplies and straitened means of this humble minister.

" Impelled by an unseen, but, as she believes, a divine presence and power, after asking counsel and guidance of the Lord, she took twenty-five dollars which were at her own disposal, and requested her husband to give it to the Rev. Dr. H—— for the writer of the above communication, if he could devise any way to obtain the writer's address.

" Doctor H—— is a prompt man, who does not let gold destined to such an end rest in his pocket   Familiar with the various organizations of the benevolent societies, and only too happy to have an agency in supplying the wants of a laborer in Christ's vineyard, he soon started the money on its appointed errand.   Early in April, the lady in her rural home had the happiness of receiving the following note, of which we omit nothing, save the names of persons and places ·

" ' DEAR MADAM.—I have just received a draft for twenty-five dollars, as a special donation from you.   This I do with profound gratitude to you for this unselfish and Christ-like deed, and to Him who put it into your heart to do it.   How you, *a lady a thousand miles away, could know that I was, and had been for some time, urged by unusual need to pray for succor and worldly support with unwonted fervency, is a matter of more than curious inquiry.   It is an answer to my prayer, for the Lord employs the instrumentality of his children to answer prayer, and, when it is necessary, he moves them to it.   This is not the first nor second time that I have been laid under special obligation by Christian sympathy and timely aid.*   May He who said, He that giveth a cup of cold water to a disciple, in the name of a disciple, shall not lose his reward, repay you a thousand-fold for this favor.'

" Does not this little incident illustrate the power of prayer? The man of God, weary and heavy-laden, in his closet in Indiana, spread his case before the Lord.   A disciple in Eastern

Massachusetts, *a thousand miles away* from the spot where the prayer was offered, who did not know anything about him or his need, is touched with his wants, and moved to send him immediate aid."

Mr. Spurgeon's Cow.

" My grandfather was a very poor minister, and kept a cow, which was a very great help in the support of his children— he had ten of them ;—and the cow took the " staggers " and died. ' What will you do now ? ' said my grandmother. ' I cannot tell what we shall do now,' said he, ' but I know what God will do : God will provide for us. We must have milk for the children.'

" The next morning, there came £20 to him. He had never made application to the fund for the relief of ministers ; but, on that day, there were £5 left when they had divided the money, and one said, ' There is poor Mr. Spurgeon down in Essex, suppose we send it to him.' The chairman—a Mr. Morley of his day—said, ' We had better make it £10, and I'll give £5.' Another £5 was offered by another member, if a like amount could be raised, to make it up to £20 ; which was done. They knew nothing about my grandfather's cow ; but God did, you see ; and there was the new cow for him. And those gentlemen in London were not aware of the importance of the service which they had rendered.

CHARLES SPURGEON."

"Trust in the Lord."

"A poor negro woman, after the death of her husband, had no means of support for herself and two little children, except the labor of her own hands ; yet she found means out of her deep poverty to give something for the promotion of the cause of her Redeemer, and would never fail to pay, on the very day it became due, her regular subscription to the church of which she was a member. In a hard Winter she had found great difficulty in supplying the pressing needs of her little family; yet the few pence for religious purposes had been regularly put by.

"As one season for the contribution came round, she had only a little corn, a single salt herring, and a five-cent piece remaining of her little store. Yet she did not waver; she ground the corn, prepared her children's supper, and then, with a light heart and cheerful countenance, set out to meeting, where she gave joyfully the five cents, *the last she had in the world.*

"Returning from the church, she passed the house of a lady to whom, a long time before, she had sold a piece of pork, so long indeed that she had entirely forgotten the circumstance. But, seeing her this morning, the lady called her in, apologized for having been so tardy in the settlement, and then inquired how much it was. Old Sukey did not know, and the lady, determined to be on the safe side, gave her two dollars, besides directing her housekeeper to put up a basket of flour, sugar, coffee, and other luxuries for her use. Poor Sukey returned home with a joyful heart, saying, as she displayed her treasures, "See, my children, the Lord is a good paymaster, giving us ' a hundred-fold even in this present life, and in the world to come life everlasting.'"

Exactly Eighty Dollars.—"They are Safe that Trust in Thee."

A clergyman somewhat advanced in years recently related to a correspondent of *The Messenger* an incident in his own life, which well illustrates the provident care of our heavenly Father over his children.

"His first church was at V——, and, though he labored diligently, working with his own hands for his support, he became eighty dollars in debt. It was a grievous burden, and all his efforts to remove it proved unavailing. One day, when

he felt especially cast down, he retired to pray over the matter, and on his knees he besought the Lord to aid, as he despaired of help from any other source.   He felt strengthened
and hopeful when he left his closet, and entered his church on
Sabbath morning with a lighter heart than usual.   As he
passed the door a young lady met him, and placed in his
hand *fifty dollars,* saying that *twenty* was to go for the Sabbath-school library, and the remaining *thirty* was for himself.
He was so surprised that he scarcely trusted his senses, and
asked her not less than three times, that he might not be
mistaken.   As he preached that day, God seemed 'a very
present help.'   At the close of the service, a young man,
noted for his free-hearted, impulsive character, stepped up
and requested that he would perform a marriage ceremony for
him the next week.   He did so, and received for his services
a bill, which he placed in his pocket, and, on looking at it
afterwards, found it *fifty dollars,* thus making up *exactly the
eighty* he had prayed the Lord to send him."

We too often forget that God is as willing to listen to our
temporal wants as to our spiritual, and that " no good thing
will He withhold from them that walk uprightly."

A Prayer for Four Dollars.

A Home Missionary from Brooklyn called one day upon an
editor to gather some tracts for distribution which he had
published.   The editor became interested in the story of his
visits among the poor, and though at first not specially moved
to give money at that time, yet toward the last, putting his
hand into his pocket he pulled out all the bills there were
there, $4, and gave them to the missionary with these words:
"There is something which may come useful."   The gift was
all forgotten until a few days afterward the missionary returned and said to the editor, "After I left you I received a
letter from a poor lady who had been owing money for rent
for several months, which she could not possibly pay.   That

very morning the landlord came and said that if she could only raise $4 he would excuse the rest; but she did not have the $4. I did not know where to get it. I happened to drop in to see you; did not tell you anything of the need, and asked for nothing; yet you gave me the exact $4 to answer that poor woman's prayer."

An infinite ·Creator and God had brought these circumstances together in this exact way. Neither the editor nor missionary had ever met before. The missionary did not know that the lady was in distress. Who was it that sent the landlord to the lady and fixed that amount of $4 in his mind? Who was it that sent the home missionary to the office of a person he had never seen or known? Who was it that knew of the $4 waiting in that pocket and prompted that hand to take it out and give it away? Who was it that led that missionary to obtain and send relief just as she was praying for that special amount?

Was it chance or science? No, No. It was the will of a loving God.

"Aunt Sally's" Faith.

"'Aunt Sally,' says the *American Messenger*, was a devout, working, trustful Christian. Her husband was a cripple, almost helpless, an unbeliever, and to some extent an opposer of religion They lived alone. The severity of a northern winter was upon them, and in spite of her best exertions their stock of fuel was scarcely a day's supply.

"'What can be done?' was the anxious inquiry of the unbelieving husband as they were rising from their bed. 'The Lord will provide,' was 'Aunt Sally's' cheerful reply. 'I know you always say so. and so it has always proved,' was the answer of her unbelieving companion; 'but I see no way in which we can be provided for now.' 'Nor do I,' said 'Aunt Sally' 'But help will come. God will not desert us.'

"That winter's morning had not passed when their son,

who had been a soldier in the Mexican war, entered the door.
It had been long since they had heard from him, and they
feared he was not alive. The sun went down upon an abundant supply of fuel, cut in the forest by the strong arms of the
soldier-boy, and drawn to the door by means of his procuring
The unbelieving husband and father declared he would never
be distrustful again.

God Careth for You.

"Nearly forty years ago I was given up by the doctors for
a dying man from consumption. I had a wife and five children dependent on me, and for many months was unable to
provide for them by my own labors   All our earthly resources
were gone, and one Sabbath morning, when breakfast was
over, we were entirely destitute; there was no meal in the
barrel nor oil in the cruse. In family worship I read the
fortieth chapter of Isaiah. I think up to that time I had
never found the word of God so sweet and precious. I had
very near access in prayer, and was enabled to lay my burden
at the Saviour's feet. I closed with the Lord's Prayer; it
seemed made on purpose for me. I think the petition, 'Give
us this day our daily bread,' was offered in faith.

"*Within an hour there was a rap at the door.* When I
opened it a young man stood there who had come three miles
to bring us bread, sugar, and money. He apologized for
coming on the Sabbath morning, but said an aunt of his was
at their house the evening before, and felt so anxious about
us she could not go away till he promised her he would come
and bring us those things."

A Prayer Not Answered.

"Many years ago, a man then recently married, settled
in my native town. It was then quite new, destitute of religious privileges, and given to all manner of wickedness.

There was no Sabbath, and no sanctuary. The man was pious. The thought of bringing up a family in such a place distressed him. He wished to remove; and he used to retire daily to a little grove, and *pray that God would send some one to buy his farm.* This prayer was not answered. Better things were in store. A neighbor was taken sick. He visited and conversed with him. In the midst of the conversation, one sitting by interrupted him and said, 'Sir, if what you say is true, I am lost.' This gave new interest to the occasion. Prayer was offered, the Spirit was found out, and many were converted. A prayer-meeting was started; other revivals followed; in due time a church was organized, a house of worship built, and a pastor settled, mainly through the instrumentality of that one man; and he trained up his family there, and lived to see most of them members of the church of Christ. Do not despair, God will *either answer your exact prayer,* or *do something better for you;* He knows what is for your best good "

Trust in the Lord.

"A pious woman, who was reduced to extreme poverty and deserted by her intemperate husband, was taken sick, and lay several days without physical power to provide food for her two little children. She had directed them where to find the little that was remaining in the house, and they had eaten it all. Still she lay sick, with no means of obtaining more, as night closed upon the hungry household. The children soon forgot their hunger in sleep; but not so the mother. She saw no help for them but in God, and she spent the night-watches in spreading before him their necessities. As the morning approached her confidence in God increased, and that passage from his word rested with peculiar sweetness upon her mind, 'Trust in the Lord and do good; so shalt thou dwell in the land, and *verily thou shalt be fed.*'

" Morning came. The starving children managed by her

direction to build them a little fire, and almost before they
had commenced telling their mother of their hunger, a stranger came in. She introduced herself as Mrs. J., saying she
had known for some time that there was a new family in the
neighborhood, and intended to call and make their acquaintance, but had been prevented *During the last night she
had been so troubled and disturbed about it*, that she thought
she would run in early, lest she should again be prevented,
and see if there was any way in which she could be of service
to them. The mother in bed, with her head bound to mitigate
its pain, revealed the story of her sufferings, and the good
lady soon learned their entire destitution. They were immediately made comfortable ; and all will be glad to know
that it was the beginning of better days to that deserted wife
and mother."

The Necessity of Asking God's Blessing Every Day, upon Your Daily Work. Every Work, however Good, Needs Special, Specific, Daily Prayer for its Prosperity.

"A colporteur in the Wabash valley became quite discouraged and was almost ready to give up his work, on account of
the smallness of his sales. On every side, his ears were filled
with complaints of 'hard times ;' the wheat crop had partially failed two years in succession—the California emigra-
tion, and railroad and plank-road speculations had almost
drained the country of money. Frequently he would be
told, that if he could come after harvest they would buy his
books, but that it was impossible to do so then. His sales
were daily decreasing, and he became more and more disheart-
ened, until one night, after a laborious day's effort, he found
that he had *only sold twenty-five cents' worth '* He felt that
he could not go on in this way any longer. He was wasting
his strength and time, and the money of the Society. On

examination of the state of his heart, he found that it had, gradually and almost unconsciously, grown cold and departed far from Christ. He felt that he had not prayed as he ought to have done, especially *he had neglected each morning, and on his approach to each dwelling, to pray that then and there God would guide him, and own and bless his efforts to sell books.* He saw that probably here was at least a part of the cause why his sales had become so small. Early the next morning, before any of the family were up, he arose and retired to the adjoining woods, where he had a long and precious season of communion with God. There he anew dedicated himself and his all to the service of Christ. There, as under the eye of the Master, he reviewed the time he had labored as a colporteur, and prayed for forgiveness for the past and grace for the future. There he told the Saviour all about his work, and asked him to go with him that day, preparing the way and enabling him to succeed in the work on which he had entered. The result was what might have been expected. He went forth a new man; his heart was interested more deeply in the truths which he was circulating—they were more precious than ever to his own soul, and he could recommend his books, as he failed to do when his heart was cold and prayerless. *That first day he sold more books than during the whole week before.* In one instance, he sold several dollars' worth in a family where, as he was afterwards told by pious men in the neighborhood, the father was most bitterly opposed to everything connected with true religion. God had prepared that man's heart, so that he was ready to purchase quite a library for his family. And in many families that met him that day with the usual salutation, 'no money,' he succeeded in disposing of more than one volume by sale. As he went from family to family, lifting up his heart in prayer to God for success in the particular object of his visit, God heard his prayers and owned his efforts. And so, he assured me, it had been since; whenever he had been *prayerful— prayerful for this particular object,* and then had diligently and faithfully done his best, he had invariably succeeded in doing even more than he expected."

Prayer found the Remedy for the Disease.

"A correspondent of *The Illustrated Christian Weekly,* states that a mother of her acquaintance had a child taken alarmingly ill. She sent for the physician. The child was in convulsions. The doctor began at once vigorously to apply the customary remedies—cold water to the head, warm applications to the feet, chafing of the hands and limbs. All was in vain. The body lost nothing of its dreadful rigidity. Death seemed close at hand, and absolutely inevitable. At length he left the child, and sat down by the window, looking out. He seemed, to the agonized mother, to have abandoned her darling. For herself, she could do nothing but pray; and even her prayer was but an inarticulate and unvoiced cry for help *Suddenly the physician started from his seat. 'Send and see if there be any jimson weed in the yard,'* he cried. His order was obeyed; the poisonous weed was found. The remedies were instantly changed. Enough of the seeds of this deadly weed were brought away by the medicine to have killed a man. The physician subsequently said that he thought that in that five minutes every kindred case he had ever known in a quarter century's practice passed before his mind Among them was the one case which suggested the real, but before hidden, cause of the protracted and dreadful convulsions. And the child was saved.

"Now, is there anything inconsistent or unphilosophical in the belief that. at that critical moment, a loving God, answering the mother's helpless cry, flashed on the mind of the physician the thought that saved the child? Is it any objection to that faith to say, the age of miracles is past? If the mother may call in a second physician, to suggest the cause and the cure, may she not call on God? What the doctor can do for a fellow-practitioner, cannot the Great Physician do? Though the doctor had often tried and thought, yet it was not till the last prayer and call on God, brought the remedy to his mind."

Prayer Instantaneously Answered for Conversion.

On the evening of the 'fifty-first daily prayer-meeting in Augusta, Ga., a large gathering assembled in the St. John's M. E. Church, at which Dr. Irvine presided, and some very touching communications were read. One was from a widowed mother, asking thanksgiving for the salvation of her youngest daughter, recently from a boarding-school in New York city, where she had finished her education. Some weeks ago she had sought the prayers of the daily prayer-meeting for the conversion of her precious child, who was spending a few weeks with some friends seventy miles from Augusta. Prayers were offered accordingly, but without intimation of any change. The loving mother sent in a second application or prayer to Dr. Irvine, to be read on a recent Monday morning; all this without her daughter's knowledge. On Tuesday the mother received a letter from her daughter, dated two o'clock on Sabbath, informing her that on that day, and at that hour, she had resolved to give her heart to Christ, intending to ask admission to the church at the next communion. Strange to say, at the very moment when the faithful mother was writing her application for prayers for that child, she was announcing her own conversion.

What a verification of the blessed promise: "Before they call I will answer; and while they are yet speaking I will hear."

Help for the Shipwrecked.

Admiral Sir Thomas Williams, a straight-forward and excellent man, was in command of a ship crossing the Atlantic Ocean. His course brought him in sight of the Island of

Ascension, at that time uninhabited, and *never visited by any ship*, except for the purpose of collecting turtles, which abound on the coast. The island was barely descried on the horizon, and was not to be noticed at all; but as Sir Thomas looked at it, he was *seized by an unaccountable desire to steer toward it.*

He felt how strange such a wish would appear to his crew, and *tried to disregard it; but in vain.* His desire became more and more urgent and distressing, and foreseeing that it would soon be more difficult to gratify it, he told his lieutenant to prepare to "*put about ship*" and steer for Ascension *The officer to whom he spoke ventured to respectfully represent that changing their course would greatly delay them*—that just at that moment the men were going to their dinner—that at least some delay might be allowed.

But these arguments seemed to increase Captain Williams' anxiety, and the ship was steered toward the uninteresting little island All eyes and spy-glasses were now fixed upon it, and soon something was perceived on the shore. "It is white—it is a flag—it must be a signal!" And when they neared the shore, it was ascertained that sixteen men, wrecked on the coast many days before, and suffering the extremity of hunger, had set up a signal, though almost without hope of relief. What made the captain steer his ship in the very opposite direction to what he and his crew wanted to go, but the *superhuman Spirit of God.*

Samuel Harris's Lawsuit, and How the Lord Settled it for Him.

"When Samuel Harris, of Virginia, began to preach, his soul was so absorbed in the work, that he neglected to attend to the duties of this life. Finding, upon a time, that it was absolutely necessary that he should provide more grain for his family than he had raised upon his own farm, he called upon a man who owed him a debt, and told him he would be glad to receive the money.

"The man replied . 'I have no money by me, and cannot oblige you.'

"Harris said: 'I want the money to purchase wheat for my family; and as you have raised a good crop of wheat, I will take that of you instead of money, at a current price.'

"The man answered· 'I have other uses for my wheat, and cannot let you have it'

" 'How then,' said Harris, 'do you intend to pay me ?'

" 'I never intend to pay you until you sue me,' replied the debtor, 'and therefore you may begin your suit as soon as you please.'

"Mr. Harris left him, meditating. Said he to himself, 'What shall I do ? Must I leave preaching, and attend to a vexatious lawsuit ? Perhaps a thousand souls may perish in the meantime, for want of hearing of Jesus ! No; I will not. Well, what will you do for yourself ? Why, this will I do: I will sue him at the Court of Heaven.' Having resolved what he would do, he turned aside into a wood, and on his knees laid the matter before the Lord. Mr. Harris felt such an evidence of Divine favor,—he felt, to use his own express-ive language, that Jesus would become bondsman for the man, and see that he was paid if he went on preaching. Mr. Harris arose from prayer, resolved to hold the man no longer a debtor, since Jesus had assumed the payment. He there-fore wrote a receipt in full of all accounts against the man, and dating it in the woods, where he had prayed, signed it with his own name. Going the next day by the man's house, on his way to meeting, he gave the receipt to a servant, directing him to give it to his master. On his return from meeting, the man hailed him, and demanded what he meant by the receipt he had sent him in the morning.

"Mr Harris replied 'I mean just as I wrote.'

" 'But you know, sir,' answered the debtor, 'I have never paid you'

" 'True,' said Mr. Harris, 'and I know you said that you never would unless I sued you. But, sir, I sued you at the

Court of Heaven, and Jesus entered bail for you, and has agreed to pay me; I have therefore given you a discharge!'

"'But I insist upon it,' said the man; 'matters shall not be left so.'

"'I am well satisfied,' answered Harris. 'Jesus will not fail me. I leave you to settle the account with him at another day. Farewell.'

"This operated so effectually on the man's conscience, that in a few days he *came and paid the debt.*"

A Wagon-Load of Food.

"A young minister and his wife were sent on to their first charge in Vermont about the year 1846. On the circuit were few members, and most of these were in poor circumstances. After a few months the minister and his wife found themselves getting short of provisions. Finally their last food had been cooked, and where to look for a new supply was a question which demanded immediate attention.

"The morning meal was eaten, not without anxious feelings; but this young servant of the Most High had laid his all upon the altar, and his wife also possessed much of the spirit of self-sacrifice; and they could not think the Saviour who had said to those he had called and sent out to preach in his name · 'Lo! I am with you alway,' would desert them among strangers. After uniting in family prayer he sought a sanctuary in an old barn, and there committed their case to God ;—his wife met her Savior in her closet and poured out her heart before him there

"That morning a young married farmer, a mile or two away, was going with a number of hands to his mowing-field. But as he afterward told the minister, he was obliged to stop short. He told his hired help to go on, but he *must go back —he must go and carry provisions to the minister's house.* He returned to the house, and telling his wife how he felt, asked her help in putting up the things he must carry. He

harnessed his horse into his wagon ; put up a bushel of potatoes, meat, flour, sugar, butter, etc. He was not a professor
of religion. The minister's wife told me there was a good
wagon-load. He drove it to the house, and found that his
gifts were most thankfully received. This account was received from the minister himself,—David P.—, who died in
Chelsea, Mass , in Dec. 1875,—and subsequently from his
wife,—and communicated to a correspondent of *The Christian.*'"

"God's Raven."

"A lady who lived on the north side of London, set out
one day to see a poor sick friend, living in Drury Lane, and
took with her a basket provided with tea, butter, and food.
The day was fine and clear when she started : but as she
drew near Islington a thick fog came on, and somewhat
frightened her, as she was deaf, and feared it might be
dangerous in the streets if she could not see. Thicker and
darker the fog became ; they lighted the lamps, and the omnibus went at a walking pace. She might have got into another omnibus and returned ; but a strong feeling which she
could not explain made her go on. When they reached the
Strand they could see nothing. At last the omnibus stopped,
and the conductor guided her to the foot-path. As she was
groping her way along, the fog cleared up, just at the entrance to Drury Lane, and even the blue sky was seen. She
now easily found the narrow court, rang the number 5 bell,
and climbed to the fifth story. She knocked at the door, and
a little girl opened it.

"'How is grandmother ? '

"'Come in, Mrs. A——,' answered the grandmother.
'How did you get here ? We have been in thick darkness
all day.'

"The room was exceedingly neat, and the kettle stood
boiling on a small clear fire. Everything was in perfect
order ; on the table stood a little tea-tray ready for use. The

7

sick woman was in bed, and her daughter sat working in a corner of the room.

" 'I see you are ready for tea,' said the lady; 'I have brought something more to place upon the table.'

" With clasped hands the woman breathed a few words of thanksgiving first, and then said, ' O, Mrs. A——, you are indeed God's raven, sent by him to bring us food to-day, for we have not tasted any yet. I felt sure he would care for us.'

" ' But you have the kettle ready for tea ? '

" ' Yes, ma'am,' said the daughter; ' mother would have me set it on the fire ; and when I said, ' What is the use of doing so ? you know we have nothing in the house,' she still would have it, and said, ' My child, God will provide. Thirty years he has already provided for me, through all my pain and helplessness, and he will not leave me to starve at last : he will send us help, though we do not yet see how.' In this expectation mother has been waiting all day, quite sure that some one would come and supply our need. But we did not think of the possibility of your coming from such a distance on such a day. Indeed, it must be God who sent you to us.'

" ' The righteous cry, and the Lord heareth, and delivereth them out of all their troubles.' "

How the Stolen Sleigh was Returned by a Thief.

The widow of a minister of the Gospel sends to " *The Christian* " the following instance illustrating God's faithfulness in hearing and answering prayer:

" About the year 1829, my husband, who died January 2d, 1854, lent his sleigh and harness to a man calling himself John Cotton, to go some twenty miles and be gone three days. Cotton was quite a stranger among us, having been in our place but six weeks. During that time he had boarded with my husband's brother, working for him a part of the time, and the rest of the time selling wooden clocks, of which he had bought a number. Three days passed, but he did not return. The fourth went by, and we began to think he had absconded. On inquiry, Mr. P. found that the clocks had been purchased on credit, and all sold for watches or money; that Cotton owed sixty dollars toward his horse, and had borrowed of the brother with whom he boarded, horse-blanket, whip, and mittens. Now it seemed sure that he was a rogue, but what could be done? Pursuit was useless after such a lapse of time.

"My husband felt his loss severely, for we had little property then, and what we had was the product of hard labor. But he was a Christian, and, I believe, always made his business a subject of prayer.

"About three weeks passed away. One evening, having been out longer than usual, he came in, and, with his characteristic calmness, said: 'I shall not worry any more about my sleigh and harness, I think I shall get them again.' 'Why do you think so?' His answer was: 'I have been praying to God to arrest Cotton's conscience, so that he will be obliged to *leave them where I can get them,* and I believe he will do it.'

"From this time, which was Wednesday evening, he seemed at rest on the subject. The next Tuesday morning, as he stepped into the post-office, a letter was handed him from Littleton, N. H. It was written by the keeper of a public house, and read thus:

"'*Mr. P.—Sir, Mr. John Cotton has left your sleigh and harness here, and you can have them by calling for them.*
Yours, etc.,   J—N N——N.'

"He returned home with the letter, and started for L——; went there the same day, some forty miles; found sleigh and harness safe, with no encumbrance. The landlord informed him that, a few nights before, at twelve o'clock, a man calling himself John Cotton came to his house, calling for horse-bait-

ing and supper; would not stay till morning, but wished to
leave the sleigh and harness for Mr. S.— P.— of Marshfield,
Vt.   He said he could not write himself; and requested the
landlord to write for him, saying he took them on a poor debt
for Mr. P., in one of the towns below! He started off at two
o'clock at night, on horseback, with an old pair of saddle-bags
and a horse blanket, on a saddle with one stirrup and no crup-
per, on one of the coldest nights of that or any other year.
He took the road leading through the Notch in the mountains, left nothing for either of those he owed, and we have
never since heard from him."

"None of the Lord's Children Left Deso-
late."

" *The Christian Era* tells of a Dutch preacher who held a
meeting one evening in a strange city.   While he was preaching, and enforcing upon the hearts of his hearers the doctrine
of the Cross, a police officer came into the room and forbade
him to go on.   He even commanded him to leave the city.
As he was a stranger in the place, and the night was dark, he
wandered around the city gates.   He was not, however, without consolation; for he remembered Him who had said, ' Lo,
I am with you always.   I will fear no evil, for thou art with
me; thy rod and thy staff, they comfort me.'

" He had long been in the school of Christ, and had learned
to watch for the slightest intimations of His will.   While he
was thus wandering around, suddenly he saw a light in the
distance.   'See,' he said to himself, 'perhaps the Lord has
provided me a shelter there,' and, in the simplicity of faith,
he directed his steps thither.   On arriving, he heard a voice
in the house; and, as he drew nearer, he discovered that a
man was praying.   Joyful, he hoped that he had found here
the home of a brother.   He stood still for a moment, and
heard these words, poured forth from an earnest heart: 'Lord
Jesus, one of thy persecuted servants may, perhaps, be wan-

dering, at this moment, in a strange place of which he knows nothing. O, may he find my home, that he may receive here food and lodging'

"The preacher, having heard these words, glided into the house, as soon as the speaker said, 'Amen' Both fell on their knees, and together thanked the Lord, who is a hearer of prayer, and who never leaves nor forsakes His servants."

The New Coat that Fitted Exactly.

"A few years since, a young preacher in the State of Massachusetts, who was laboring in a field which yielded no great pecuniary returns, had laid aside the sum of fifteen dollars from his scanty income, with which to purchase himself a coat, of which he stood in need. Before he had time to obtain it, there was presented to him a certain charitable object which seemed to demand a portion of his little store. After some consideration as to whether it was his duty to give as much as the ten dollars, which first presented itself to his mind as the proper sum to bestow, he concluded to follow his convictions, and thus assist one who was more needy than himself, and trust in the Lord to provide the coat.

"Within two or three days afterwards, he was visiting at the house of his mother, in another town, and she, as mothers will, noticed that his coat had arrived at that condition which usually affords the preacher of the Gospel evidence that he is shortly to have a new one, and she made some remarks about its worn appearance, saying, 'It seems to me you need a new coat.' 'I know it,' he replied, 'and I shall get me one as soon as I get the means.' She said, 'There is a coat up stairs which your brother had made for him not over two weeks ago, which he never has worn but once, because it was *made too small*, and he said that you might have it, if you wanted it.'

'The coat was accordingly brought down and tried on, and it fitted exactly. The young man gladly accepted the coat, wondering a little at the wisdom of the Lord in clothing him at the expense of his brother, who was not particularly interested in the Lord's work, and who was so much larger than he was, that nothing short of the wisdom of Providence could have made a coat that was measured for one of them ever to fit the other."

This was the return that God made to him for his sacrifice to the Lord. *Never withhold from the Lord.*

Praying to Stop the Wind and the Sailing of a Vessel.

The late aged and venerable Rev. Dr. Cleaveland, of Boston, relates the following incident:

"In a revival of religion in the church of which he was pastor, he was visited one morning by a member of his church, a widow, whose only son was a sailor. With a voice trembling with emotion, she said, 'Doctor Cleaveland, I have called to entreat you to join me in praying *that the wind may change.*' He looked at her in silent amazement. 'Yes,' she exclaimed, earnestly, 'my son has gone on board his vessel; they sail to-night, unless the wind changes.' 'Well, madam,' replied the doctor, 'I will pray that your son may be converted on this voyage; but to pray that God would alter the laws of His universe on his account, I fear is presumptous.' 'Doctor,' she replied, 'my heart tells me differently. God's Spirit is *here.* Souls are being converted here You have a meeting this evening, and, if the wind would change, John would stay and go to it; and, I believe, if he went he would be converted. Now, if you cannot join me, I must pray alone, for he must stay.' 'I will pray for his conversion,' said the doctor.

"On his way to the meeting, he glanced at the weather-vane, and, to his surprise, *the wind had changed,* and it was blowing landward. On entering his crowded vestry, he soon observed John, sitting upon the front seat. The young man seemed to drink in every word, rose to be prayed for, and attended the inquiry meeting When he sailed from port, the mother's prayers had been answered; he went a Christian. The pastor had learned a lesson he never forgot. The Lord had said, ' O, woman, great is thy faith; be it unto thee, even as thou wilt.' God answered that prayer because the mother was seeking to advance His own kingdom. God always hears a prayer that will in any way bring a soul to the Lord."

Insanity Cured and Suicide Prevented.

"*Augusta Moore*, writes *The Christian*, of a young lady called home by the illness of her widowed mother, who died before she could reach her. This alone was a terrible shock to the delicate daughter, who, having been reared in luxury, was ill-fitted for firm endurance of calamity. But, when it became known that a relative, in whom she had placed confidence, had managed, in ways that need not be explained, to defraud her out of her inheritance, her mind gave way and *she became insane*.

"For years, her distressed husband strove in every way to restore her reason, but she seemed rather to become worse, and showed signs of intentions to commit suicide; and her family and friends lived in a wretched state of apprehension. In spite of the most faithful watchfulness, she twice succeeded in securing the means for self-destruction, but something prevented her from accomplishing her design. At last, it occurred to a friend to present this woman's case in the prayer-meeting, to the Lord, and earnest prayer was offered for her restoration.

"No immediate result appeared ; but the friends *persevered*. During the Winter, a revival of religion occurred in the town where she dwelt, and, with much difficulty, the insane woman, who declared that she was utterly and finally forsaken by God, was prevailed upon to attend the meetings. They began

immediately to have a good effect upon her. She could sleep
better; she grew more cheerful, and, in a short time, her reason returned to her. A happier, or more grateful woman than
she now is, no mortal eyes ever beheld, and she affords one
more instance of the Lord's willingness to hear and answer
fervent prayer."

Answers to Prayer.

Dr. Newman Hall, minister of Surrey Chapel, London,
gives the following instances of answers to prayer from his
own experience :

"The writer's brother, when superintendent of a Sunday
School, felt a strong impulse, one Saturday evening, to call
on a member of his Bible-class, whom he had never visited
before, and to inquire if he was in any need. He found him
very ill. Though the mother and sister seemed in comfortable circumstances, he felt constrained to inquire if he could
aid them in any way. They burst into tears, and said that
the young man had been asking for food which they had no
power to supply, and that, on Monday, some of their goods
were to be taken in default of the payment of rates. When
he knocked at the door *they were on their knees in prayer for
help to be sent them.* By the aid of a few friends, the difficulty was at once met—but the timely succor was felt to be
the divine response to prayer.

" With that brother, the writer was once climbing the Cima
di Jazzi, one of the mountains in the chain of Monte Rosa.
When nearly at the top, they entered a dense fog. Presently,
the guides faced right about, and grounded their axes on the
frozen snow-slope. The brother—seeing the slope still beyond,
and not knowing it was merely the cornice, overhanging a
precipice of several thousand feet — rushed onward. The
writer will never forget their cry of agonized warning. His
brother stood a moment on the very summit, and then, the
snow yielding, began to fall through. One of the guides, at

great risk, rushed after him and seized him by the coat. This tore away, leaving only three inches of cloth, by which he was dragged back. It seemed impossible to be nearer death, and yet escape. On his return home, an invalid member of his congregation told him that she had been much in prayer for his safety, and mentioned a special time when she particularly was earnest, as if imploring deliverance from some great peril. *The times corresponded!* Was not that prayer instrumental in preserving that life?"

Bishop Simpson's Recovery.

Bishop Bowman gives the following instance from his own experience :

"In the Fall of 1858, whilst visiting Indiana, I was at an annual conference where Bishop Janes presided. We received a telegram that Bishop Simpson was dying. Said Bishop Janes, 'Let us spend a few moments in earnest prayer for the recovery of Bishop Simpson.' We kneeled to pray. William Taylor, the great California street preacher, was called to pray, and such a prayer I never heard since. The impression seized upon me irresistibly, *Bishop Simpson will not die.* I rose from my knees perfectly quiet. Said I, 'Bishop Simpson will not die.' 'Why do you think so?' Because I have had an *irresistible impression* made upon my mind during this prayer' Another said. '*I have the same impression.*' We passed it along from bench to bench, until we found that a very large proportion of the conference had the same impression. I made a minute of the time of day, and when I next saw Simpson, he was attending to his daily labor. I inquired of the Bishop, 'How did you recover from your sickness?' He replied, '*I cannot tell.*' 'What did your physician say?' '*He said it was a miracle.*' I then said to the Bishop, 'Give me the time and circumstances under which the change occurred' He fixed upon the day, and *the very hour,* making allowance for the distance—a thousand miles away—that the preachers were engaged in prayer at this conference. The physician left his room and said to his wife, '*It is useless to do anything further, the Bishop must die.*' In about an hour, he returned and started back, inquiring, '*What have you done?*' '*Nothing,*' was the reply. 'He is recovering rapidly,' said the physician; '*a change has occurred in the disease within the last hour beyond anything I have ever seen; the crisis is past, and the Bishop will recover.*' And he did."

The doctor was puzzled; it was beyond all the course and probabilities of nature and the laws of science. What was it that made those ministers so sure—what was it that made the patient recover, at the exact hour that they prayed? There is only one answer, "*The ever living Power of a Superior Spirit which rules the world.*"

The Seven Letters.

The following incident is given by "*The Presbyterian,*" on the authority of a private letter from Paris:

"At a Bible reunion, held at the house of an English Congregationalist minister, where several colporteurs, teachers and others meet for devotional reading and conversation, a brief anecdote was related by a clergyman living in La Force, who established there an institution for epileptics, where he has now three hundred, supported entirely on the principle of faith, like Muller's orphanage.

"At one time, he found himself in debt to the amount of five hundred pounds. After a sleepless, anxious night, he found, on his table, seven letters. Opening five, he found them to be all applications, some of them most painful in their details, for the admission of new inmates. His excited mind could not bear it. Without opening the other two letters he threw them to his wife. 'Put them into the fire,' he said, and turned to seek relief in the open air. 'John,' said a sweet voice, 'this won't do. Come back.' So he did, taking up the sixth letter, which proved to be from a stranger, enclosing a check for three hundred pounds. The other envelope gave him just what was needed, just that and no more. He thanked God, and took courage. Will he ever again hear the sweet, sad voice, 'Wherefore didst thou doubt?'"

The Lord Did Not Forget the Potatoes.

"A correspondent of *Arthur's Magazine* tells of a poor woman who had been washing for us, who said: 'Seems as if the Lord took very direct ways to reach people's feelings sometimes. Now, I was astonished once in my life. I lived away out West, on the prairie, I and my four children, and I couldn t get much work to do, and our little stock of provisions kept getting lower and lower. One night, we sat hovering over our fire, and I was gloomy enough. There was about a pint of corn-meal in the house, and that was all. I said, 'Well, children, may be the Lord will provide something.' '*I do hope it will be a good mess of potatoes,*' said cheery little Nell; 'seems to me *I never was so hungry for 'taters before.*' After they were all asleep, I lay there tossing over my hard bed, and wondering what I would do next. All at once, the sweetest peace and rest came over me, and I sank into such a good sleep. Next morning, I was planning that I would make the tinfull of meal into mush, and fry it in a greasy frying-pan, in which our last meat had been fried. As I opened the door to go down to the brook to wash, I saw something new. *There, on the bench, beside the door, stood two wooden pails and a sack. One pail was full of meat, the other full of potatoes, and the sack filled with flour.* I brought my hands together in my joy, and just hurrahed for the children to come. Little dears! They didn't think of trousers and frocks then, but came out all of a flutter, like a flock of quails. Their joy was supreme. They knew the Lord had sent some of his angels with the sack and pails. Oh, it was such a precious gift! *I washed the empty pails, and put the empty sack in one of them, and, at night, I stood them on the bench where I had found them, and, the next morning, they were gone.* I tried and tried to find out who had befriended us, but I never could. The Lord never seemed so far off after that time,' said the poor woman, looking down with tearful eyes."

The Prayer in the Woods.

A friend relates the following incident, as received from the lips of a poor afflicted, crippled orphan boy, whose own experience is a practical illustration of the words: " When my father and my mother forsake me, then the Lord will take me up." Ps. xxvii 10.

" Out of many instances of answered prayer I will tell the following one : In August, 1874, I wished to go to Lowell, a distance of some thirty miles, or more. I had no money, and did not know how to get there. I asked the station-agent and the conductor, but each refused, saying it would not be consistent with their duty. Knowing of no human help, I left the depot and went into the woods, some ways from the station, where I could be alone, and tell that Friend who is able to provide, and who is rich unto all that call upon Him. I knelt down beside the stump of a tree and prayed, and told the Lord all about it, and asked Him either to give me money, or provide some way that I could go where I desired. I felt that the Lord heard and answered me, and filled my soul with praise and joy. The language of my heart was, 'Bless the Lord.'

" As I turned and was going out of the woods, I heard a voice saying, ' Halloo.' As I had seen no one, and knew not that any human being was near, I was surprised at this greeting. ' Halloo!' said the stranger, ' I never heard such a prayer in my life. Why did you go and pray ?' I told him that I felt heavy, burdened, and I took the burden to the Lord He said, 'I heard you pray—you want money, do you ?   The

Lord has opened the way; here is five dollars. It is the best way to go to the Lord, and trust Him to open the way. Go. and use the money.' I thanked him, and I thanked the Lord, and went on my way rejoicing in Him whose promise is, 'My God shall supply all your needs,' and who himself had heard and answered my request."

The Lord Can Do It.

"In one of the mountainous towns—says *The Christian*—in the north-western part of Connecticut, there lived, some time since, an aged couple who had seen some eighty years of earthly pilgrimage, and who, in their declining days, enjoyed the care of a son and daughter, who resided with them at their home.

"In process of time, the son became sick, and drew nigh the gates of death. The doctor pronounced him incurable, saying that one lung was consumed, and that he could live but a short time.

"The fear of her brother's death, and the thoughts of being left alone to bear the responsibility of the aged parents' care, burdened the sister's heart exceedingly, and led her to cry mightily to the Lord to interpose for his recovery, and spare him still to them; and her importunate supplications ascended to God, until the answer came to her heart as a sacred whisper,—'I have heard thy cry, and have come down to deliver thee.'

"Comforted by this sweet assurance, she rejoiced exceedingly, knowing that what our Heavenly Father promises he is abundantly able to perform, and that He will fulfill his word, though heaven and earth shall pass away. But her faith was destined to be tried, and, on the very day after she had obtained the assurance of her brother's recovery, in came some one, saying, 'The doctor says S—— can live but a little time.' For an instant, these words were like a dagger to the sister's heart, but she still held fast her confidence, and replied : ' If *men* can't cure him, the *Lord* can.'

"From that very moment, the brother began to amend. On the next day, when the physician came, he looked at him, commenced examining his symptoms, and exclaimed in astonishment : 'What have you been doing? You are evidently better, and I don't know but you will get up, after all.'

"His recovery was so rapid, that in two weeks' time he was out about his customary duties on the farm ; and that in weather so damp and foggy that it would have kept some stronger men in-doors. But he was well ; the prayer of faith was answered, and it had saved the sick."

Answer to Prayer in all the Little Temporal Anxieties of Life

The question having been asked, "Does God answer Prayer, in even all the little anxieties and cares of daily life." *The Illustrated Christian Weekly*, called in 1876, for testimonies of the surety of God in fulfilling his promise, and giving answer in little things as well as great things Many, even good Christians have believed that they should not pray for anything for themselves, but only for those things which were to be used for God's work. The following instances show that those who are devoted to God's good work and helping in his service can ask for anything needed for their personal comfort, and expect the Lord to grant them. In truth the Lord *has commanded* all his disciples, '*Ask and receive, that your joy may be full.*" "*Anything that ye shall ask in my name, I will do it.*"

BREAD TO THE HUNGRY.

"God was pleased to deprive me totally of my hearing in early boyhood. By the late war I lost all of my earthly possessions. I have a wife and family totally dependent on me for a support. A man employed to attend to my little manufacturing business as manager, by imprudent management, deprived me of every earthly dependence for a support. I had no refuge but God. This feeling was intense beyond expression—God was my only hope. I laid my case before him. Then this came to me, 'Seek first the kingdom of God and his righteousness, and all these things shall be added unto you.' 'Now,' I said, 'I am deeply conscious that I and my wife seek and desire the kingdom of God above all things; God then will give us temporal help.' Then a feeling came over me, a feeling of waiting upon God. It was sweet waiting. I was at rest. I had thought frequently if I could get *two hundred dollars* I could start my little business again. While thus trusting, and waiting, and praying, a package was handed to me by the express-agent containing $200 from a stranger in a distant county, against whom I held an old note dated 1856; and for many years I had forgotten the note, and would have taken twenty-five cents for it any time. The man was bankrupt, and did not fear the Lord, nor know anything of my situation in life. He was under no legal obligation to pay the note."

NO "IFS."

"A number of years ago I went West to better my condition. . . . After a little time I went into business of my own, had but little capital, and my good name to be punctual in paying for what I bought on credit was of great importance to me. I had promised to pay on a certain day a note of about $60. I thought I was sure to get the money, but was disappointed; I went to the Lord for help, not knowing how he could send me the money, but convinced that he was able to do it. At about noon the same day a man inquired for me I knew him by sight; he had the name of being a hard man, took all the interest he could get, and never put any money out without security. He had not the note, but he asked me if I wanted to hire any money; if so he had

sixty dollars he would like to let me have.   The man took
my note and never did ask for any security.

"At another time, being away from home some 2,000
miles, was at the house of an uncle ; same evening I received
a letter from my wife that the children were very sick and
but little hope of recovery.   The letter had been written for
over a week.   I communicated the contents of the letter to my
aunt ; went up in my room and prayed the Lord to be their
physician.   I felt so sure that my prayer would be answered
that I could not help singing ; when they heard me they
thought what a cold-hearted man I must be to sing if the
children were dying at home.   *But from that day the children did get better, and in a short time were out of danger.*

"In my younger years I had a good many ifs, but those
are all gone; I know that the Lord has the means at his command to answer all my prayers if I come believing, asking in
the name of Christ."

THE HORSE IS HIS.

"The writer was preaching Sundays at a little country
church, about 70 miles by rail from the institution where he
attended.   He went Saturday, returning on Monday   One
Saturday the train ran off the track.   All day long they
worked at the wreck.   At last, finding it too late to make
connection with the other railroad, he took the down train
back to the institution.   What should be done ?   A promise
to preach forty miles across the country had been made.
There was also an appointment six miles beyond for an afternoon service   It was now night.   To drive across the country
was the only way open or stay at home.   Two disappointed
congregations the result in the latter case.   But the roads
were heavy from recent rains.   'Twill be so late that none can
direct.   Friends said, 'Stay, you can't go forty miles across,
to you, an unknown country'   But the writer felt it duty to
go.   Hiring a horse noted for endurance, at nine o'clock at
night—dark, threatening—he set out.   As he headed the

horse in the direction of the village—for he could find none who could tell him the exact road—he prayed. 'O God, starting out to preach thy word to-morrow, direct the way— guide this horse.' The night wore on; as cross-roads came, dropping the lines over the dashboard, the same prayer was offered. When the horse chose a road, the driver urged him on. As day began to break, emerging from some wood in an unfrequented road, they entered the village they sought The sermon that morning was from the text, 'Son, go work to-day in my vineyard' The largest congregation of the Summer had gathered. It will not do to say that the horse knew the road. Returning in broad daylight the next day, though directed and directed again, we lost the way and went seven miles out of our course. A scientist might laugh at this way of driving, or at asking God to guide in such trival matters. But we shall still believe that God led the horse and blessed us in our attempt to serve him."

ALL OUR NEEDS.

"About eight years ago, while a student in college, I became embarrassed for want of funds. Debts began to accumulate. Anticipating money from usual sources, promises had been made to pay at a certain date.

"The time to make these payments approached. The anticipated money did not come. A student in debt is most dependent and hopeless. In great distress, locking the study-door, I sat down to think First came visions of an auction sale of a few books and scanty furniture; then of notes and protests; finally the promises of God came into mind. I knew he had promised to supply my wants. 'All things whatsoever ye have need of,' came home in great power I am needy, I have given up business, all, to preach the gospel. I remember as 'twere yesterday the feelings, the struggles, of that hour. With all earnestness I asked for help in my hour of distress. At last I felt confident that the aid needed would come in time, Saturday; this was Monday I thanked God

8

for the answer—and being questioned by a needy creditor of that afternoon, assured him that his money would be ready.

"Tuesday, Wednesday, Thursday passed—no sign, but faith said God will not fail. Friday morning—heart beat fast as I went to the post-office—it seemed as if through its agency the help would come. Nothing. But it must be here to-day. Returning from the office Friday evening, wondering how God would send deliverance, I saw on my table a long official envelope. A classmate preceding me at the office had brought it. A letter from a gentleman in Wall street whom I have never seen. On Monday, he casually asked of a tea-broker, an acquaintance, if he knew of any one in H——. The broker mentioned, after a little thought, my name.

"The letter contained a request for service of a peculiar sort, connected with some legal matters, contained money and promise of more. *Over three times the sum I asked God for was finally given. More than enough for a term's expenses.*

"I never mentioned the matter of my need at that time to a human being, nor spoke of the prayer. I have always thanked God for that, and am sure he provides for me in accordance with his promise."

HE HEALETH THE SICK.

"The wife of Deacon W. was sinking rapidly with pneumonia. Friends gave up all hope of her recovery, and even the hopeful physician felt that he was hoping against hope In his despair the husband bore the case directly to God; he sought the prayers of his minister and of the church; and he asked all Christians to pray that the mother of his little children might be spared. She lingered between life and death for several days, when unexpectedly to many, she began to gain strength, and in due season was about again This was several years ago, and she has been an active worker in the church and Sunday-school ever since."

A POWERFUL DREAM.

"My father, a minister of the gospel, was prostrated by sickness. A large family of little ones was dependent upon him for support Funds ran low. One evening my mother remarked that she had broken the last dollar My father lay awake most of the night, praying to his God for help in this emergency. That same night a man in a parish not many miles distant was much impressed by a dream He dreamed that a minister who preached in his church not long before, was sick and in want He knew neither his name nor his place of residence He arose at the first dawn of day, and going to his own pastor inquired the name and address of the stranger who had recently preached for them. These obtained, he mounted his horse, and knocked at our door just as my mother drew up the window-shades. She answered the knock, when, without a word, a stranger placed an envelope in her hand and immediately rode away. The envelope contained a ten-dollar bill, which we all believed was the Lord's answer to our father's prayer. Afterwards these facts were disclosed by the pastor to him whom the Lord chose to disperse his bounty "

ASK AND YE SHALL RECEIVE.

"In 1874, through Providence, I became sore pressed to provide for myself and family ; two of my children had just begun to learn to read I was desirous to procure for them the 'N.—,' (a children's journal,) but I could not see how I was to pay for it and meet other obligations. So I carried it to our Father in heaven, asking if it was best and according to his will my children should get the 'N.—.' In about ten days afterward I received a note from a lady friend, with whom I or none of our family had had any communication for weeks, and in that note she advised us that her little daughter, the same age as our second, had sent as a Christmas gift a subscription for the 'N.—,' to be sent to our

Mary's address. ' If ye abide in me, and my words in you, ye shall ask what ye will and it shall be done unto you. ' '

CASTING ALL YOUR CARE ON HIM.

" Once, soon after the death of my husband and the loss of all his large property, I had a bill of *fifty dollars* to pay, and was notified two weeks beforehand that not a day's grace would be given. Besides what I was earning by my pen, I had due me, in a neighboring city, just the amount I should need—the income on my only remaining piece of real estate ; and, as my tenant was always prompt, I wrote to him where to send me the money, and gave the subject no farther thought. But, when the time for his response was already past, and I heard nothing from my debts, and but a few days to the time of my own need yet remained, I felt anxious and sought divine direction as to the course I ought to pursue. Rising from my knees, I took up my Bible, and the very first words my eyes rested upon, were these : ' Casting all your care upon Him, for he careth for you.' All anxiety from that hour left me ; but I felt impelled to apply to a certain editor for the payment of *twenty dollars* he owed me, and I felt sure the other thirty would come from somewhere.

" So the days passed until the morning of the day upon which I should be called on for the fifty dollars, and *still I had not a single dollar* on hand to meet the claim. At ten o'clock my creditor came, but half an hour before him the postman had put into my hand a letter containing a check for *fifty dollars*, the exact amount I needed. It had come from the editor to whom I had applied for twenty dollars, and lo! he had sent me fifty. The thirty advanced he said I could give him credit for on my next MS. He did not know my need, but God did, and thus He had answered my prayer."

IN EVERYTHING MAKE KNOWN YOUR WANTS.

" Six years ago, on the low country of South Carolina, a friend asked me to go with him to a camp-meeting. I was delighted with the idea, for, in my estimation, a good camp-meeting comes nearer heaven than any other place on earth.

"Just three days before we were to go, an unexpected circumstance connected with his business, made it impossible for him to leave. It was with real heartfelt sorrow I heard of it. The day before we were to have started, as I saw another member of the family, who was going with a friend, packing her trunk, it seemed to me I could not bear it. I carried my trouble to my dear heavenly Father, begging him to send me a way to go.

"I rose from my knees with the sweet assurance in my heart my prayer was heard—packed my trunk and waited patiently. When night came and the men came home, in the place of the expected buggy came a small spring-wagon, and a seat for me. What may seem more remarkable, the change between buggy and spring-wagon was made ten miles away, while I was praying.

"I believe I enjoyed the meeting more for the feeling of thankfulness that pervaded my whole being while there."

THE GREAT PHYSICIAN.

"Nearly five years ago, after a decline of almost two years, I was brought very near to the grave. Medical aid availed nothing. I was fearfully emaciated, and my death was daily expected. A devoted mother and a sister, who had watched over me tenderly during my long illness, were completely exhausted.

"I determined to apply to the Great Physician, as directed in James 5.14. As I united with others in prayer, unconsciously I uttered these words, 'I shall yet praise Thee in the great congregation.' All present felt assured that it was the will of God to restore me to health. Appearances were against me; for some time I could sleep but very little, and there was no perceptible gain. But trusting in the sure promise, the next Sabbath I rode a short distance to church, and, as I thus ventured out little by little, my strength gradually returned. A few months later, my mother, who through disease had been in a state of despair for some years, was enabled again to hope in God's mercy."

SHALL SAVE THE SICK.

" I was desperately ill. My physicians had done all in their power, without success—and yet I lived! For my father's sake, the hearts of hundreds waited the issue, and prayed for me! For his sake, the bells in the neighborhood were tied—the criers did not come within sound of the house—nor was the sound of wheels heard upon the street.   There was a death-like stillness without and within.

"The physicians sat with folded hands and wept, because the blow seemed too heavy for my father to bear—the thought that I was going to die without any assurance that I trusted in my Saviour!

"'It cannot be,' he said, 'I will wrestle with my God until He hears me!' Sunday came. In almost every church a special prayer was offered for my recovery. After morning service, a band of devoted women met, and offered fervent prayers that God would spare my life. Evening came—the weary doctors went home, leaving the last sacred moments to my parents   Early next morning they came again, and exclaimed, as they entered the room, 'She is better! Prayer has saved her!' I still live, 'a spared monument of God's mercy.'"

ALL-SUFFICIENT FOR ALL NEED.

"I am a mother of seven children. By the help of our Father in heaven, we have all of us gone regularly to church and Sunday-school. We are poor; and at length the time came we were not clothed so we could comfortably go to church. I earnestly asked our Father to show me, within a week, which was right for us to do: to go in debt for clothes, or stay at home. Within that week, I received a large package of ready-made clothing. The clothing came from a source I never thought of receiving anything from."

A VERY PRESENT HELP IN TROUBLE.

"At one time, during a season of adversity, there was urgent occasion for a certain sum beyond the income of the family, and there was no way of borrowing it. I took the matter to the Lord in prayer, asking Him, if the money were really needed, as it appeared to be, to send it, and, if it were not, to remove the distressing circumstances. The answer came in a sum five times the amount asked for, and in a manner totally unexpected."

"At another time, the mother of the family was very ill, and, when apparently near death, the physicians had ordered a remedy which was to be constantly employed, as her life, so far as they could judge, depended on its use. · One night, her symptoms became so alarming as to compel the writer (who had charge of the nursing) to use this remedy more freely than ever, and, about midnight the supply was exhausted. There was no possibility of obtaining any more before morning, and the rest of that night, while attending to the other directions of the doctors, I spent in one earnest, agonizing prayer that God would so overrule natural causes that death would not occur in consequence of what I felt to be my own culpable carelessness in not having provided a larger quantity of an article so necessary. In His great mercy, He granted the prayer, the dangerous symptoms did not increase during the seven or eight hours that intervened before the remedy could be procured. One proof that it was a special mercy, is found in the fact that there was no other such standing still of the disease, either before this or afterward. And the doctors were astonished when they saw that the disease had made no progress, under conditions that rendered that progress inevitable in the usual law of cause and effect. And when, on her final recovery, Doctor Parker told her that she owed her life to the good care I had taken of her, my thoughts went back to the long hours of that night of anguish, and I said, 'It was the Lord that took care of her.' 'I meant your care, under Providence,' was the reply."

HE SHALL DIRECT THY PATHS

"I am a teacher by profession, and, a few years ago, I found myself placed in a school whose every surrounding was utterly repugnant to my tastes, and to all my ideas of right and wrong and what good teaching should be. At first, I kept hoping that things would grow better, and that I should, at least, be able to have some influence on the modes of teaching; but I soon found that everything connected with the establishment was directed by the iron will of an unscrupulous and tyrannical woman, whose laws were as irrevocable as those of the Medes and Persians. I at once decided I could not stay there long, but I had no other position in view, and it was not easy to secure one in the middle of the term. As usual, I made it a subject of prayer, and the result was that, in a short time, I was most unexpectedly, and without the least solicitation on my part, offered a much better position, in every respect, which, of course, I was only too thankful to accept. That is only one instance, out of thousands I could name, where God has heard and answered my prayers, and I believe He will do so to the end."

How the Lord is Constantly Caring for His Trusting Poor.

A city missionary recently found, in this city on the streets, a refined Englishwoman with her children, who had been turned out of her home for non-payment of rent. With the aid of a few friends he installed her in a new domicile, and procured work for her. From time to time he visited her, and rejoiced with her that God had sent him to her in the hour of extremity. At length, pressure of business kept him away for some time, until, one evening, he started out to look up a few dollars owing him, in order to procure some delicacies for a sick wife. One dollar was all he could procure, and with that in his pocket he was returning homeward, when he became so impressed with the idea that he should visit the English-woman that he turned aside and did so. He found her in tears, and asking the cause, heard the sorrowful tale of no work, no food in the house for to-morrow, which was Sunday. He was in doubt whether to give her the dollar and suffer his sick wife to go without something palatable, but in a moment, " Blessed is he that considereth the poor, the Lord will deliver him in time of trouble," presented itself to his mind, and— the dollar dried the widow's tears.

Upon reaching his home he found a lady had called on his wife and brought with her three or four kinds of jellies, fruit, home-made biscuit, various relishing things ; three times more than the dollar would have purchased.

The same gentleman, while calling on a poor family one day, discovered a little house in the rear, which he visited, finding a neat, cleanly room, occupied by an old lady, crippled with rheumatism. He found she had no one in the world but a sister, a monthly nurse, to care for her. When first setting out on his tour that morning, the missionary had fifty cents given him by a gentleman, who expressed the hope that "it might do some good during the day." Although a number of visits had been made, he had not felt called upon to bestow it until then, nor could he tell why he should want to put it in the old lady's hand at parting, but he did so.

She was too much overcome by her emotions to speak, but she took his hand and led him to a little table, on which lay a Bible, opened at the passage, " Whatsoever ye shall ask the Father in my name, He will give it you." She said, "Please tell me if any one sent you here ? " " No." " Did you ever hear that I lived here ? " " I did not " " Then the Lord sent you in answer to my prayer this morning For the first time in my life, I am without food. My sister was to have come home yesterday, but has not.   I was just asking the Lord to provide for me when you knocked at the door."

Such scenes as these amply repay our missionaries for all the toils and weariness, all the anxieties and perplexities of the work.

A Prayer for Bread.

"Washington Allston, who stood at the head of American artists a half century ago, was, at one time, so reduced by poverty, that he locked his studio, in London, one day, threw himself on his knees and prayed for a loaf of bread for himself and wife.   While thus engaged, a knock was heard at the door, which the artist hastened to open.   A stranger inquired for Mr. Allston, and was anxious to know who was the fortunate purchaser of the painting of the 'Angel Uriel,' which had won the prize at the exhibition of the Royal Academy.   He was told that it was not sold.   'Where is it to be found ?'   'In this very room,' said Allston, producing a painting from a corner and wiping off the dust.   'It is for sale, but its value has not been adequately appreciated, and I would not part with it.'   'What is its price ?'   'I have done affixing any nominal sum.   I have always so far exceeded any offers, I leave it to you to name the price.'   'Will four hundred pounds be an adequate recompense ?'   'It is more than I ever asked for it.'   'Then the painting is mine,' said the stranger, who introduced himself as the Marquis of Stafford, and, from that time, became one of Mr. Allston's warmest friends and patrons."

The Daughter's Prayer.

The late Doctor Krummacher, chaplain to the king of Prussia, in referring to faith and prayer, writes as follows:

"A little incident occurs to me which I can hardly withhold, on account of its simplicity and beauty.   The mother of a little girl, only four years of age, had been, for some time, most dangerously ill. The physician had given her up. When the little girl heard this, she went into an adjoining room, knelt down, and said : 'Dear Lord Jesus, O make my mother well again.'

"After she had thus prayed, she said, as though in God's name, with as deep a voice as she could . 'Yes, my dear child, I will do it gladly!' This was the little girl's amen. She rose up, joyfully ran to her mother's bed, and said : 'Mother, you will get well!'

"And she recovered, and is in health to this day. Is it, then, always permitted for me to pray thus unconditionally respecting temporal concerns ? No; thou must not venture to do so, if, whilst you ask, you doubt. But shouldst thou ever be inclined by God's Spirit to pray thus, without doubt or scruple, in a filial temper, and with simplicity of heart, resting on the true foundation, and in genuine faith, then pray thus by all means! None dare censure thee; God will accept thee."

The Lord Will Provide.

"A city missionary, one Saturday night, was going home with a basket of provisions on his arm. Meeting a policeman, he asked him if there had any families moved in the bounds of his beat during the week. He answered, 'Yes,' and, pointing to a building up an alley, said, 'a woman and some children are living there now.'

"The missionary went to the house, rapped at the door, and was admitted. The woman was sitting by a small light, sewing. In the corner of the room, were two little girls, apparently from nine to twelve years of age, playing.

"The missionary said, 'Madam, I am here to see if you will allow your girls to attend Sunday-school to-morrow morning.' 'I would, sir; but what you see on them is all the clothing they have, and you would not wish them to go as they are now.' 'The Lord will provide, madam. Have you no money?' 'Not yet, but I have committed my case into the hands of the Lord' 'Have you anything to eat?' 'Nothing, sir!' 'What will you do for breakfast?' 'O, sir, I once had a husband; he provided when he could. These children had a father; he supplied their wants; but he is dead now. Yet my Maker, even God, is my husband, and He has promised to be a father to the fatherless We have committed all to Him, have called upon Him in this our day of trouble. I am trusting in God to take care of a poor widow and her children in a strange place, and I know He will provide.' 'Thank God for such faith,' said the missionary; and, handing her the basket, said ' here is your breakfast, and you shall have the clothing for your children.' With tears streaming down her face, she replied. ' Oh, thank God for his faithfulness! He heareth and answereth prayer. May He bless you!' And, said our dear brother to us, ' I felt the promise was sure, for she was blessed in receiving, I was more so in giving.' "

A Prayer for a Load of Wood.

Here is an illustration of the way in which God sends relief in trouble. The story is told by the Christian woman to whom it happened, in her own language:

"About the month of January, 1863, I was living in Connecticut, alone with two little boys, one of them four years old, and the other about a year and a half old. My husband was away in the service of his country. When the coldest weather came, I was nearly out of wood I went down into the village, one day, to try and get some, but tried in vain; so many men were away in the army that help was scarce. Very little wood was brought into market, and those living on the main street, got all that came, while those who lived outside the village could get none I tried to buy a quarter of a cord from two or three merchants, but could not get any. One of them told me he could not get what he wanted for his own family. Another said he wasn't willing to yoke up his team for so small a quantity ; but, as I only had a dollar and seventy-five cents, I could not buy any more, and so I was obliged to go home without any. I went back to my little ones, feeling very sad. But while I sat there, almost ready to cry, the words of Abraham came into my mind, 'Jehovah-Jireh, the Lord will provide.' Then I went up to my chamber. There I knelt down and told God of my trouble, and asked him to help me and send the relief that we needed. Then I went to the window and waited, looking down the street, expecting to see the wood coming. After waiting a while, without seeing any come, my faith began to fail. I said to myself, 'The Lord did provide for Abraham, but He won't provide for me' Our last stick of wood was put in the stove. It was too cold to keep the children in the house without fire. I got the children's clothes out, and thought I would take them to the house of a kind neighbor, where I knew they could stay till we got some wood. But, just as I was going out with the children, in passing by the window, I saw the top of a great load of wood coming up the road towards our little house. Can that be for us ? I asked myself. Presently I saw the wagon turn off the road and come up towards our door. Then I was puzzled to know how to pay for it. A dollar and seventy-five cents I knew would only go a little way towards paying for all that wood. The oxen came slowly on, dragging the load to our door. I asked the man if there wasn't some mistake about it. 'No, ma'am,' said he, 'there's no mistake.' 'I did not order it, and I cannot pay for it,' was my reply. 'Never mind, ma'am,' said he, 'a friend ordered it, and it is all paid for' Then he unhitched the oxen from the wagon, and gave them some hay to eat When this was done, he asked for a saw and ax, and never stopped till the whole load was cut and split and piled away in the woodshed.

"This was more than I could stand My feelings overcame me, and I sat down and cried like a child. But these were not bitter tears of sorrow. They were tears of joy and gladness, of gratitude and thankfulness. I felt ashamed of myself for doubting God's word, and I prayed that I might never do so again. What pleasure I had in using that wood! Every stick of it, as I took it up, seemed to have a voice with which to say 'Jehovah-Jireh.' As Abraham stood on the top of Mount Moriah he could say, 'The Lord *will* provide.' But every day, as I went into our woodshed, I could point to that blessed pile of wood sent from heaven, and say, 'The Lord *does* provide.'"

"A Refractory Man Compelled to Pay a Debt.

A refractory man who owed a small debt of about $43, refused to pay it all, but offered to do so if ten dollars was taken off. His creditor, feeling that it was just, declined to abate the amount.

For more than a year the creditor waited, after having no attention paid to his correspondence or claim by the debtor, who exhibited unmistakable obstinacy and want of courtesy. At last it was put into the hands of a lawyer. The lawyer, too, was fairly provoked at the faithlessness of the debtor in his promises or his attention to the subject; thus matters dragged wearily for months, yet exercised leniency in pressing the claim.

The creditor, whose forbearance had now reached the extremity of endurance, at last was led to take it to the Lord in prayer; saying he would "willingly forgive the whole debt if in anything he was wrong, but if the Lord thought it was right, hoped that his debtor *might be compelled to pay the amount he so obstinately withheld.*"

To the astonishment of all, a letter received from the lawyer four days after, informed him *that his debtor had called and paid the claim in full* with interest to date. "In doing so, he said he paid it *under protest,*" thus showing he was *compelled by something he could not resist to pay it all.*

A Hurricane Passes Around a Ship.

A Sea Captain relates to the editor of the *Christian*, a remarkable incident, whereby in one of his voyages his ship was unaccountably held still, and thereby saved from sailing directly into the midst of a terrible hurricane —" We sailed from the Kennebec on the first of October, 1876. There had been several severe gales, and some of my friends thought it hardly safe to go, but after considerable prayer I concluded it was right to undertake the voyage. On the 19th of October we were about one hundred and fifty miles west of the Bahamas, and we encountered very disagreeable weather. *For five or six days we seemed held by shifting currents, or some unknown power, in about the same place. We would think we had sailed thirty or forty miles,* when on taking our observations we would find we *were within three or four miles of our position the day before.* This circumstance occurring repeatedly proved a trial to my faith, and I said within my heart, ' *Lord, why are we so hindered, and kept in this position ?'* Day after day we were held as if by an unseen force, until at length a change took place, and we went on our way. Reaching our port they inquired, ' Where have you been through the gale ? ' ' *What gale ?'* we asked. ' *We have seen no gale.'* We then learned that a terrible hurricane had swept through that region, and that all was desolation. We afterwards learned that *this hurricane had swept around us, and had almost formed a circle around the place occupied by us during the storm. A hundred miles in one direction all was wreck and ruin, fifty miles in the opposite direction all was desolation ; and while that storm was raging in all its fury, we were held in perfect safety, in quiet waters,* and in continual anxiety to change our position and pursue our voyage. *One day of ordinary sailing would have brought us into the track of the storm, and sent us to the bottom of the sea.* We were anxious to sail on, but some unseen power held us where we were, and we escaped."

The Captain was a prayerful man, trusting in his Lord, though his faith was tried, and he thought the Lord was not helping him.   Yet the Lord was keeping his promise to him, *" The beloved of the Lord shall dwell in safety by him, and the Lord shall cover him all the day long."*

Recovery from Spinal Disease.

"Miss M—— is the daughter of a respectable farmer, an elder in a Presbyterian church in Western Pennsylvania. When a young girl her spine was injured while nursing her aged and helpless grandmother, and she has been a great sufferer for many years.   For eleven years she has not been able to attend church nor to go from home, and for a long time was unable to leave her chamber or her bed.   Two years ago she was so ill that hopes of her recovery were abandoned, her mind was thought to be seriously, even hopelessly impaired.   Her physician acknowledged that her disease baffled his skill.

"A few months ago, being near her residence and hearing that her health was better, I called on her, and to my surprise, found her able to sew, walk about, and even go down stairs.   She informed me that she suffered so intensely from the remedies used for her cure, and constantly grew worse, that she determined to do nothing more, it seemed like fighting against God; she would put herself into His hands to do with her as He pleased   Then it seemed to her that the Saviour came to her and said, 'M——, what aileth thee?' She told Him all her case, and He soothed and comforted her. From that time she began to improve; the paroxysms of pain grew less, and disappeared; her nervousness was relieved, she could sleep, her mind was full of peace.   She said, 'I am not cured, and do not expect to be well, but I can bear what I have to suffer, and am willing to depart whenever it is the Lord's will to take me away to himself.'"

Prayer for a Pair of Boots.

In the Fall of 1858, H——, a student in the Theological Seminary at Princeton, N. J., was in great need of a new pair of boots. His toes were sticking out of his old ones, and he had no money to purchase new ones. All the money he could command was barely enough to pay his fare to his home, where he had promised a dear friend to be present on the approaching communion Sabbath.

H—— was a man of great faith, and was accustomed to carry all his wants to God in prayer. To God he carried the present emergency, and earnestly importuned Him, that He would send him a pair of boots, and that He would do it before the approaching Sabbath. He was persuaded that God heard, and would answer his petition, yet his faith was sorely tried. Saturday morning came and still there was no answer; he resolved, however, to go to his home, fully persuaded that God would in good time grant his request. He took the morning train at the Princeton depot, and reached home about eleven o'clock. It was a hard trial for him to go to "Preparatory Lecture" with his boots in the condition they were in; yet at two o'clock he went, still praying that God would send him a new pair of boots. During the service, a merchant in the town took a seat in the same pew with him, and at the close of the service, without a word being spoken on the subject, the merchant, after shaking hands with H—— and inquiring of his welfare, asked him if he would do him the favor of going down town to a certain boot and shoe store and select from the stock as good a pair of boots as he could find, and, said the merchant, "have them charged to me." It was, as H—— said to me on his return to the seminary, a direct answer to prayer. Indeed, it might be said of H—— that he went through college and seminary *on prayer*. He laid all his plans before God, pleaded his promises, and never was disappointed.

Under Garments in Answer to Prayer.

Among the students in the Theological Seminary at Princeton, N. J., in 1860, was my intimate friend L——. He was at the time poorly clad, but was a devoted Christian, and is at present a successful foreign missionary.

One day when on the Seminary campus, I heard two of the students very thoughtlessly criticising the exceeding shabbiness of L——'s wearing apparel, his short pants, old shoes, and socks with no heels in them   At almost every step L—— took when playing ball, his bare heels could be seen.   That day, after evening prayers, I took L—— by the arm, for a walk to "Orthodox point," a tree about a mile distant from the Seminary.   During our walk, I gently told him of the criticisms I had heard, and learned more fully than I had ever done of his destitution of wearing apparel, especially of under garments   I offered him a share of mine, or the loan of money, so as to meet his present wants, but this he declined to receive, saying, that he "would take it to the Lord in prayer," and that God would in good time supply all his wants.   I, too, bore his case to the throne of grace.   The next day after this, on going into his room, he laid before me an empty envelope, and a five dollar bill, and asked me the question, "Did you throw that envelope with that bill in it, through that ventilator?"   I assured him that I did not.   "Well," said he, "when I came in from recitation a short time ago, I found this envelope on the floor and that five dollar bill in it.   It has evidently been thrown in through the ventilator."   We both recognized God's hand in the provision made and mentally gave thanks to our Heavenly Father.   Soon after this, " a missionary box " was sent to the Seminary, and my friend was therefrom well supplied with under garments.   Frequently afterward did he say to me, in substance, " Prayer is the key to God's treasury.   Trust in Him and the Lord will provide."

Unexpected Relief.

Henry Badgerow was a man about seventy years of age at the time of the incident, and a resident of Steuben county, State of New York. This was in the year about A. D. 1830–31. He had been for many years an invalid—so much so that he couldn't walk—the result of a horse running away with him. In a forest, isolated from neighbors, the old man resided alone with an aged wife. They were quite poor, and wholly dependent upon the labor of a son who worked away from home for others. This son was at length taken sick with a fever, and unable to minister to his parents' wants. This was in mid-winter, when storms were frequent and the snows deep and lasting. One evening when the storm was at its highest, this old couple found themselves without a particle of food in the house. Matters were desperate with them. They could see but starvation staring them in the face They resolved upon prayer, having a firm trust in their Heavenly Father, whom for many years they had been humbly serving. They did not retire, but continued in fervent prayer that God would send them food. About two and a half miles distant lived a young married man in comfortable circumstances, by the name of Joseph Clason (the author of the story). He was not at this time a Christian, although it was not long after this he was converted, and has since lived an eminently active and godly life About 12 o'clock on the night of the snow storm above mentioned, young Clason awoke. His first thoughts were of old Mr Badgerow and his condition in that storm. His mind became so impressed with the thought of him, and so wrought upon that he could not again go to sleep, although trying so to do. At length he awakened his wife, told her that he was in trouble about Mr B., for fear he and his wife were starving. She replied that if he would get right up and make a light, she would prepare something, and that he had better take it right down. Young C. did so, taking with him a pail of provisions. After a jaunt through the storm and snow in the dead hour of night, he reached the old man's cabin. There he found a light burning. He knocked; the door was opened by the wife. The old man was fervently praying; but when he saw young C. with the pail of provisions, he held up both hands and said, "Now I know that God heareth prayer Not one mouthful have we in the house to eat. I know that God sent you here." Young C. staid with the old couple until day-light. The conversation revealed that about midnight the old man perceiving that a storm had arisen, and that unless relief came, which was not likely, they would starve, resolved to appeal to his Heavenly Father, saying that God who sent the ravens to feed Elijah would feed him if he went to him in faith, and now God had heard his prayer, and he blessed God that he could do so in all trouble and trial.

The old man having asked C. how he came to visit them, he replied he didn't know, but supposed God had sent him, as he had awoke and couldn't again sleep on account of thought of him.

The incident made a serious and lasting impression on young C.'s mind.

In the morning, as C was returning home, he came by his father's house; his mother, espying his pail, wished to know where he had been. He replied, "To feed the hungry." His father spreading the incident, the neighbors all turned out and brought in enough provision to last them during several weeks, the old man being greatly loved and respected by his community on account of his sterling Christian life and character.

Mr. Joseph Clason is still living, now seventy-five years of age, in Bazine, Ness county, Kansas.

That Beautiful Christmas Gift. How the Lord Used it.

A lady and gentleman were walking up Madison avenue, New York City, from church, when incidentally the lady said,

"We are trying to get up Christmas decorations and entertainment for our Mission School."

"*Well, put my name down for anything you like,*" and then came into his mind a certain sum to give.

A day passed on, it seemed forgotten; but a note from the lady reminded him of his promise, and he responded, giving the exact sum originally thought of, $25. Notice, now, the most singular disposition of it, which, by the hand of Providence, was made to go on its circuitous way to meet those who needed it most.

The next Sabbath, the lady and gentleman again meeting each other, she said, "Your gift was too large I cannot take so much from you I shall give you back part."

"But I won't take it."

"Well, you must. I can't keep it."

It resulted in the lady taking $15 from her muff and forcing it back into the gentleman's hand.

The gentleman felt badly. "*I intended this for the Lord, and now it is refused. It is the first time I ever heard that money ever given to a Sunday school was not wanted. I meant the whole for the Lord.* If she don't want it and wont keep it, I will give the rest away. *It does not belong to me.*" Before night he had enclosed it in a letter and sent it out of the city to an invalid as a *Christmas present* He had occasion not long after to visit the invalid, and was fairly astonished at the extraordinary circumstances connected with its use; and this is his story, told in his letter to the lady who returned the $15.

"The sequel to the $15 is far more beautiful and wonderful than anything I have ever known. This invalid had been praying for some money for a needed article of dress to protect her from cold. *The $15 came the very next morning in answer to her prayer. But it was more than enough.* As a consistent Christian, having asked the Lord only for enough to meet but one need, she felt as if the rest belonged to the Lord and must be used for Him. So in wondering how to use it, she thought of a poor woman who needed a new calico dress, and at once bought it and gave it to her. She had but $5 left. A dear friend was in distress; his horse and carriage had been seized for failure to pay the livery bill of their keeping; he could not collect any money of the debts due him, to pay his bill, and had nothing. His wife and children were in New Britain, and here he was, no means to get there. The little Christian invalid sent him her $5, the last money she had, not knowing where her next was to come from, with these words: "*The Lord has sent you this,*" and though he offered to return, or use only part, she said, "*No, the Lord meant this for you. You must keep it, I will not take it back.*" Now see how beautifully all these incidents have been made to work for the good of many, by the managing hand of Providence.

"My original gift of $25 to you was *more than enough.* You did not need it all for your Sunday-school, and the Lord made you force back the $15 upon me. I could not keep it, because I felt it belonged to the Lord. So I sent it to the little invalid.

"She, too, had only needed a part, and used only what she asked the Lord for, and then she, in her turn, gave the rest away. The most wonderful part of it is, that the money you gave back to me, and I gave to the Lord, was *three-fifths of the amount you received,* and the money the little invalid gave away *to the Lord* was also *three-fifths the amount she received. The money which you kept for your use was just two-fifths, and the money that the invalid kept for her own use was just two-fifths also. The very next day after she had given her money away,* a lady called and gave her some money, which *was precisely the same amount* which *the poor woman's calico dress* had cost, (though she knew nothing of the circumstances), and in return for the $5 which she gave her friend in distress, and refused to take back, the Lord remembered her and gave her a good home.

The Widow's Wood and Flour.—The Unbelieving Ones Made Speechless.

The following instance is known to *The Christian* as true, and to a remarkable degree indicates how thoroughly God knows our minutest needs, and how effectively He makes those who ever reproach his name ashamed of their unbelief.

"A friend and relative of the one who was 'a widow indeed,' one who trusted in God, and continued in supplications and prayers day and night, was once brought into circumstances of peculiar straitness and trial. She had two daughters who exerted themselves with their needles to earn a livelihood; and at that time they were so busily engaged in trying to finish some work that had long been on their hands, they had neglected to make provision for their ordinary wants until they found themselves one Winter's day in the midst of a New England snow storm, with food and fuel almost exhausted, at a distance from neighbors, and without any means of procuring needful sustenance.

"The daughters began to be alarmed, and were full of anxiety at the dismal prospect, but the good old mother said, 'Don't worry, girls, the Lord will provide; we have enough for to-day, and to-morrow may be pleasant,' and in this hope the girls settled down again to their labor.

"Another morning came, and with it no sunshine, but wind and snow in abundance. The storm still raged, but no one came near the house, and all was dark and dismal without.

"Noon came, and the last morsel of food was eaten, the wind was almost gone, and there were no tokens of any relief for their necessities.

"The girls became much distressed, and talked anxiously of their condition, but the good mother said, 'Don't worry. the Lord will provide.'

"But they had heard that story the day before, and they knew not the strong foundation upon which that mother's trust was builded, and could not share the confidence she felt.

" 'If we get anything to-day the Lord will have to bring it himself, for nobody else can get here if they try,' said one of the daughters, impatiently, but the mother said, 'Don't worry.' And so they sat down again to their sewing, the daughters to muse upon their necessitous condition, and the mother to roll her burden on the Everlasting Arms"

Now mark the way in which the Lord came to their rescue, and just at this moment of extremity, put it into the heart of one of his children to go and carry relief. *Human Nature* at such a time would never have ventured out in such a storm, but waited for a pleasant day. But Divine Wisdom and power made him carry *just what was needed, in the face of adverse circumstances, and just at the time it was needed.*

"Mr. M. sat at his fireside, about a mile away, surrounded by every bounty and comfort needed to cheer his heart, with his only daughter sitting by his side.

"For a long time not a word had been spoken, and he had seemed lost in silent meditation, till at length he said, 'Mary, I want you to go and order the cattle yoked, and then get me a bag I must go and carry some wood and flour to sister C.'

" ' Why, Father, it is impossible for you to go. There is no track, and it is all of a mile up there. You would almost perish.'

"The old man sat in silence a few moments and said, 'Mary, I must go.' She knew her father too well to suppose that words would detain him, and so complied with his wishes While she held the bag for him, she felt perhaps a little uneasiness to see the flour so liberally disposed of, and said, ' I wish you would remember that *I* want to give a poor woman some flour, if it ever clears off.' The old man understood the intimation and said, 'Mary, give all you feel it duty to, and when the Lord says stop, I will do so.'

"Soon all things were ready, and the patient oxen took their way to the widow's home, wallowing through the drifted snow, and dragging the sled with its load of wood and flour. About four o'clock in the afternoon, the mother had arisen from her work to fix the fire, and, looking out of the window, she saw the oxen at the door, and she knew that the Lord had heard her cry

"She said not a word—why should she? She was not surprised!—but, presently, a heavy step at the threshold caused the daughters to look up with astonishment, as Mr. M. strode unceremoniously into the room, saying, '*The Lord told me, Sister C., that you wanted some wood and flour.*'

"'*He told you the truth,*' said the widow, 'and I will praise Him forever.'

"'*What think you now girls?*' she continued, as she turned in solemn joy to her unbelieving daughters.

"*They were speechless;* not a word escaped their lips; but they pondered that new revelation of the providential mercy of the Lord, until it made upon their minds an impression never to be effaced.

"From that hour they learned to trust in Him who cares for *His needy* in the hour of distress, and who, from His boundless stores, supplies the wants of those who trust in Him."

A Pair of Shoes.—The Lord's Rebuke to those who "Didn't Believe."

The following incident occurred in Connecticut: In an humble cottage two sisters were watching over and caring for a much-loved brother, who, for many long months had been upon a bed of sickness. At length, the younger of them began to be discouraged. She was dependent, for her clothing, upon her labor; her shoes were worn out, and how should she get another pair, unless she could leave the sick bed and go away from home and work and earn some money.

"Well," said the mother, "I know you need a pair of shoes, but don't worry, the Lord will provide"

"*Do you think that* THE LORD *will come down from heaven and buy me a pair of shoes?*" said the younger sis-

ter, with an expression of discouragement and vexation on
her countenance.

"No," said the mother, "but perhaps he will put it into
somebody's heart to buy you a pair."

"Perhaps He will, *but I don't believe it,*" said the discouraged girl.

"Well," said the other sister, who was a little more hopeful, "you won't get them any quicker by fretting, so you
might as well be quiet." Then the subject dropped and the
day passed as usual.

As the shades of evening were gathering, a brother who
lived at some distance, and who knew nothing of their previous conversation, called to inquire after their prosperity.
After the customary salutations, he said, "You have been sick
here a long time, and I thought I would come round and see
if I could not do something for you; thought perhaps by
this time the girls needed something." Then turning to the
younger sister, he said, "*How is it, aren't your shoes worn
out?*"

She dropped her eyes, blushed deeply, and, perhaps, a little
conscience-smitten, answered not a word. Nothing was said
of the previous conversation, though it was not forgotten by
those who heard it. The brother soon saw for himself enough
to satisfy him, and said no more, but went away. The next
day *two pairs of shoes* were sent around to her, and with
them came to her heart a lesson which she never forgot.

She lived many years after that, but was never heard to
murmur in that way again, and often said that the two pairs
of shoes taught her to *wait, hope and trust,* and thereby learn
implicit confidence in Him who sendeth all blessings. The
last time she alluded to the occurrence, she said, "*I was speechless then, but, by the grace of God, I will not be in the world
to come.*"

The Lame Healed.

Rev. Charles G. Finney, during his life-time, was familiar with the circumstances connected with the remarkable healing of a sick lady in Oberlin, O., the wife of Rev. R. D. Miller, and these facts were vouched for as unquestionably authentic. Mr. Finney says:

"Mrs. Miller is the wife of a Congregational minister, and a lady of unquestionably veracity. However the fact of her healing is to be accounted for, her story is no doubt worthy of entire confidence, as we have known her for years as a lame, suffering invalid, and now see her in our midst in sound health. This instantaneous restoration will be accounted for by different persons in different ways. Mrs. Miller and those who were present regard the healing as supernatural and a direct answer to prayer. The facts must speak for themselves. Why should not the sick be healed in answer to the prayer of faith? Unbelief can discredit them, but faith sees nothing incredible in such facts as are stated by Mrs. Miller. Mrs. Miller's own statement is as follows, and it is fully endorsed by the most reliable citizens and members of the First church at Oberlin:

"From my parents I inherited a constitution subject to a chronic form of rheumatism. In early life I was attacked with rheumatic weaknesses and pains, which affected my whole system. For nearly forty years I was subject to more or less suffering from this cause, sometimes unable to attend meeting for months at a time. For seven years, until the last three months, I have been unable to get about without the aid of crutch or staff, generally both. I have used many liniments and remedies, but with no permanently good result. I have been a Christian from early life, but last Spring, in our revival, I received a spiritual refreshing from the Lord, which gave a new impulse to my faith. Since then my religion has been a new life to me.

"Last Summer, several of us Christian sisters were in the

habit of spending short seasons of prayer together, that the
Lord would send us a pastor. Some of our number had read
the narrative of Dorothea Trudel, and had spoken to me on
the subject of healing in answer to prayer. My faith had
not then risen to this elevation. I had in fact accepted what
I supposed to be the will of God, and made up my mind to
be a lame and suffering invalid the rest of my life. I had
long since ceased to use remedies for the restoration of my
health, and had not even thought of praying in regard to it,
for I regarded it as the will of God that I should suffer in
silent submission.

"Notwithstanding what had been said to me, I remained in
this opinion and in this attitude until the 26th of September,
1872, when several ladies met at our house, by appointment,
for a prayer-meeting. I had been growing worse for some
time, and was at that time unable to get out to attend a
meeting. I was suffering much pain that afternoon; indeed,
I was hardly able to be out of my bed. Up to this time none
of the sisters who had conversed with me about the subject
of healing by faith, had been able to tell me anything from
their own experience. That afternoon, one lady was present
who could speak to me from her own experience of being
healed in answer to the prayer of faith. She related several
striking instances in which her prayers had been answered
in the removal of divers forms of disease to which she was
subject. She also repeated a number of passages of Scripture,
which clearly justified the expectation of being healed in
answer to the prayer of faith. She also said that Jesus had
shown her that he was just as ready to heal diseases now as
he was when on earth; that such healing was expressly
promised in Scripture, in answer to the prayer of faith, and
that it was nowhere taken back. These facts, reasonings,
and passages of Scripture, made a deep impression on my
mind, and, for the first time, I found myself able to believe
that Jesus would heal me in answer to prayer. She asked
me if I could join my faith with hers and ask for present

healing. I told her I felt that I could. We then knelt, and called upon the Lord. She offered a mighty prayer to God, and I followed. While she was leading in prayer I felt a quickening in my whole being, whereupon my pain subsided, and when we rose from prayer I felt that a great change had come over me, that I was cured. I found that I could walk without my staff or crutch, or any assistance from any one. Since then my pains have never returned; I have more than my youthful vigor; I walk with more ease and rapidity than I ever did in my life, and I never felt so fresh and young as I now do, at the age of fifty-two.

"Now, the hundred and third psalm is my psalm, and my youth is more than renewed, like the eagle's. I cannot express the constant joy of my heart for the wonderful healing of my soul and body. I feel as if I was every whit made whole."

The testimony of eye-witnesses to this healing is as follows:

" We were all present at the time of the healing, and know the facts to be true. We are all Christians, and have no interest in deceiving anybody, and would by no means dishonor God by stating more than the exact truth. Since the healing, Mrs. Miller is still with us, and in excellent health. Neither the severe cold of last Winter, nor the extreme heat of this Summer, has at all injured her health. From our first acquaintance with her, she has been so lame as to be unable to walk, except by the aid of crutches. Since which time she has been able to walk without help, and appears perfectly well."

Her husband, also adding his testimony, says:

" She has been unable to walk without crutches for a series of years. A long time ago, we tried many remedies and physicians, with no lasting good results, and were expecting she would remain an invalid. Of late, she had applied no remedy, nor taken any medicine. At the time of her cure, she was much worse than for a long while before, being in great pain continually, until the moment she fully believed, and, *in an instant,* she was restored to perfect soundness. From that moment to this she has not felt a particle of her former complaint.

"She can now walk for miles as fast as I wish to, without feeling very much fatigue, does all her own housework, and attends seven meetings during the week. In short, she is stronger, and seems as young and spry, as when we were married, thirty-two years ago. The work of the dear Savior in her cure seems to be perfect, and she is an astonishment to all who knew her before and see her now. To *His* name be all the praise.

"Another lady, the same week my wife was healed, a member of the First Congregational Church, confined to her bed with a complicated disease, was prayed for, and restored at once to soundness."

The Wonderful Cure of Mrs. Sherman.

Although there are so many cases of healing in answer to prayer, yet the incident of the healing of Mrs. Sherman is so minute, and resulted in such a radical change of the physical constitution, that it is necessary to relate it in full detail. It is too well proven to admit the possibility of a doubt.

"Mrs Ellen Sherman is the wife of Rev. Moses Sherman, and, at the time of this occurrence, in 1873, they were residents of Piermont, N. H. She had been an invalid for many years. In the Winter after she was fifteen, she fell on the ice and hurt her left knee, so that it became weak and easy to slip out of joint. Six years after, she fell again on the same knee, so twisting it and injuring the ligaments that it became partially stiff, and, the physician said, incurable.

"The next Summer, by very fast walking, one day, she brought on special weakness, which no physician was able to cure. From that moment she was subject to severe neuralgia, sick-headaches, at least monthly, and sometimes even weekly.

"In December, 1859, while stepping out of doors, she slipped, by reason of her stiff joint, and fell, striking near the base of the spine, directly across the sharp edge of the stone step. This caused such a sickness that she was obliged to leave the school she was attending.

"Three years after (in January, 1862), she fell at the top of a stairway, striking just as before, and sliding all the way down to the foot. This nearly paralyzed the spinal cord, and caused deep and permanent spinal disease. After this she was up and down for many years, attended by various physicians, yet nothing bettered, but, rather, growing worse It may be said, for short, that every organ of the lower body became chronically diseased, and that the headaches increased in violence

"In September, 1872, through a severe cold, she took her bed, where she lay, except when lifted from it, till the night of August 27, 1873. She was unable to walk a step, or even stand. She could sit up only a short time without great distress. The best medical skill that could be procured gave only temporary relief. The spine grew worse in spite of every appliance, and the nervous sensitiveness and prostration were increasing. During the two or three weeks immediately preceding her cure she was especially helpless, two persons being required to lift her off and on the bed. On the Monday before, one of her severest neuralgia sick-headaches came on. During Wednesday she began to be relieved, but was still so sick that when, in the evening, she tried to have her clothes changed, she could only endure the change of her night-dress "

It will be seen from this her utter physical helplessness, and not the slightest hope of any amelioration. During the night of August 27th, she enjoyed a blessed time of communion with her Lord, giving herself, in all her helplessness, wholly to Him to do as he wills

With feelings beyond all expression, she *felt* the nearness of her mighty Savior, and the sense of receiving a new and most delicious pulsation of new life. At last, though she had been bed-ridden for twelve months, and incapable of any bodily assistance, she felt an uncontrollable impulse to throw off the clothes of the bed with her left arm, and sprang out of bed upon her feet, and started to walk across the room.

"Her husband's first thought was that she was crazed, and would fall to the floor, and he sprang towards her to help her. But she put up her hands against him, saying with great energy, 'Don't you touch me! Don't you touch me!' and went walking back and forth across the room speaking rapidly, and declaring the work which Jesus had been working upon her.

"Her husband quickly saw that she was in her right mind, and had been healed by the Lord, and his soul was filled with unutterable emotion.

"One of the women of the household was called, also their son, twelve years old, and together they thanked God for the great and blessed wonder he had wrought.

"In the morning, after a sleep of several hours, she further examined herself to see if entirely healed, and found both knees perfectly well; and though for sixteen years she had not been able to use either, now she lifted the left *foot* and *put it upon the right knee*, thus proving the completeness of her restoration.

"At the end of two years from her healing, inquiry having been made as to how thorough had been the work, Mrs. Sherman gave full and abundant evidence. ' I cannot remember a Summer when I have been so healthy and strong, and able to work hard. I am a constant wonder to myself, and to others, and have been for the two years past. The cure exceeded my highest expectations at the time I was cured. I did not look forward to such a state of vigor and strength No words can express my joy and gratitude for all this.'

"The parents of Mrs. Sherman also testify of the wonderful change physically which occurred with the cure.

"Before, her appetite was always disordered, but on the very morning of the healing it was wholly changed, and her food, which distressed her formerly, she ate with a relish and without any pain following; and she so continues. For years before a natural action of the bowels was rare. From that day since, an unnatural one is equally rare.

"For fifteen years, with few exceptions, she had had severe neuralgic sick headaches monthly or oftener. From that time she has been natural and without pain, with no return of the headaches, except a comparatively slight one once, from overdoing and a cold taken through carelessness.

"There was also at that time an immediate and radical change in the action of the kidneys, which had become a source of great trouble before. Moreover the knee which had been partially stiff for so many years was made entirely well In fine, her body, which had been so full of pain, became at once free from pain, and full of health.

"The week after she was healed she went fifty miles to attend a camp-meeting, riding five miles in a carriage, the rest by cars. A near neighbor said, 'She will come back worse than ever.' Though the weather was especially bad, she came back better than when she went."

These are but few out of many expressions respecting her extraordinary recovery, which fully satisfy the believing Christian that *the Great* Physician is with us now, " *healing the lame,*" and curing the sick. It is faith only, unyielding, which the Lord requires ere he gives his richest blessing.

The unbelieving one simply sees in it " *something strange,*" which he can not understand, but the faith-keeping Christian knows it is the sign of his *Precious Lord,* in whom he trusts and abides forever.

Dr. Newman Hall's Testimonies to the Value of Prayer.

Dr. Newman Hall, of London, in his wide experience has met with many incidents of answered prayer, and thus relates several:

10

A Prayer for Thirty Pounds.

"On a recent evangelizing visit to Newport, one of its citizens said to me, 'In yonder house dwell a man and wife, who recently needed a sum of £30 to meet some payment the next morning. Having failed in their efforts to collect it, they earnestly prayed God to provide it. The store was being closed for the night when a sea-captain knocked at the door and asked for some seamen's clothes. The gas was relighted, and various articles were selected; the purchaser then asked for the account, and the money was paid—*a little more than* £30. The man and his wife thanked their Heavenly Father for sending it in this way in answer to prayer.'"

Recovery from Dangerous Illness.

Dr. Newman Hall was once visiting, on his dying bed, John Cranfield, son of the great originator of ragged schools, under the ministry of Rowland Hill.

"We were conversing on prayer. He said, 'A remarkable instance occurred in connection with my father. The former organist of Surry Chapel, Mr Howard, was dangerously ill He was greatly beloved, and his friends met for special prayer that God would spare his life. My father on that occasion was remarkably earnest in asking that the life of his friend might be lengthened, as in the case of Hezekiah. The next day he began to recover; and during fifteen years was a blessing to his friends and the church.'"

A Sunday School Teacher in Distress.

"My brother," says Dr Hall, "told me that when superintendent of a Sunday school he felt a strong impulse, one Saturday evening, to call at the home of one of his teachers whom he had never visited before. He found his mother and sisters in such evident distress that he inquired the cause.

With much reluctance they explained that, being unable to pay their taxes, their goods were to be taken on the coming Monday, and they had been asking special help from God to save them from a disaster which they felt would be a dishonor to religion. By the aid of a few friends the difficulty was at once met, but the timely succor was regarded as the divine answer to their prayer."

Rescued in Peril.

" With my brother I was once climbing the *Cirrha di Jazze,* one of the mountains in the chain of *Mount Rosa.* When nearly at the top, we entered a dense fog Presently our guides faced right about and grounded their axes on the frozen snowed slope. My brother, seeing the slope still beyond, and not knowing it was merely the cornice overhanging a precipice of several thousand feet, rushed onward I shall never forget their cry of agonized warning. He stood a moment on the very summit, and then, the snow yielding, he began to fall through. One of the guides, at great risk, had rushed after him, and seizing him by the coat, drew him down to a place of safety.

"No one could be nearer death and yet escape. On his return home, an invalid member of his congregation told him that she had been much in prayer for his safety, and mentioned a special time when she was particularly earnest, as if imploring deliverance from some great peril. *The times corresponded.* His life was saved in answer to her prayer."

A Physical Impediment Removed.

" A clergyman, of great scholarship and genius, has told me of a remarkable answer to prayer, authenticated by three missionaries known to himself, who are personally acquainted with the facts.

" A Prussian, the master of a hotel in India, was anxious

to relinquish his large income, and labor as a missionary among the Santil tribes. Objection was made to him on account of an impediment in his speech which would render him, in speaking a foreign language, incapable of being understood. Believing in the efficacy of prayer, he called together his friends, specially to ask that his impediment might be removed. The next morning, he presented himself again at the Mission House—*the impediment had gone!* He was accepted, relinquished his business, and is now preaching the gospel to the Santils in their own tongue."

Restoration from Death.

"My father, the author of the *Sinner's Friend*, narrates in his autobiography a circumstance which he often used to speak of with great emotion.

"My mother was very ill, and apparently dying. The Doctor said that now, if at all, the children might be brought for her to look at them once more. One by one we were brought to the bedside, and her hand was placed on our heads.

"Then my father bade her farewell, and she lay motionless as if soon to breathe her last.

"He then said to himself, 'There is yet one promise I have not pleaded, "If ye ask anything in my name I will do it." He stepped aside, and in an agony of soul exclaimed, '*O, Lord, for the honor of thy dear Son, give me the life of my wife!*'

"He could say no more, and sank down exhausted. Just then the nurse called him to the bedside saying, 'She has opened her mouth again as if for food.' Nourishment was given, and from that time she began to recover. The doctor said it was miraculous. My father said it was God, who had heard his prayer."

The Help of the Lord in Little Things.

The Rev. Dr Patton, of Chicago, in receiving many letters from clergymen, received one from Mr. F., a pastor in Massachusetts.

In it he speaks of his unsuccessful search for a valuable knife, prized as a present from a friend, which he had lost on a hillside covered with laurels. He paused in prayer, asked to be guided, commenced his search, and was almost immediately successful thereafter.

The same letter also mentions the case of a friend in a responsible position under the government, whose accounts failed to balance by reason of an error, which, after long search, he could not detect.

In great distress he betook himself to prayer, and then opening his books, *on the very first page,* which he happened to glance at, and at the top of the column, he saw instantly the looked for error, standing out so plainly that he wondered he had not seen it before.

The writer also speaks of a rubber shoe being lost and promptly found after mention in prayer.

These may seem little matters, but they are the privileges of the righteous to ask " anything " of " Him who careth for them."

A Boy's Faith in Prayer.

In a letter to Dr. W. W. Patton, by Mr. T. I. Goodwin, M. D , of Staten Island, he describes a little incident which happened to him when only thirteen years old.

" He lost a choice penknife while collecting and driving several cows from a pasture covered with grass two inches high. Having read Huntington's Book of Faith, he thought of prayer, and in child-like trust he knelt under a tree, outside the bars, and prayed for his lost treasure; for he was a farmer's boy, and his spending money amounted to only about fifty cents a year. 'I rose up, cast my eyes down on the ground, and without planning my course or making any estimate of probabilities, walked across the meadow centrally to near its farther edge, saw the penknife down in the grass directly before me, and picked it up all as readily as I could have done had any one stood there pointing to the exact place. *Had I gone ten feet to the right or left* I could not have seen the knife, for the grass was too high.' "

A Prayer for Five Dollars.

One of the City Home missionaries in New York city received on a certain day five dollars with special directions that it be given to a certain poor minister in Amos street. In the evening the missionary called and gave him the money.

For a moment the good man stood amazed and speechless. Then taking down a little journal he turned to the record made in his diary of that morning, and showed it to the missionary. "*Spent two and a half hours in earnest prayer for five dollars.*"

"And now here it is," said the man, with a heart overflowing with gratitude. "The Lord has sent it." Both giver and receiver had their faith strengthened by the incident.

Go to the Post-Office.

A correspondent of "*The Guiding Hand*" relates this incident:

"In the year 18—, having a brother living in the city of R., I went to see him. Going to the store where he had been at work, I found that the firm had suspended, and that he was thrown out of employment, and had broken up housekeeping, but could not ascertain where he was, only that he was boarding somewhere out in the suburbs of the city. I searched for him all day, but in vain.

"It was *absolutely necessary* that I should find *him*. What more to do I knew not, except to *pray*. Finally, I was impressed to write a line and drop it into the post-office, and I obeyed the impression, telling him, if he got it, to meet me at a stated place, the next morning, at ten o'clock. *I prayed earnestly* that the Lord would cause him *to go to the post-office*, so that he might get my letter. I felt full of peace, and at rest about the matter. The next morning, at ten o'clock, I went to the place appointed for him to meet me, *and he soon came in.*"

This incident might seem one of ordinary or chance occurrence, but for the following unusual circumstances:

" As they were returning to their home, his brother said: ' There is something *very strange* about my going to the post-office this morning—*I had my arrangements all made to go with a party, this morning early, to the bay, fishing; but, when I awoke, I had such an impression to go down to the post-office, that I had to forego the pleasure of going to the bay, and went to the post-office and found your letter.*'

"I replied, ' *It was the Lord* that impressed you in answer to my prayer, for I have prayed earnestly for the Lord to send you to the office this morning,' and, although but young in years and religion, I gave God the praise for his guidance and His grace."

The Widow's Tree.

Not many years ago a violent storm, with wind and thunder, spread devastation all through the valley of Yellow Creek, Georgia. For a mile in width, trees were uprooted, barns and fences were prostrated, and all the lands were desolated.

Right in the center of the tornado stood a small cabin. Its sole occupants were an aged widow and her only son. The terrible wind struck a large tree in front of her humble dwelling, twisting and dashing it about. If it fell it would lay her home in ruins. Desolation, death itself, might follow. The storm howled and raged. The great trees fell in all directions. When it seemed her tree must also fall and there was no remedy, she knelt in fervent supplication to Him who gathereth the wind in his fists, that he would spare that tree. Her prayer was heard. The tree was spared, and was the *only one* left within a considerable distance of the widow's cabin.

The Lord Paid His Interest.

A most curious answer to prayer occurred in the experience of a home missionary in Brooklyn. It illustrates how God, in his trials of faith to see if His people do really cling to the promises, compels them to march right into the scene of danger, and into the mouth of the cannon, that apparently is open specially to shoot them down.

The interest on the mortgage of his property was due in a few days Its amount was $300. He did not have the money—did not know where to obtain it. With anxious heart during the day, he kept up his faith and courage by thinking of the Lord's promises, and, the last night before the eventful day, was spent in prayer, until the assurance came that all was well. Often he pleaded, often he reminded the Lord that, as his life was *His*, to save him from reproach, and not let his trust in the Lord suffer dishonor before others.

The last moment came—no money—no relief. With sinking heart he went to the holder of the mortgage to announce his utter inability to meet his demand. While there, just at the last moment, when he was about to leave, the gentleman said, "*By the way, here is an envelope I was told to give you*"

The missionary opened it, *and out came six fifty dollar bills*, just the *three hundred dollars prayed for*. The Lord met and delivered him in the very jaws of the enemy.

Will the Lord Deliver from Bad Habits of Tobacco, Rum, Liquor, Licentiousness, etc., in Answer to Prayer.

This question having been asked by a clergyman of Brooklyn, Rev. S. H. Platt, he received a large number of communications, which evidently prove that the Lord is *willing* and *does*, either *instantaneously* or gradually in answer to prayer, deliver and take away wholly the bad *habits* and *appetites* of those who are willing to forsake their sinful ways and cleave only to Him. *The Lord's salvation cleanses and delivers the body as well as the soul.*

We quote a few extracts from his correspondence, which is but a small portion out of many published in his volume, " *The Power of Grace.*'

Cured of Tobacco Appetite.

"A little more than a year has elapsed since I left off the use of tobacco. This further time has more fully developed the thoroughness of the case spoken of and the completeness of the victory over an evil habit. I am filled with wonder, for I expected a terrible fight with an appetite, strengthened by an indulgence of about thirty-five years, but the enemy has not shown his head. *Not only has the desire for smoking been effectually squelched,* but a perfect hatred of smoking has been developed on account of the offensiveness of the odor of tobacco. I frequently cross the street, or change my seat in a car to escape the puff of smoke, or the fetid breath of a smoker. 'Thanks be unto God who giveth us the victory.'"

Bad Habits Wholly Overcome.

"A physician of extended practice was converted and reclaimed while I had charge of the place in which he lived. He had acquired the habit of using large quantities of whisky and brandy, and withal more or less given to licentiousness. Since that time he has been steadily advancing in morals and moral power, till he now preaches the gospel as a local preacher, side by side with the best of the district."

Was it Instantaneous?

"Yes, as respects tobacco; he became convicted of its sin-fulness by a voice saying, 'That is not the way to glorify God; stop, and stop now' And from that moment he says he has never used it, neither does he in any way like the smell, or even the sight of tobacco."

The Lord Delivers from Bodily Sins.

"I had used tobacco from my childhood, and the love and use thereof grew upon me. I became convicted of its sinful-ness, went to God and said, '*Destroy the appetite, and give me power over it.* Save me that I may glorify thee as a God of power for our present sins, and I will glorify thee ever more' I wrote out the contract and signed it, and from that blessed afternoon have no recollection of ever desiring it even."

Another Deliverance.

"Tobacco was a great trouble to me; and I had tried a number of times to leave it off, but could not do so. One night as I was retiring to rest, I thought I would kneel by my bed and ask *Him*, who never refuses to answer prayer, to take from me the desire for tobacco, and from that moment it has been impossible for me to use it.

Not Your Own Strength Can Break the Habit.

"I smoked tobacco excessively for fifteen years, commenc-ing when I was about twenty years old. I often strove to break off from the use of it; indeed I determined time and again to desist from it, sometimes abstaining for a few months or weeks, once for twelve months, *but the desire never left me,* and whenever I tasted it I was sure to take to it again I sometimes vowed whilst upon my knees in prayer, to abstain from it and never touch it again, but I always attempted to do this in my own strength; hence I failed, being overcome by the almost irresistible influences it had upon my appetite, so long accustomed to the use.

"One Sunday morning, I retired to a secluded place, got down upon my knees, and asked the Lord to help me quit it, determining then and there that I would, God being my helper, never touch the accursed thing again by any kind of use in the way of consumption, and from that day to this, I have never had any desire to smoke or chew tobacco, or to use it in any way; I lifted my heart to God, imploring his assistance in abstaining from it. I have now been clear of the desire of it for nearly twenty-three years."

A Double Cure.

"At the age of twelve years I commenced to use tobacco, and continued to use it, both smoking and chewing, till five years ago, when in answer to prayer the appetite was instantly removed.

"The circumstances were as follows I had tried many ways to leave off the use of tobacco, but the appetite was so strong that I could not withstand it. At one time I left it off for a month, but not a day passed but I craved it, and when I did begin again it tasted as good as ever. I found that tobacco was injuring my health. My nervous system was much deranged

"For more than a year before I left it off there was scarcely a night but I lay for two or three hours, before I could go to sleep. I resolved a great many times I would leave off, but always failed. I had also acquired the habit of drinking, and became a confirmed drunkard.

"I knew the habits were killing me, but I was powerless to stop. One evening a prayer-meeting was appointed at my house. The minister in his remarks spoke about habits, and said that religion would cure all bad habits, such as tobacco, &c., and that by prayer God would remove all evil appetites.

"I thought but little about it that night; was very careless and trifling about it. The next morning I took out my tobacco to take a chew, and thought of what the minister had said the night before. It was a new idea to me. I put the tobacco in my pocket again, and said, '*I'll try it.*'

"*I was alone in my barn, I kneeled down and asked God to remove the appetite from me. It was done. I was cured.* I felt it. I knew it then. I have never had a desire for it since. There has been no hankering for it or for strong drink since. My sins were all forgiven, and I was made a new man all over, inside and outside.

" When I go into company where they are smoking, I have no desire for it at all, neither have I for drinking, any more than if I had never had those habits. *My nervous difficulty was also instantly cured.* No more trouble about sleeping, and I know that Jesus can heal and remove and destroy all evil habits."

A Special Word to all Seeking to Escape Evil Ways.

Should these words meet the eye of any one so troubled over any evil way or bad habit from whose bondage he would gladly escape, let me say to you these words of good cheer · " *The Lord can save you, the Lord can deliver you, the Lord can wholly heal you. He can take away your appetite and cleanse you thoroughly.* He has done it for many others. He can do it for you. Realize that your own strength can not do it. Forget not that it is only in answer to your own prayer. Those who want this good gift must *pray for it.* Deliverance may be instantaneous or gradual, but do not cease your prayer. Seek in the Bible for those promises which show that he can *deliver from all evil*, and plead them and then trust in Him and his strength to fulfill them.

"Forget not also to ask others to pray for you, and remember that the answer is sure to come if you add to your prayer these true thoughts of your heart, '*Deliver me and I give myself to thee forever.*'

"If you expect so great a gift from the Lord, he asks of you, '*What are you willing to do for me?*'"

Help at the Very Last Moment. Faith Rewarded.

A clergyman in the State of New York, through the influence of a disaffected member, was unfairly and precipitately deprived of his pulpit, which involved a large family in necessity. At supper the good man had the pain of beholding the last morsel of bread placed upon the table without the least means or prospect of a supply for his children's breakfast. His wife, full of grief with her children, retired to her bed. The minister chose to sit up and employ his dark hours in prayer, and reading the promises of God. Some secret hope of supply pervaded his breast, but when, whence, or by whom, he knew not. He retired to rest, and in the morning appeared with his family, and offered family prayer. It being the depth of Winter, and a little fire on the hearth, he desired his wife to hang on the kettle, and spread the cloth upon the table. The kettle boiled, the children cried for bread; the afflicted father, standing before the fire, felt those deep emotions of heart over his helplessness and impending starvation which those reared in affluence never know.

While in this painful state some one knocked at the door, entered, and delivered a letter into the minister's hand. When the gentleman was gone the letter was opened, and to the minister's astonishment it contained a few bank bills, with a desire for acceptance. So manifest an answer to prayer from Divine Goodness could not but be received with gratitude and joy, and fulfills to the very letter these promises. "Verily thou shalt be fed." Psalm 37 : 3. "I will never leave thee nor forsake thee." Heb. 13 . 5.

To ascertain how this occurrence came to take place, this remarkable coincidence of relief at the identical moment of time when there was the last appeal to God, the incident was communicated to the editor of a religious journal. Having an intimacy with the gentleman said to be the one whose hand had offered the seasonable relief, he determined the next time he made him a visit to introduce the subject, and, if possible, to know the reason that induced the generous action. The story was told with a modest blush which evinced the tenderness of his heart. On interrogation, he said "he had frequently heard that minister. On a certain morning he was disposed for a walk ; thought in the severity of the winter season a trifle might be of service, as fuel was high ; felt a kind of necessity to enclose the money in a letter ; went to the house, found the family, delivered the paper and retired, but knew not the extreme necessity of the minister and his family, either at that time nor till this very moment when his friend introduced the subject. Thus it is seen none but God knew the want or moved the hand that gave the supply, and brought them to meet at the right time.

Spinal Disease Cured.

"There was a little girl in this place that had the cerebro-spinal-meningitis ; several had died with this disease, and the physician had given her up to die. The weekly prayer-meeting met in town that night, and her parents wrote a note and sent it by their little son, requesting prayer that their little daughter might live and not die, signed with the names of both parents. From that time she began to recover, and to-day she is a bright little girl, with full use of every faculty, and not deformed as most persons are from this terrible disease. I cannot view it in any other light than a direct answer to prayer."

An Old Man's Prayer.

" I feel also like mentioning another instance. I knew an old father in Israel, a minister of the gospel, who once in speaking with a brother minister, after a revival of religion in which five of his grandchildren had professed their faith in Christ, among others with whom he had labored; said if he could only live to see his one remaining granddaughter brought into the fold, and the two Presbyterian churches, then called the Old and New school, united, he could say, like Simeon of old, 'Lord, now lettest thou thy servant depart in peace, for mine eyes have seen thy salvation.' About three years after, the two Presbyteries met near this place in Germantown, Mo., and he seemed as if he could not contain himself till the time came for the meeting, so anxious was he for this great desire of his heart to be fulfilled. On the day of meeting he took sick and could not be present at any of the sessions, but many of his brethren were with him, among whom was this one he had been conversing with. The sessions lasted three days, and upon the last evening his wishes were gratified, the two Presbyteries merged into one, singing ' Blest be the tie that binds;' and his youngest granddaughter united with the church, and after the meeting adjourned this brother came to watch with the aged servant of God. He was permitted to convey the glad news to him, and see a heavenly smile light up his countenance as he passed away with his earnest prayer gratified."

The Mysterious Leadings of Providence.

The following incidents are contributed to the book by a prominent clergyman :

" A period, ever memorable in the life of the writer, occurred in the Autumn of 1832, while attending a protracted meeting of more than ordinary interest and power, held under the auspices of the Baptist church in the city of Scheneotady, under the then pastoral charge of Rev. Abraham D. Gillette, this being his first settlement. It was in one of the meetings that the Holy Spirit impressed my mind of its sinfulness and the need of a Savior, not only to cleanse my soul of sin and sinful stains, but to save me. These impressions caused me to humble myself at the feet of sovereign mercy; and in the midst of my pleadings, God answered my prayer, and opened to me new views, views of the heavenly kingdom, which so electrified my soul, that with a full heart I could say, 'Blessed be the Lord who has shown me marvelous works in this lonely place beneath the star-lit sky.'

"This great change was, and is, to me the most wonderful interposition of God in my behalf in answer to prayer   This answer to prayer the promised result of faith in Him."

"Again, in the year 1836, the writer in the year mentioned was employed by a transportation company, in the city of Troy, in the character of an employe having direction of a portion of the business of the company which brought me into close relation with the many boatmen connected with the company. Association with the boatmen was painful to my religious nature, compelled, as I was, to hear all manner of offensive talk. The latter led me to indulge a wish that I might free myself from such company, in order to form associations with persons of my own religious turn of mind. But God willed otherwise, as will be learned from the recital of God's dealings with me on an occasion of a journey alone in a carriage from Troy to Schenectady. It was on the occasion alluded to that most of the time was occupied in prayer, and the burden of my prayer was 'that God would open up a way for me wherein I could find more congenial company, where in fact my religious feelings would not meet with the trials incident to my present associations' But He who knew my needs better, came to my relief in words seemingly distinct enough to be heard. This was the answer· 'I have placed you just where I want you.' Instantly my prayer for a change of location or separation from my business and its connections ceased, and since, instead of looking for easy positions, wherein the principles of the faith which is in me may be undisturbed, I deem it suited to my growth in grace and increase in devotion to my Master's cause, to covet the association of men whose only tendency is to evil continually. I have found by experience in the latter direction, that although many tongues are loose in the habit of profanity, I am roused more and more by grace to impart words of counsel. I know that efforts at consistency in Christian conduct and converse will stop the mouth of profaners of the name of our Redeemer, God."

Another instance of the presence of God with his children is clearly manifest in the following sketch of a meeting of two brethren, of whom the writer was one, held in the conference room of the First Baptist church in Troy, N. Y., of which church he was a member. The meeting alluded to occurred in the early spring of 1840 or '41. We were accustomed to meet almost every day for the purpose of arranging the Sunday school library, but would occupy a portion of the time, usually at noon, in prayer for such persons or objects as were presented to the mind. On the particular occasion we propose to mention, it was mutually agreed that we pray for one of the brethren, whose gifts were of a high order, and his usefulness hindered by a lack of spirituality. We mutually bowed in prayer for this brother, and while thus engaged the door of the room was opened, and a person entered and knelt between us, but who he was, or the purpose of his visit we knew not until we had ended our prayer, at which time the person spoke and requested us to continue praying for him.

At the conclusion of the service, the question was mooted how he came there. His reply was in substance as follows: "When standing on a stoop on the corner of Fourth and Congress streets, cogitating which way I should go, I was impressed by a voice within which directed my course to the Conference Room. I debated with the impression, taking the

11

position that it being noon no meeting was then in progress. Still the impression remained, and could not be removed. Noticing this, I gave way to the voice and here I am." Neither of the three thus brought together could doubt for a moment that our prayer for this brother was answered. His joy was great in view of being thus called from his delinquency to share in the fullness of his Savior's love.

"Another instance in the experience of the writer very clearly shows the power and worth of prayer. About the year 1840, in the Autumn thereof, he experienced a lack of vital, spiritual energy. This had been of months' continuance, but to his joy, culminated after retiring to rest. After this manner, before sleep overcame him, he was impressed to present his case before the mercy-seat. To do so he arose from his bed, retired to a quiet part of his home and bowed in prayer, seeking to occupy the entire night if need be in prayer for the bestowal of the Holy Spirit, and the consequent revival influences of other days. This season of prayer was of short continuance; but not by reason of disrelish for the exercise, but because my prayer was answered and a complete breaking away of the previous hindrances to my spiritual enjoyment. Since the event alluded to, now more than thirty-six years, I have not been afflicted by doubts, and counsel brethren and sisters not to allow themselves to be made unhappy by this evil to our spiritual progress."

Life Spared for Two Weeks.

" On the 8th of January, last, I was called upon to visit a dying man in Jersey City, whom the doctors had said could not live but a few hours. I found him in severe bodily sufferings and a terrible agony of mind. He had lived a moral and upright life in the eyes of the world, but careless and neglectful of all religious duties, and now with eternity before him he felt his life a failure and his imperative need of help.

"In his agony he would cry out, 'Lord, help me,' and

perhaps the next moment blaspheme the name of God. I sought to show him his great sin in having so long neglected God and his salvation, and at the same time assured him that Jesus was a great Savior, 'able to save to the uttermost all who would come unto Him' I went from his bedside to the union prayer-meeting, held in our city during the week of prayer, where I presented his case and asked the brethren to pray that God would save this poor man even at the eleventh hour, and spare him to give good evidence of his conversion. His case seemed to reach the hearts of all present, and most earnest prayers were offered in his behalf; so strong was the faith that many came to me at the close of the meeting and said that young man will certainly be saved before he is taken from this world.

"In answer to prayer he was spared nearly two weeks, and for some six or seven days before his death, gave much clearer evidence of being truly converted than could have been expected of one in his condition."

A Missionary's Experience in Mexico.

"While laboring with my wife as a missionary in Northern Mexico, we supported ourselves for nearly four years by teaching and such other ways as the Lord opened up to us.

"But our schools being decidedly Protestant, and I preaching regularly, the opposition from Romanists was very strong; this, together with the extreme poverty of the people, made our income very small. Frequently the opposition would rise to that pitch that only the children of the poorest would be permitted to come, but we never turned these away, though they could pay no tuition, trusting that God would provide for us in some other way.

"Early in the year 1869, we were much exercised to know the will of the Lord concerning us, whether he would have us continue or not. We brought our case before the Lord and prayed him to make known his will and provide for our necessary wants. In about three weeks we received a check for eighty dollars, sent us, as we felt, truly by the Lord in answer to our prayer through a friend in New York, who knew nothing of our circumstances or prayer.

"In August the same year, our condition became such that it seemed as if in a few days we would be wholly without the necessaries of life. We laid our case before the Lord, and as he did not appear to open up any way for us to leave the field, we went forward with our work as faithfully as we knew how, believing that the Lord would provide in his own time and way, when one evening, just after family worship, a rap came to the door. I opened it, there came in quite a company of persons, all bearing something, and just exactly the things we needed most, and to the amount of over fifty dollars worth, and about a sixth of it was, as we learned, given by Romanists who had opposed us very strongly all the time we had been there. Truly the Lord answers prayer and turns the hearts of men to do his will."

The Greatest of Physicians.

Miss X. of Brooklyn, had suffered long and severely from a distressing tumor. One physician after another had plied his skill, but to no purpose; even the celebrated Doctor Simms of New York, corroborated their verdict, that there was no help for her but in the knife. She finally consented to that terrific method, but was in no condition of strength to bear the operation. It was decided to postpone it till the 22d of June. Twelve doctors were invited to be present. Meanwhile a diet nurse sent from New York, remained with her to prepare her system for the ordeal.

Three days preceding the one appointed for the operation, she was attacked by severe nausea, which lasted two days, and so weakened her that again the doctors were all notified by the attending one, that a further postponement was imperative, and a certain date fixed in November.

All this time her own prayers were unceasing, those of her friends added to her own, and many a remembrance in the Fulton Street meeting, cheered and encouraged her.

By November, the tumor had totally disappeared! That was two years ago. She is still well, strong; able to walk three miles any time.

She is as certain that the whole cure was performed by the Lord in answer to all those fervent prayers, as she is certain she lives and moves.

How the Lord Paid Back the $5.

Mr. H., missionary, was appealed to by a poor man who seemed almost distracted. He had a wife and five children; one of them ill; had been sick himself for three months, and owed rent for the whole of that time. The landlord had served him with a writ of ejectment, and he could get no other tenement, unless he could pay five dollars on the rent. He had applied to a well-known society in Brooklyn; but they were entirely out of funds and gave him a note to the missionary, hoping he might have or find the desired help. But missionaries' pockets are more often depleted, than those of benevolent organizations, and the one in question was fain to take the applicant to a friend, whom we shall call Q

The poor man told his story, asked the five dollars only as a loan, and, having an order for the painting of two signs, said he should be paid for them when done, and could return the loan the next Saturday, one week from that time.

Mr. Q. saw, at once, that the utter destitution of the family, and the need of *everything*, would prevent the man returning the money, however much he might wish to, and so refused to lend it. The case was urged, but without avail; and the missionary sent the man away, promising to see him again that night or on Monday After his departure, the following conversation passed between the gentlemen:

Q.—"Now, H., I don't take any stock in that man. Can

you not see that his paying that money back, is a simple impossibility?"

H.—"Well, perhaps so; but the question with me in such cases, is this: What is duty? Admit that he cannot pay it, or even that he will not try; is it not better to relieve his desperate need, than to have him perhaps turn criminal and prey upon society? He *must* leave the house he is in; he *cannot* get another without the money, and he is desperate; feels that five dollars he must have, by fair means or foul. Moreover, think of his wife and children, leaving him out of the question. Now let us open this little Bible, and see what meets our eye first."

Q.—"Oh, pshaw! You know I do not believe in that kind of thing! Do you go to the Bible for everything?"

H.—"Why not? Can we have any better guide?"

Q.—"Oh! well, I don't work that way. Now about that man and his money. I will toss up a penny with you, whether I lend or not."

H.—"No you won't! You know I don't believe in chance, but in the Lord. And would you sooner rest your decision on a gambler's test, than on God's promise? Now just let us open the book."

Q.—"Well; what do you see?"

H.—"'The wicked borroweth, and payeth not again; but the righteous sheweth mercy, and lendeth.'" 37th Psalm, 21st verse.

As there was no hunting up of passages, nor leaves turned down to open easily, the coincidence was impressive, as well as amusing, and H., following it up, said, "Lend him the money, and if he does not pay you next Saturday night, I will."

It was so agreed upon, and, when the man called on the missionary on Monday morning, he was sent to Q. for the relief.

The week passed on, as they all pass, weighted and freighted with human ills; some capable of alleviation, some not; but of the former, a full share had come under the notice and care of the missionary, and Saturday found him stepping into the Fulton street prayer-meeting, N. Y., for fresh encouragement and benediction on his labors.

At its close, a gentleman said to him, "Mr. H., I have known you by sight for years; know your work; but have never given you anything; and I promised myself the next time I saw you, I would do so. Have you any special need of five dollars now? If so, and you will step to the bank with me, you shall have it." Instantly it flashed through the mind of H that this was the day when, either the borrower or he, must pay his friend It may be supposed that he went to the bank with alacrity. Going back to B. and meeting the friend, he learned that neither man nor money had appeared, and at once tendered the five dollars, telling the story of the Lord's care in the matter.

Q. was so interested in this manner of obtaining supplies, that he refused to take the money, and instructed H. to use it in the Lord's work.

Praying for Money for a Journey.

A lady, Miss E., residing in New Bedford, received a letter telling of the serious illness of her mother, in New York Sick herself, from unremitted care of an invalid during eight years, poor as Elijah when his only grocers were the ravens, too old for new ambitions, too well acquainted with the gray mists of life to hope for many rifts through which the sunshine might enter, she had no sum of money at all approaching the cost of the trip between the two places

" He shall cover thee with his feathers, and under his wings shalt thou trust," is a text bound over her daily life, as a phylactery was bound between the eyes of an ancient Hebrew. She lives literally, *only one day at a time,* and walks literally by faith and not by sight So then as ever, the Lord was her committee of ways and means; but for three days the answer was delayed. Then, an old lady called to express her indebtedness for Miss E.'s services three years before, and ask her acceptance of ten dollars therefor, "no sort of equivalent for days and days of writing and searching law papers, but only a little token that the service was not forgotten."

There was the answer to her prayer; there the redemption of the pledge: "As the mountains are round about Jerusalem, so the Lord is round about his people from henceforth, even forever."

Employment Found.

A man and wife were out of employment, and in very great trouble. Mr. H. (missionary) had added his efforts to theirs, and sedulously sought among the families he knew, for positions for them. After two weeks' fruitless endeavor, he said to the man, "Well, John, let us go into the Fulton street meeting and leave it with the Lord." They did so; the request was read and remembered

The very next day, Mr. H. received a note from one of the families to whom he had already applied, and without success, requesting him to send the man and wife of whom he had spoken. Very joyfully he did so, and they were both engaged! Mr. H. considered it a very marked answer to prayer, inasmuch as it was quite difficult to find a family who wanted a man as well as woman servant; and that particular family was, of all others, the least likely to make such an arrangement!

A Barrel of Flour.

For the "Faith Home for Incurables" Mr. H. received, one day, five dollars. A barrel of flour was terribly needed. He went to a large house in New York, hoping the Lord would incline the proprietor to sell him a barrel for that sum. He felt too poor, was not willing; and with a heavy heart, Mr. H. returned, asking the Lord what next he should do He called at the store of a friend, where the following conversation took place. "Well, did you get the flour?" "I did not; they feel too poor, and I am terribly disappointed. It is almost dark now; I have lost my time going over there, and at this hour, the flour merchants here are closed." "Well, Mr. —— called here, and I told him you were in, and on what errand you had gone to New York. He said he would send a barrel to my store if I would send it up to the Home; and I did so, about an hour ago."

Wonderful Ways of the Lord in Guiding His People.

Our missionaries move amidst the reality of scenes which religious fiction vainly strives to equal. Remarkable proofs of genuine and vivid piety, triumphs of patience and grace, lifting their possessors above the most painful and distressing circumstances, are met with in all their explorations, and more than repay them for toil or privation.

Wonderful Conversion of a Roman Catholic.

A frame dwelling in an alley, two rooms on the first floor, in the smaller one a bed-ridden old colored man, who had fought the battle of life for ninety years, fifteen of them on his bed, with eyes so dimmed by age that he could not even read; and a wife who was eye, ear and solace to him, are the salient points of our first picture.

They were both earnest, exultant Christians, around whom the angels of God encamped day and night. The wife was brought up in the West Indies, as a Catholic, but her ideas of religion consisted mostly in counting beads on a rosary. After coming to Brooklyn, she became a servant in the family of a well-known naval officer, and was always a favorite on account of her vivacity. One day, a young painter who was working there, and proved to be one of the Christians whose light shines for all in the house, spoke to her, and invited her to a prayer-meeting in a Protestant chapel. She refused, laughing ; but the painter's assurance next day, that she had been prayed for in that meeting, made her restless, uneasy and sick. In a few days, she was confined to her bed and pronounced by some doctors, a victim to consumption. One, more sagacious than the rest, said her trouble was of the mind, not the body, and a minister would be better than a doctor.

It proved to be the case ; she was soon led into a glimmering hope, though feeling that she literally carried a burden on her back. Starting out, one night, to look for a place of worship, she turned her feet to a Methodist meeting from whence the sound of singing had reached her. In the prayer and exhortation, however, there were words which revealed to her the secret of faith and salvation. She felt the burden loosen and fall from her shoulders, so sensibly, that involuntarily, she turned and looked for it on the floor. In a few moments she began to realize the freedom she had gained, and started to her feet in joy and wonder.

Her work then began in her own home, and through her prayers of faith, five members of the Commodore's own family and an Irish Catholic servant girl, were brought to " Christ, the living way." For years her faith was proved by her works ; her daily example in the household, her watchings and waitings by the bedside of her helpless husband—poverty, sickness, perplexities of every sort, but made her hope the brighter, her hold the firmer. With no dependence for their daily bread but the benefactions of one and another person, sometimes entire strangers, they never knew what it was to suffer actual want, nor did Frances ever believe that her friend would forget her.

Remarkable Preservation of Life from Lightning in Answer to Prayer.

I was riding on top of the Boulder Pass of the Rocky Mountains, in the summer of 1876, when a sudden storm of rain, wind, and furious tempest came up. There was no shelter from rocks, no trees or buildings to be seen—a lonely, wind-swept summit. I knew that the lightning on those high elevations was fearful in intensity. I was appalled at the prospect before me, but feeling that God had promised to care for his children—"No evil shall befall thee or come nigh thy dwelling"—I composed myself, and though on horseback, with the rain beating in torrents, I offered simple prayer to God that he would save me from the rain and stop it. But *No*, it came harder than ever; then I prayed that I might be protected from all danger, "*for I trusted in Him!*"

I rode on and on for miles, chilly, cold, wet through, the clouds hanging low and the lightning flashing above me, around me, striking near me, constant flashes, peals of thunder, but I was not terrified. "God must keep me." *Twice I was distinctly struck* with the electric flash, detached portions or sparks from the electric cloud, directly in the center of the forehead, but it had no more force than just to close my eyes, shake my head a little, obscure my sight a moment, and then it was all over, and I was clearer, cooler, calmer, happier, and more self-possessed than ever before. I attribute my protection from peril entirely to prayer, and the fierceness of the tempest and the proximity of danger were permitted by the Lord to try my trust. Those portions which struck me, if in ordinary times had been given me from an electric battery in a school-room, a shock with sparks only one-hundredth the size, would have killed me.

I can thus say with thanks, faith was then made perfect in danger, and the Lord *was faithful* in hearing his child's cry, and delivered him.

God Never Failed Her.

An aged colored woman, lived that life of faith which shines brighter and brighter unto the perfect day. Born a slave, on Long Island, she was never taught to read, never enjoyed any social privileges; but the God of the widow of Sarepta, who had neither "store-house nor barn," was her God, and brought her out of the house of spiritual bondage.

She outlived all her early associations; all her children and grandchildren, husband and brother passed on before, leaving her alone in poverty and sickness. Yet she sat in her little hut, a cheerful, happy Christian, a living witness for God as a covenant-keeper. Doubting, despondent souls were always glad to visit her, to listen to her simple words of wisdom and gather strength from her invincible trust. Roman Catholic neighbors persecuted and even threatened her; but in reply to a missionary who remarked that it must be very trying and somewhat dangerous, she said, " Don't you know the Lord has a hook in the jaws of the wicked, so they shan't hurt us if we belong to him ? Jesus is always with me; so I'm never alone and never afraid."

His Mother's Prayer.

A poor sailor, leading a most profligate and abandoned life, whose praying mother followed him like a shadow into and out of his drinking saloons and gambling houses, at last absented himself from home, whenever he was in port. Her burden, finally, seemed too great to bear, and she resolved to make a stronger effort than ever before, to cast it upon the Lord. As she knelt, with her heart well-nigh bursting with this desire, she felt a powerful conviction that, at last, she was answered. For several years the son went on in his wicked career, and the mother sorrowed that it was so, but her soul was no longer laden with fear; she felt the assurance of his conversion, sooner or later. Again, for several years, she never heard of him, and thought him dead; then she ceased praying for him, and was steadfast in the faith of meeting him in heaven. But sight was to be given her, as a reward for faith. He returned, at last, only thirty years of age, but broken down in health, and worn out by dissipation and hardship. Still unconverted, but, to satisfy his mother, he consented to remain in the room during a visit of the missionary of that district; a man with sufficient tact not to make his efforts obnoxious. He did not tell the young man he was a sinner and must flee from the wrath to come; he merely presented the *love* of Jesus; the love that saved to the very *uttermost*; that waited more patiently than any earthly friend, and forgave more royally. At first, he listened indifferently, but, at last, burst into tears, saying, " I thought I was so bad He didn't want anything to do with me." A long conversation, and others at intervals followed, and, before his death, which occurred several months after, his mother's heart was gladdened by the account of his change, and the knowledge that, in farthest lands, his thoughts were back with her. The deeper he went in sin, the more unsatisfactory and abhorrent it became, and he would have turned, long before, to the Lord, had he believed there was the least hope for him. When he closed his eyes to earth, a few friends enabled his mother to give him respectable burial, in the same grave where, years before, his father was laid.

The Heart of Stone Relents.

Another consumptive in the neighborhood, was thoroughly an infidel. Mr. A. visited the house three times a week, and, at last, succeeded in overcoming his objections to a weekly prayer-meeting in his house. In his hearing, earnest supplication was always made for him, and, at the end of four months, the heart of stone relented. He had not, at first, the courage to appropriate the promises to himself; but one morning very early he sent for the missionary to reveal the news that he felt all his sins forgiven, and had "Christ *in him*, the hope of glory." Four months more he lived to bear witness continually to God's amazing mercy, and then joyfully expired, declaring himself saved by grace alone.

A Discouraged One Revived.

Mr. C——, walking home one Saturday afternoon, fell into a discouraged train of thought because he appeared to have done so little for the Master that whole week. At that moment a young man took him by the hand saying—"You do not know me, but I know you. A few weeks ago I was on the high road to destruction, but now through your instrumentality I am in the narrow path which leads to everlasting life. I attended your prayer-meeting one evening in company with a friend of mine. You spoke with great earnestness, and after we sang the last hymn you remarked, 'How can I bless whom God has cursed? For he declares, If any man love not the Lord, he shall be accursed.' I cannot describe my sensations. For several days I could find no peace, but when at last my faith rested on Jesus, I found that peace which flows like a river; and now, like Moses, I have chosen rather to suffer affliction with the children of God than to enjoy the pleasures of sin, for I know if I have to face any trouble on account of my religion, I can look forward to a glorious reward."

The Prisoner Loosed.

On the third floor of a tenement house, a missionary, Mr. B., found a comely, intelligent young English woman in great distress. Her heart seemed wrung by grief. A few kind words of sympathy drew from her the story of her woe. She came to this country with her husband and three young children. He was employed as book-keeper in a large mercantile house; but soon became addicted to drink, and the story is ever the same; loss of position, poverty, disgrace, suffering and recklessness. On the day of the missionary's visit, he was in a prison cell, committed as a vagrant and common drunkard. The wife was bitterly weeping in her cheerless home, and the children around her fretting with hunger. Mr B. was so touched he could scarcely find words with which to console her, but turned to Isaiah and read, "For thy maker is thy husband; the Lord of Hosts is his name." "For a small moment have I forsaken thee, but with great mercies will I gather thee." After his prayer, she felt calmer, and entreated him to come the next week, on the day her husband would be released. He complied; found a prepossessing and cultivated man; and upon telling him how earnestly his wife and himself had prayed for him, was rejoiced to learn that in that lonesome cell the Spirit of God had visited him, filled him with a sincere wish to reform the future and redeem the past. The missionary called again and again, and witnessed the strong determination of the young man to fight against his pernicious habit. He was soon employed again in a large house, became a regular attendant at the Lord's house, and began to pray both publicly and privately for help from on high Only a few months, and both husband and wife united with a church and became teachers in the Sabbath school Their own home, once laid waste, again blossomed like the rose.

Praying for Tea.

On a top floor in a street of tenements lives a colored woman one hundred and ten years old! Her son, a man over seventy, lost his wife, a neat, active Christian woman, very suddenly, and his aged mother was plunged in despairing grief. "Why, why was I left, old and rheumatic and useless, and Mary, a smart, busy, capable woman taken away without a minute's warning?" was her continual cry. But the son was left desolate, and the two rooms were to be kept clean, the meals provided before he left for his work in the morning, and after his work at night; there was no one else to do it, and love for him called out new effort. With cane in one hand she treads the rooms back and forth, performing the household duties. Eyes undimmed, faculties unimpaired, she *does what she can*. Upon receiving a call a few months after the death of her daughter-in-law, she said — "You've brought me a whole pound of that nice tea! Well, honey, *I asked the Lord for some good tea last night, and I knowed well enough it would be along some time to-day, cos He never keeps me waiting long.* I found out why he took Mary instead of me ; old as I was, I wasn't half so fit to go, and he was so full of mercy he let me stay long enough to see it! You know, honey, I've got no one to talk over old times with. There ain't none of 'em left that I was young with, and not many I was old with ; but I'm never lonesome, for I'm too busy thinking of all the Lord's watching and waiting for me. I'm dreadful little use, but my son couldn't get along very well without me, and then I tell you I'm so busy thinking, I ain't got any time to be lazy or lonesome. Good many little things we want, too, and I have to be runnin' to the Lord for 'em."

"Do they come every time, auntie?" "Every single time, honey! He never fails, no matter who else does. He knows I don't ask for no nonsense ; only for the things we really need, and he has promised them all the time" "But, are there not times, auntie, for instance, when your son is sick, when you cannot see where rent and food is coming from?" "Don't want to see, honey! What's the use seein'? Believin's the thing! Believin's better than money." And so, all the revolving months, this relic of the last century walks by faith in the unseen.

Giving Her Last Dollar to the Lord.

A poor woman, sitting in a little church, heard the minister make an urgent appeal for money enough to pay a debt of two hundred dollars, contracted by the church the previous Winter. She had one dollar in her pocket ; half drew it out; thought of the improbability of having any more for several days, put it back. Thought again, "Trust in the Lord for more;" drew it wholly out, and deposited it in the basket. The next morning, a lady called to settle a bill of two dollars, so long unpaid that it was, long before, set down among the losses.

The Danish Girl's Blessing.

A very poor Danish girl, broken down in health, utterly unable longer to labor for her own support, was provided with the means, and urged to go to Denmark, as her friend felt sure there was some good in store for her there, meaning, more definitely, the restoration of her health. She could not be induced until, thoroughly satisfied by several tokens that it was the Lord's will, and then she consented

A devout, humble Christian missionary became acquainted with her soon after her arrival, and, being struck with the beauty of holiness in every action and conversation of her life, asked her to marry him, that he might have the constant satisfaction of rendering her life comfortable, and finding his own encouragement in her unfailing faith. His letters are full of his saintly wife, and her signally blessed efforts in winning people to put their trust where it need fear no betrayal.

The Swedish Girl Blessed.

A Christian Swedish girl, who had, for three years, done the washing of a certain family, had so interested them by her care of an aged father, and gained their esteem by her humble piety, that, wishing to go to Europe for six months, they offered her two rooms in their house for that time, that she might not only save the labor necessary to pay her rent, but, also, take charge of their effects. The offer was gladly accepted, and recognized as a token especially from the Lord.

12

In times when the father was yet able to work a little, they had economized to a degree that resulted in saving twenty dollars. It was laid by for three months' rent, when he should be no longer able to earn it. That time had come; as yet the money had not been touched; but Satan sent a wicked woman to hire the next room, and, while the father was asleep, and his poor daughter at church, she stole it. Their grief was great, but they reminded the Lord how hardly it was earned, and how faithful he had always been to His promises. It can be easily understood with what emphasis this unexpected offer came to them.

Saved from Drowning.

A poor German woman rushed frantically through the street and into the house of a countrywoman, very little better off than herself, declaring she would drown herself that very night if *no* one would give her work. A family on the same floor gave her the use of a very small, bare room for one week, free of charge; after that, it would be eighty cents per week rent. Her countrywoman shared with her, such as she had for the evening and the morning, and after the breakfast, sent for a good, ever-ready missionary to talk and pray her into a better frame of mind. He did so, but confirmed and rested her faith on substantial works. He procured employment for her before the sun set; enough to pay the rent and get a little common food. Then obtained coal sufficient to last a couple of months; and so, leading her little by little into light and hope, drew her into regular attendance at the Mission chapel in her neighborhood.

The Widow in Want.

A home missionary in Brooklyn, who has an enviable reputation for his entire consecration to the work of helping the poor, one day when engaged in his benevolent works, entered a restaurant, kept by a Christian friend, a man of like spirit with himself, who, in the course of conversation, related to him the following circumstances, illustrative of the power of prayer.

He had, on a certain day, cleared a large sum, part of which consisted of *Mexican dollars*. Returning home in high spirits, he felt as if he could go to sleep sweetly on this silver pillow. But a thought suddenly intruded, which gave a new turn to his feelings. It related to a poor woman in his neighborhood, the widow of a very dear friend of his, whom he knew to be in want "Shall I take all this money to myself?" thought he. "Does not the Providence who gave it to me say, *No! Give some of it to the widow of your friend.*"

With this impression he retired, as was his habit, quite early, but he could not sleep. The thought of the needy widow haunted him. "I will go to-morrow," said he to himself. "and see what I can do for her." But this good intention proved no opiate to his disturbed mind. "Possibly she or I may not live to see to-morrow" Something seemed to say *go now*. He tossed from side to side, but could not sleep. *Go now* kept ringing in his ear. So at length the restless man had to dress himself and go

At this late hour, not far from eleven, he sallied forth to find the widow Seeing a dim light in the upper story where she resided, and following its lead, he crept softly along on the stairway, until he reached the room from which a low sound issued. The door was slightly ajar; through which he could hear the voice of prayer, scarcely audible, but deeply earnest. He dared hardly stir, lest he should disturb the praying widow. But he came on an errand, and he must accomplish it. But how? Recollecting at the moment, that he had in his pocket a few of the *Mexican dollars,* he gently pushed at the door, and it opened just wide enough for his purpose. So taking each piece of money between his fingers, he rolled it in along the carpet, and withdrew as noiselessly as he had ascended. Returning to his home, he fell asleep and slept soundly, as well he might, after this act.

The widow at length arose from her knees, and was struck on seeing the shining money lying about her floor. Where had these pieces of silver come from? Here was a mystery she could not solve. But she knew it was from the Lord, and that he had answered her prayer. So with tears of gratitude, she gave thanks to Him, "whose is the silver and the gold"

Shortly after this event, she attended prayer-meeting, where she felt constrained to make known this wonderful interposition in answer to prayer. The Christians present were as much astonished as herself. The silence which ensued was broken by a brother of that church, who rose and said, "What this good woman has told you, is strictly true. These dollars came from the Lord. They came in answer to her prayer." He then detailed the circumstances before related. "God deputed me to carry this money, and providentially I am here to night to testify to the fact that God hears and answers prayer."

It seems, from a subsequent statement, that this widow owed a certain sum, that she was obliged to pay immediately, and having nothing in hand, she was pleading, that night, that her Heavenly Father would send her the needed amount.

The Sewing Girl Relieved Just in Time.

A sick Scotch girl was found lying on a narrow bed in a close, uncomfortable room, her sobs audible to the missionary, when half-way up the stairs. Her story was short. When about, she earned three dollars and a half a week, at a business that was killing her. Of that, she paid three dollars for her board; leaving but the half-dollar for clothing or incidentals. But now—she had been lying there two weeks; six dollars were due for board, and still she was unable to rise, and, when she did, how could she ever pay the back indebtedness?

The woman with whom she lived, was too poor herself to give her the lost time, and, moreover, was one of the class whom struggle and battle hardens. The missionary came just in time to quell the poor girl's fears, and paid her debts; mind and body were set at rest, and, one or two Christian ladies being made acquainted with the case, attended to the comforts which hastened her recovery; and, when once more pursuing her avocation, her "mither's God" seemed very near, not as one afar off.

Praying for a Home.

A young Southern girl, who had lost a position through five months' sickness, and found herself, at last, in the street and penniless, turned her steps to a daily prayer-meeting. She said her earliest impressions from her mother were, that the Lord never failed those who really put their trust in Him. She had sought work for food and shelter, though destitute of sufficient covering to keep her from trembling with cold, and, so far, sought in vain; but she was sure it was waiting for her somewhere, and she thought perhaps God's people could tell her where. She was right. A sweet-faced lady, who had listened, said she wanted some young girl who might help her a little when she left for her summer residence, and she had been waiting to find a child of pious parents. Bessie went home with her from that very meeting, and, in two weeks, came back, with bright eyes and warm, good clothing, to say good-by to the ladies who had spoken to her so kindly, and, in whose midst, she had found a second mother. They were to leave town the next day, and she asked permission to come to the meeting once more and tell what the Lord had done for her.

How Much Good Two Dollars Did.

A lady sent two dollars to a brave-hearted sister—who, by faith alone, and not by money, had gathered some sick and poor about her, and lived only by prayer—and a note of apology and half-contempt that it was such a miserable pittance. She received, in reply, the following little financial statement:

"MY DEAR FRIEND :—Remember the five loaves and two fishes, and listen to the message of your two dollars. This is the way I expended it:

Corned beef, ...	$0 80
Chop and egg for sick aunty, ...	13
Sweet potatoes, ...	25
White potatoes, ...	10
Cabbage and bread, ...	30
Tea, milk and sugar, ...	30
	$1 88

The balance bought the coal with which it was cooked, and *fifteen* people were fed!"

Saved from Starvation.

On the second floor of a rear house lived a lady well known once as among the foremost members of a wealthy church. The first blow of adversity opened a wide passage for a succession of disasters. She passed through the whole sliding scale, until the missionary found her in the poor, dilapidated tenement where, for two days and nights, she had lain in bed to keep warm; or as nearly so as her scanty covering would admit.

It was Saturday, and the only food she had to keep her alive until Monday, was two soda biscuits! She had sold everything comfortable in the way of furniture; all her clothing but one respectable suit for the street, and the only thing remaining, that pointed to the history of better days, was a pair of gold eye-glasses, given her by her dying mother. Within a few months her dire necessity had often pointed to the glasses; but she could not see without them, nor could she sell the gold frames unless she had means to have the glass set in commoner ones. Moreover, the harpies who feed and thrive on the miseries of the poor, would in no case have given her more than twenty-five cents for them; and the short respite derived from that amount would not have compensated for the sacrifice. She had looked at them that morning; felt that starve she must and would, but that souvenir of her mother should never leave her. She went back to bed and prayed fervently that the Lord would show her some way of escape, or take her that day to himself. She slept an hour or two, and then awakened, strong in the conviction that he would show her some way before night, and though it was six o'clock P. M., before the missionary called, no doubt had arisen to trouble her mind; and as soon as he entered and introduced himelf, she said—"You are a messenger from the Lord, sir; I have been expecting you."

God With Us.

An old woman was taking home some sewing the night before, and passing through a narrow and dark street, was knocked down by a runaway horse. Taken up senseless and unknown, she was carried into the house of a kind family who sent for a physician It was not till next morning that she recovered consciousness, and was able to give her address. A messenger was at once despatched to her husband, who was supposed to be wild with terror. He was truly thankful to hear from human lips of her whereabouts; but said he knew she was not dead, and he would see her in the morning, for the Lord had been with him all night and assured him of it. He had also kept the fire from going out; and now that she would be brought home in a few hours, he was ready to trust his Father, as he had been through the night. His hourly friend was Immanuel, God *with* us; not God somewhere or other in infinite space.

A Vessel Saved.

A vessel was six months making the passage from Liverpool to Bermuda Island. Fogs enveloped it; winds sent it hither and thither; captain and mate lost their reckoning, lost their senses; and when, added to the rest, the vessel sprung a leak, gave up in despair. Crew and passengers were finally reduced to a few drops of water and one potato a day, and they merely waited death from starvation or drowning. All but one! One man; a minister, whose faith and belief in their final escape burned but brighter and brighter, as the others sank in the gloom of silent despair. A few days before they made the land, the leakage suddenly ceased; no one could account for it; but a week after their arrival, when the vessel had been condemned by the authorities as unseaworthy, it was proposed to turn it bottom upward and see what stopped the leak. God seemed to have performed a miracle for them, when it was discovered that that end of the vessel was entirely covered with barnacles !

A Remarkable Prayer Concerning a Remarkable Text.

A clergyman, accustomed to preach regularly in his journey through Fleming Circuit, Kentucky, was preparing on one Saturday for the labors of the next day. He was then staying at the residence of a family named Bowers, from which he was to journey the next day five miles to preach at 11 A. M., at a church called Mt. Olivet. On this Saturday, as he relates the incident, as soon and as privately as practicable, I pored over the Bible in quest of a suitable subject for the next day at Mount Olivet, and strange to tell! not one passage in the whole Book, that afternoon and night, could I fix upon, as, in my estimation, suitable for the next day. There was one passage, (two or three clauses of which I had by some means got fixed in my memory), that early that afternoon appeared in my mind as though each word was written in CAPITAL LETTERS. I turned to the whole passage as soon as I could find it; Heb. 6:4-6; and read, "For it is impossible for those who were once enlightened," etc., etc. I had previously studied that whole subject, as recorded in the original, and as disposed of by learned Commentators of different creeds. I had settled in my own mind the import of the passage. But it seemed unsuitable for me, not then three years old in the ministry, to attempt the settlement of a theological question, about which the best and most learned of modern days had differed. I therefore tried to dismiss it from my mind, and to find some passage more suitable for the coming morrow. But my constant effort proved unsuccessful; and the said passage in Hebrews often recurred to my mind. Thus passed my time till I had to go to bed, resolving to attempt an early settlement of the growing difficulty next morning. But the morning studies produced no change in the unsettled state of the question, what shall I preach from to-day? Thus matters remained until I reached Mount Olivet, and had to begin service without a text. But I concluded if a suitable text did not occur while singing, praying and reading some Scripture lesson, rather than have no text, I would take Heb. 6:4-6. And, cornered in this dilemma, so I did, and used it as well as I could.

I then passed around the circuit as usual, and the fourth Saturday thereafter, I arrived again at Brother Bowers', preached, met the class, etc. Then, when all the class had left the room except their own family, Brother and Sister Bowers said to me, each manifesting intense feeling and interest, "Have you heard of the *strange* thing that happened when you were here four weeks ago?" Said I, "No! what was it?" They said, "Did you see a man sitting in the house while you was preaching to-day?" describing his dress, looks, etc. I answered, "Yes." Said they, "Did you see a woman sitting over there," describing her? I said, "Yes." Said they, "They are husband and wife—their name is—(I have long since forgotten the name)—they are good members of the Presbyterian church, their children are members of our class, as you have called their names every time you have examined us. The man and his wife were here and heard you four weeks ago—they know our rules, and when those not of our church were dismissed, they left their children with us, as usual, and their parents started home. And, as they themselves tell us and others, as they went along, said the woman to her husband, 'Does not Mr. Akers preach to-morrow at Mount Olivet?' And he answered, 'I believe he does.' Said she, ' *Well, if I thought he would take a certain text I would like very much to go and hear him.*' Said her husband, ' *What text?* ' And she repeated the whole passage in *Hebrews* 6 : 4–6. Said her husband, 'Well, I reckon he will take some subject that will be interesting, and if you say so we will not go to our own church to-morrow, we will go to Mount Olivet.' She answered, '*Agreed*, and I do pray the Lord that he may take that text.' And she says, she continued to pray all that evening and next morning, until sitting in the church at Mount Olivet, she heard *you read out the said text, when she knew the Lord had answered her prayer*, and she could scarcely help from loud crying of thanks to God."

I then told Brother and Sister Bowers my troubles about that text, as above stated. The Lord answers prayer.

How She Learned to Love the Bible.

The Rev. Frederick G. Clark thus writes of an answer to prayer, from one who wanted to love the Bible more :

"Twenty-seven years ago, in the congregation of my first charge, was a lady whose love for the Bible was something remarkable. In the confidence of a pastoral visit, she told me of her joy in the divine word, and also recited the incidents of her experience in this regard. She had formerly read her Bible as so many do—a chapter now, and a half-chapter then, without much interest or profit. She was, even then, most interested in religious things. But her chief sources of spiritual strength were in such writings as those of Baxter, Payson and Robert Phillips. It was her custom to read the Bible from duty, and then turn to these uninspired volumes for the kindling of a higher devotion. For a good while this satisfied her; but, at length, she came to feel grieved about it. She thought it a dishonor to God's word that any book should be as interesting to her as the Bible. She tried to change this, but, at first, with little success. The Bible was still duty—Baxter was pleasure and spiritual elevation.

"*At length, she could bear it no longer; so she took the case to God, with strong crying. She told her Heavenly Father how grieved she was that any book should rival the Bible in her affections. She asked this one thing—and she renewed her prayer every day—that her first delight might be in reading the word of God.* I think it was some time before she felt that her request was granted. But, at length, the answer to her prayer was complete and marvelous. A strange light came over the sacred page. A fascination held her to her Bible. She discovered a depth, a meaning, a curiosity, a charm, which were all new and most wonderful. Sometimes, when she had finished reading her Bible for the night, and had closed the book and had moved towards her bed, she would go back again and enjoy the luxury of a few more verses.

The Blind Restored to Sight.

At the age of twenty years, a lady in Winchester, Iowa, began to lose her health, and in a short time was confined to her bed. And she writes:—"In addition to this I lost the use of my eyes, and was blind and helpless, a greater portion of my time for five years.

"I enjoyed the blessing of prayer and trust some six months before feeling a liberty to pray for the healing of my body;

fearing I should desire it without due submission to God's will. It was with *fear and trembling* that I first made known this request. Though my pleadings in this direction were earnest, and often agonizing, yet I could say with a fervor as never before, 'Not my will, but thine be done.'

" About the end of November, or early in December, 1873, I realized that my faith was perfect, that I was ready *now* to be healed, that my faith was momentarily waiting on God, resting without a doubt on the promises. From this time forward my faith remained fixed with but one exception. During the time between December, 1873, and July, 1874, I was healed to such an extent that I could walk some, and see more or less every day, though sometimes with only one of my eyes. A portion of this time I felt as though in a furnace of fire; but amid the flames I realized the presence of the Son of God, who said, '*I have chosen thee in the furnace of affliction.*' This for a time seemed an answer to my petition, and so thought it my life-work to suffer; for a while my faith became inactive, and I almost ceased praying for my health. Though I felt submissive, yet somehow I was soon crying, and that most instinctively, 'Thou Son of David, have mercy on me.' After this, my faith did not waver. Oh, the lesson of patience I learned in thus *waiting* on *God's* good time. And with what comfort could I present my body an offering to Him, realizing that as soon as at all possible with His will, I should be healed; I had an assurance of this, but did not know whether it would be during life, or accomplished only at death.

" In this manner I waited before God until the morning of the 29th of July, when, without ecstacy of joy, or extra illumination, came a sense of the presence of Jesus, and a presentation of this gift, accompanied with these words: 'Here is the gift for which you have been praying; are you willing to receive it?'

" I at first felt the incoming of the Divine power at the parts diseased, steadily driving out the same. until death was swallowed up in victory. I at once arose from my bed, and proceeded to work about the house, to the great astonishment of my friends, some of whom thought me wild; but I continued my work, assuring them that Jesus had healed me. Realizing the scrutiny and doubt with which I was observed, I said to my father, 'What do you think?' He replied, 'It is supernatural power; no one can deny it.'

"My healing took place on Wednesday; on Saturday was persuaded to lie down, which I did, but found the bed was no place for me; thought of Peter's wife's mother, who 'arose and ministered to them;' knew that to her, strength, as well as health, was instantly given, as in the case of the palsied man, who rose, took up his bed, and departed. I returned to my work, backing my experience with those in God's word, and since then have not lain down during the day time.

"My friends could not realize the completeness of the cure, until I read a full hour, and that by lamp-light, and until asked to desist, the first opportunity after being healed.

"A week from this time, I discharged the hired girl, taking charge of the household work, which I have continued with perfect ease. About four weeks after my healing, had occasion to walk four miles, which I did with little or no weariness. Let me add to the praise of God, that I have no disease whatever. Am able to do more hard work with less weariness, than at any other period in my life, and faith in the Lord is the balm that made me whole."

The Widow's Shoes.

A poor woman—a widow with an invalid son—a member of the church, could not attend church, or the neighborhood prayer-meetings, for the want of shoes. She asked the Lord for the shoes. That very day the village school-master called in to see her son. Meanwhile he noticed that the boy's mother had very poor shoes. He said nothing, but felt impressed, and inwardly resolved to purchase the poor woman a pair of shoes forthwith. He accordingly hired a horse, rode two miles on horseback to a shoe-store, bought the shoes, and requested them sent to the widow's cottage without delay. They proved a perfect fit; and that very night the overjoyed woman hurried to the prayer-meeting to announce that in answer to prayer the Lord had sent her the shoes.

The young school-master, who, I suspect, was my informant himself, now a venerable, white-haired man, heard the poor woman's testimony; and his pillow that night was wet with tears of gratitude and joy because God had used him thus to bless the poor widow, and to answer her prayers.

A Remarkable Dream.

The late Dr. Whitehead was accustomed to repeat with pleasure the following fact: In the year 1764, he was stationed as an itinerant preacher in Cornwall. He had to preach one evening in a little village where there was a small Methodist Society. "The friend," said he, "at whose house we preached, had at that time a daughter, who lived with one of our people about ten miles off. His wife was gone to attend her daughter, who was dangerously ill of a fever; and her husband had that day received a message from her, informing him that his child's life was despaired of. He earnestly and with tears desired Mr. Whitehead to recommend his daughter to God in prayer, both before and after preaching. He did so in the most warm and affectionate manner. Late that evening, or very early next morning, while the young woman's mother was sitting by her daughter's bedside (who had been in a strong delirium for several days), she opened her eyes and hastily addressed her mother thus: 'O mother! I have been dreaming that I saw a man lifting up his eyes and hands to heaven, and fervently praying to God for my recovery! The Lord has heard his prayers, and my fever is gone; and what is far better, the Lord has spoken peace to my soul, and sealed His pardoning love on my heart. I know it, I feel it, my dear mother; and His Spirit bears witness

with my spirit, that I am a child of God, and an heir of
glory.' Her mother, thinking that she was still in delirium,
desired her to compose herself, and remain quiet. The
daughter replied, ' My dear mother, I am in no delirium now;
I am perfectly in my senses; do help me to rise, that upon
my bended knees I may praise God' Her mother did so,
and they both praised God with joyful hearts, and from that
hour the young woman recovered so fast, that she was soon
able to attend to the affairs of the family where she lived.
She had never seen Mr Whitehead, previous to this remarkable time; but some weeks after, she saw him, and the
moment she beheld his face, she fainted away. As soon as
she came to herself, she said, ' Sir, you are the person I saw
in my dream, when I was ill in a violent fever; and I beheld
you lift up your hands and eyes to heaven, and most fervently
pray for my recovery and conversion to God. The Lord, in
mercy, heard your prayers, and answered them to the healing
of my wounded spirit, and to the restoration of my body. I
have walked in the light of His countenance from that time
to the present, and I trust I shall do so as long as I live.' How
remarkably does this circumstance illustrate the words of St.
James, ' The prayer of faith shall save the sick, and the Lord
shall raise him up, and if he have committed sins, they shall
be forgiven him!'"

"You Must Not Go."

A remarkable instance of deep impression occasionally
made by the Holy Spirit on the mind of the Rev. William
Bramwell during prayer, occurred in Liverpool. A pious
young woman, a member of Society, wished to go to her
friends, then living in Jamaica. She took her passage, had
her luggage taken on board, and expected to sail on the following day. Having the greatest respect for Mr. Bramwell,
she waited upon him, to take leave and request an interest in
his prayers. Before parting, they knelt down, and he recom-

mended her to the care of God.   After he had been engaged
in prayer some time, he suddenly paused, and thus addressed
her, " My dear sister, you must not go to-morrow.   God has
just told me you must not go." She was surprised, but he
was positive, and prevailed upon her to postpone her voyage,
and assisted her to remove her luggage out of the vessel.
The ship sailed, and in about six weeks intelligence arrived
that the vessel was lost, and all on board had perished.

Evil Averted.

A correspondent of the *Guide to Holiness* says :
" We remember a poor woman who had had a life of sore
vicissitude which she bore with remarkable Christian cheerfulness; and after a time of the suspension of trial, a bad
prospect came in sight.   She resorted to a friend to whom
she confidingly related the threatening evil, and at parting
said, ' Oh pray for us.'   The case as it was known was taken
immediately that early morning to the throne of grace and
laid out in all its circumstances with a deeply sympathizing
heart, and a consciousness of the past sufferings of that woman
—and as the friend rose from prayer, the answer was given
that the evil was averted, and a new change would come to
that afflicted one.

" That very day a strange deliverance and opening appeared
which set that family at rest from their peculiar trials for the
rest of life."

How a Poor Little Cripple Converted a Village.

Mr. D. L. Moody relates the instance of a poor little cripple, whose prayers were answered to the conversion of *fifty-
six people.*

" I once knew a little cripple who lay upon her death bed.
She had given herself to God, and was distressed only because

she could not labor for Him actively among the lost. Her clergyman visited her, and hearing her complaint, told her from her sick bed she could pray; to pray for those she wished to see turning to God. He told her to write the names down, and then to pray earnestly; he went away and thought of the subject no more.

"Soon a feeling of religious interest sprang up in the village, and the churches were crowded nightly. The little cripple heard of the progress of the revival, and inquired anxiously for the names of the saved. A few weeks later she died, and among a roll of papers that was found under her little pillow, was one bearing the names of fifty-six persons, every one of whom had in the revival been converted. By each name was a little cross by which the poor crippled saint had checked off the names of the converts as they had been reported to her."

Please God, Give Us a Home.

Mr. Moody tells of a beautiful answer to the faith of a little child.

"I remember a child that lived with her parents in a small village One day the news came that her father had joined the army (it was the beginning of our war), and a few days after, the landlord came to demand the rent. The mother told him she hadn't got it, and that her husband had gone into the army. He was a hard-hearted wretch, and he stormed, and said that they must leave the house; he wasn't going to have people who couldn't pay the rent.

"After he was gone, the mother threw herself into the arm-chair, and began to weep bitterly. Her little girl, whom she taught to pray in faith, (but it is more difficult to practice than to preach,) came up to her, and said, '*What makes you cry, mamma, I will pray to God to give us a little home, and won't He?*' What could the mother say? So the little child went into the next room and began to pray. The door was open, and the mother could hear every word.

13

"' *O, God, you have come and taken away father, and mamma has got no money, and the landlord will turn us out because we can't pay, and we will have to sit on the door-step, and mamma will catch cold. Give us a little home.'* Then she waited as if for an answer, and then added, '*Won't you, please, God?*'

"She came out of that room quite happy, expecting a home to be given them. The mother felt reproved. God heard the prayer of that little one, for he touched the heart of the cruel landlord, and she has never paid any rent since."

God give us the faith of that little child, that we may likewise expect an answer, "*nothing wavering.*"

"Of Course He Will."

Mr. Moody also gives the story of a little child whose father and mother had died, and she was taken into another family. The first night she asked if she could pray, as she used to do.

They said, Oh, yes! So she knelt down, and prayed as her mother taught her, and when that was ended she added a little prayer of her own: "*Oh, God, make these people as kind to me as father and mother were.*" Then she paused, and looked up, as if expecting an answer, and added, "*Of course he will.*"

How sweetly simple was that little one's faith; she expected God to "do," and she got her request.

Striking Answer.

The following incidents are specially contributed to these pages by Rev. J. S. Bass, a Home Missionary of Brooklyn, N. Y.:

"While living in Canada, my eldest daughter, then a girl of ten years of age, rather delicate and of feeble health, had a severe attack of chorea, "St. Vitus's dance." To those who have had any experience in this distressing complaint, nothing need be said of the deep affliction of the household at the sight of our loved one, as all her muscles appeared to be affected, the face distorted with protrusion of the tongue, and the continuous involuntary motions by jerks of her limbs. The ablest medical advice and assistance were employed, and all that the sympathy of friends and the skill of physicians could do were of no avail. She grew worse rather than better, and death was looked to as a happy release to the sufferings of the child, and the anguish of the parents; as the medical men had given as their opinion that the mind of the child would become diseased, and if her life were lengthened, it would be an enfeebled body united to an idiotic mind.

"But God was better to us than our most sanguine hopes, far better to us than our fears.

"In our trouble we thought on God, and asked his help. We knew we had the prayers of some of God's chosen ones. On a certain Sunday morning I left my home to fill an appointment in the Wesleyan chapel in the village of Cooksville, two miles distant. I left with a heavy heart. My child was distressing to look upon, my wife and her sister were worn out with watching and fatigue. It was only from a sense of duty that I left my home that morning. During the sermon God refreshed and encouraged my heart still to trust in him. After the service, many of the congregation tarried to inquire of my daughter's condition, among them an aged saint, Sister Wilson, widow of a Wesleyan preacher, and Sister Galbraith, wife of the class-leader. Mother Wilson encouraged me to 'hope in God,' saying 'the sisters of the church have decided to spend to-morrow morning together in supplication and prayer for you and your family, and that God would cure Ruth.'

"Monday morning came. Ruth had passed a restless night. Weak and emaciated, her head was held that a tea-spoonful of water should be given her. My duties called me away (immediately after breakfast) to a neighbor's; about noon, a messenger came, in great haste, to call me home. On entering the sick-chamber, I noticed the trundle-bed empty, and my little girl, with smiling face, sitting in a chair at the window, (say eight feet from the bed.)   I learned from the child that, while on the bed, the thought came to her that, if she could only get her feet on the floor, the Lord would help her to sit up.   By an effort, she succeeded, moving herself to the edge of the bed, put her legs over the side until her feet touched the floor, and sat up.   She then thought, if she tried, the Lord would help her to stand up, and then to walk; all of which she accomplished, without any human aid, she being left in the room alone.   The same afternoon she was in the yard playing with her brothers, quickly gained flesh, recovered strength, with intellect clear and bright; she lived to the age of twenty-two, never again afflicted with this disease, or anything like it.   At the age of twenty-two, ripe for heaven, it pleased God to take her to himself.

"The sisters, led by Mother Wilson, waited on God in prayer, and God fulfilled that day the promise—Isaiah 65 : 24: 'And it shall come to pass, that before they call, I will answer; and while they are yet speaking, I will hear.'"

A Remarkable Case.

On the afternoon of Monday, August 20, 1869, I was sent for to visit Mrs. M., who was reported to be very sick.   Arriving at the house, I was told that " Mrs. M., after a hard day's work, had retired to rest Saturday night in her usual state of health, that immediately after getting in bed she had fallen asleep and had not awoke up to this time, (6 o'clock Monday evening,) that three physicians had been in attendance for 30 hours, that all their efforts to arouse her were without avail."

In the chamber, Mrs M. lay in the bed apparently in a troubled sleep, she was a woman of medium size, about 50 years of age, the mother of a large family ; around her bed stood her husband, four sons and a daughter, and relatives, about twelve persons in all. The husband and sons were irreligious, but awed in the presence of this affliction.

I felt, as perhaps I never felt before, my ignorance, my helplessness, and the necessity of entire dependence on God for guidance and inspiration, that prayer should be made in accordance with his will.

I knelt at the bedside and held the woman's hand in mine, lifted up my heart to God and prayed, "If it be thy will and for thy glory, and for the good of this family, grant that this woman may once more open her eyes to look upon her children, once more open her lips in counsel and holy admonition." While thus praying, as I believe, inspired by the Spirit of God, and with faith in Jesus Christ, I was conscious of a movement around me, and opening my eyes, I saw Mrs. M. sitting up in bed. Some of the persons in the room were weeping, others laughing; the sons came nearer the bed, and asked, "Mother, do you know me? do you know me?" She called each by name, and beckoned to her daughter, held her by the hand. I, poor faithless one, was wondering what does this mean? One of the sons took me by the hand saying, "Oh! Mr. Bass, God heard and answered that prayer." I sung the hymn, "There is a fountain filled with blood," Mrs. M. singing to the close, and then, apparently exhausted, sank back on the pillow, speechless and unconscious. The physicians were sent for, came, wondered, speculated, administered medicine, blistered the calves of the legs, and cupped the back of the neck, but to no purpose She remained in speechless unconsciousness till the next afternoon, when, while prayer was being made, she again opened her eyes, sat up and conversed with her children and friends. In a few days she resumed her household duties, enjoying a good degree of health and strength, and faithfully serving God and her generation until it pleased God to call her home to the rest prepared for the people of God, three years after the incident, the subject of this paper.

A Little Girl's Beautiful Faith.

A little German girl, who had never hitherto known the name of the Lord Jesus, was led to attend a Mission school. It was the custom at the school, before the little ones received their dinner, to lift their hands and thank God for their food.

When in course of time she spent her days at home, and her father's family were gathered around their own table, this little girl said:

"*Pa, we must hold up our hands and thank God before we eat.* That's the way we do at the Mission."

So winning was the little one in her ways, the parents yielded at once

At another time her father was sick and unable to work, and the little girl said, "*Pa, I'm going to pray that you may get well and go to work to-morrow morning.*"

At four o'clock in the morning she awoke and called out, "*Pa, don't you feel better.*" The father said, "Yes, I am better," and he went to his work in the morning, although weak and obliged to rest by the way.

There came a time once when he could not get work, and there was no food in the house for dinner.

This little girl knelt down and asked God to send them their dinner, and when she rose from her knees, she said, "Now we must wait till the whistle blows, till 12 o'clock."

At twelve o'clock the whistle blew, and the little girl said, "Get the table ready, it is coming," and just then in came a neighbor with soup for their dinner.

The Lord Helps to Pay Debts.

The author of this incident is known to the editor of "Remarkable Providences," and speaking of it says: "*God never gave me exactly what I wanted. He always gave me more.*"

"When I married I was a working man; I had not much money to spare. In about three months after my marriage, I fell ill, and my illness continued for more than nine months. At that period I was in great distress. I owed a sum of money and had no means to pay it. It must be paid on a certain day, or I must go to jail. I had no food for myself or wife; and in this distress I went up to my room, and took my Bible. I got down on my knees and opened it, laid my fingers on several of the promises, and claimed them as mine. I said, 'Lord, this is thine own word of promise; I claim thy promises.' I endeavored to lay hold of them by faith. I wrestled with God for sometime in this way. I got up off my knees, and walked about some time. I then went to bed, and took my Bible, and opened it on these words: '*Call upon me in the day of trouble, and I will deliver thee, and thou shalt glorify me.*'

"I said, 'it is enough, Lord.' I knew deliverance would come, and I praised God with my whole heart. Whilst in this frame of mind I heard a knock at the door. I went and opened it and a man handed me a letter. I turned to look at the letter, and when I looked up again, the man was gone.

"The letter contained the sum I wanted, and five shillings over. It is now eighteen years ago. I never knew who sent it. God only knows. Thus God delivered me out of all my distress. To Him be all the praise."

Praying for a Lost Pocket-Book.

A contributor to *The Christian* writes as follows:

" A few months since I lost my pocket-book, containing money and papers of a large amount—more than I felt able to lose—and which I should feel the loss of, as I was owing at that time about the same amount.

" On the day of my loss, I had been from home about a mile and a half, and it was about 9 o'clock *in the evening*, when

I returned.   And it was not till then that I ascertained my loss.

"My health was very poor, and the prospect of regaining the lost pocket-book was quite uncertain; it was so dark that I thought it would be impossible for me to find it. Consequently I determined to remain awake during the night, and at 3 o'clock in the morning search for it, and if possible, find it before any one should pass over the road.

"The seeming impossibility of finding it, and the reflections consequent upon the loss of the money were so unpleasant to me that I was led to make it a subject of prayer, fully trusting that in some way God would so direct that I should come in possession of it   If so, I determined to give him $25 of it

"As soon as I had formed this purpose, all that unpleasant feeling left me, and I did not admit a single doubt but I should get it.

"Accordingly, *at 3 o'clock in the morning* I made a thorough search, but could not find it.   Yet my faith in God's guiding hand did not fail me, and I believed that my trust would be realized.

"While I was thus thinking of the certainty of the fulfillment of the promises of the Gospel to the believer, I was called on by a gentleman, a leading business man of the place, who came to know if *I had lost anything*.

"I told him I had lost my pocket-book   He wanted to know how much it contained.   I told him.   He said his son had occasion to pass early on that morning, and had found it in the road, and that in all probability I should otherwise have lost it, as two men passed by immediately after it was found.

"Thus God found it and returned it to me."

Lives of Faith and Trust.

An Extraordinary Life of Faith and Trust.

FOR many centuries there has not been a more remarkable testimony of unfaltering trust in the faithfulness of God in supplying human wants, than is found in the life and labor of George Muller and his Orphan Home, in Bristol, England. His record is one of humility, yet one of daily dependence upon the providence and the knowledge of God to supply his daily wants. It has been one of extraordinary trial; yet never, for a single hour, has God forsaken him. Beginning, in 1834, with absolutely nothing; giving himself, his earthly all and his family to the Lord, and asking the Lord's pleasure and blessing upon his work of philanthrophy, he has never, for once, appealed to any individual for aid, for assistance, for loans; but has relied wholly in prayer to the Lord—coming with each day's cares and necessities—and the Lord has ever supplied. He has never borrowed, never been in debt; living only upon what the Lord has sent—yet in the forty-third year of his life of faith and trust—he has been able, through the voluntary contributions which the Lord has prompted the hearts of the people to give, to accomplish these wonderful results: *Over half a million dollars* have been spent in the construction of buildings—*over fifteen thousand orphans have been cared for and supported*—and *over one million dollars* have been received for their support.

Every dollar of which has been asked for in believing prayer from the Lord. The record is the most astounding in the faith of the Christian religion, and the power and providence of God to answer prayer, that modern times can show.

The orphans' homes have been visited again and again by Christian clergymen of all denominations, to feel the positive satisfaction and certainty that all this were indeed the work of prayer, and they have been abundantly convinced.

The spectacle is indeed a *standing miracle.* "*A man sheltering, feeding, clothing, educating, and making comfortable and happy, hundreds of poor orphan children, with no funds of his own, and no possible means of sustenance, save that which God sent him in answer to prayer.*"

An eminent clergyman who for five years had been constantly hearing of this work of faith, and could hardly believe in its possibility, at last visited Mr. Muller's home for the purpose of thorough investigation, exposing it, if it were under false pretenses or mistaken ways of securing public sympathy, or else with utmost critical search, desired to become convinced it was indeed supported only by true prayer. He had reserved for himself, as he says, a wide margin for deductions and disappointment, but after his search, as "*I left Bristol, I exclaimed with the queen of Sheba, 'The half had not been told me.' Here I saw, indeed, seven hundred orphan children fed and provided for, by the hand of God, in answer to prayer, as literally and truly as Elijah was fed by ravens with meat which the Lord provided.*"

Mr. Muller himself has said in regard to their manner of living. "*Greater and more manifest nearness of the Lord's presence I have never had, than when after breakfast, there were no means for dinner, and then the Lord provided the dinner for more than one hundred persons, and when after dinner, there were no means for the tea, and yet the Lord provided the tea; and all this without one single human being having been informed about our need.*"

Thus it will be seen his life is one of daily trial and trust, and he says, " Our desire therefore, is, not that we may be without trials of faith, but that the Lord graciously would be pleased to support us in the trial, that we may not dishonor him by distrust."

The question having been asked of him, " Such a way of living must lead the mind continually to think whence food, clothes, etc., are to come, with no benefit for spiritual exercise," he replies : " Our minds are very little tried about the necessaries of life ; just because the care respecting them is laid upon our Father, who, because we are his children, not *only allows* us to do so, *but will have us to do so.*

" It must also be remembered that even if our minds *were* much tried about our supplies, yet because we look to the *Lord alone* for all these things, we should be brought by our sense of need, into the presence of our Father for the supply of it, *and that is a blessing*, and satisfying to the soul."

This humble statement from the experience of one who has tried and proven the Lord in little things, as well as large, conveys to the Christian that world of practical instruction which is contained in the precepts of the Bible, viz: to *encourage all to cast their cares on God;* and teaches them the lessons of their dependence upon Him for their daily supplies.

The meaning of the Lord's blessing upon the work of Mr. Muller, is to make it a standing example and illustration to be adopted in every Christian home. *"How God supplies our needs, how he rewards faith, how he cares for those who trust in Him. How he can as well take care of his children to-day as he did in the days of the Prophets, and how surely he fulfills his promise, even when the trial brings us to the extremities of circumstances seemingly impossible."*

Mr. Muller's experience is remarkable, not because the Lord has made his an exceptional case for the bestowal of blessings, but because of the *remarkable, unwavering and persevering application of his faith,* by the man himself.

His faith began with small degrees, and small hopes. It

was painfully tried. But it clung hopefully, and never failed to gain a triumph. Each trial only increased its tenacity, and brought him greater humility, for it opened his own heart to a sense of his own powerlessness, and this faith has grown with work and trial, till its strength is beyond all precedent.

The lessons which the Lord wishes each one to take from it, is this : *"Be your faith little or weak, never give it up ; apply my promises to all your needs, and expect their fulfillment. Little things are as sacred as great things."*

In the journal kept by Mr. Muller during his many years of experience, he has preserved many incidents of answer to prayer in small matters, of which we quote the following from his book. *" The Power of Faith and Prayer."*

1. "One of the orphan boys needed to be apprenticed. I knew of no suitable believing master who would take an indoor apprentice. I gave myself to prayer, and brought the matter daily before the Lord. At last, though I had to pray about the matter from May 21 to September, the Lord granted my request, and I found a suitable place for him.

2. I asked the Lord that he would be pleased to deliver a certain sister in the Lord from the great spiritual depression under which she was suffering, and after three days the Lord granted my request.

3. I asked the Lord daily in his mercy to keep a sister in the Lord from insanity, who was then apparently on the border of it. I have now to record his praise, after nearly four years have passed away, that the Lord has kept her from it.

4 During this year has occurred the conversion of one of the greatest sinners that I had ever heard of in all my service for the Lord Repeatedly I fell on my knees with his wife, and asked the Lord for his conversion, when she came to me in the deepest distress of soul, on account of the most barbarous and cruel treatment that she had received from him in his bitter enmity against her for the Lord's sake. And now the awful persecutor is converted.

5. It pleased the Lord to try my faith in a way in which before, it had not been tried. My beloved daughter was taken ill on June 20. This illness, at first a low fever, turned to typhus, *and July 3 there seemed no hope of her recovery.*

Now was the trial of faith, but faith triumphed. My wife and I were enabled to give her up into the hands of the Lord. He sustained us both exceedingly.

She continued very ill till about July 20, when restoration began. On August 18, she was so far restored that she could be removed to Clevedon for change of air. It was then 59 days since she was taken ill.

6. The heating apparatus of our Orphan Home unexpectedly gave out. It was the commencement of Winter. To repair the leak was a questionable matter. To put in a new boiler would in all probability take many weeks. Workmen were sent for to make repairs. But on the day fixed for repairs a *bleak north wind set in.*"

Now came cold weather, the fire must be put out, the repairs could not be put off. Gladly would I have paid one hundred pounds if thereby the difficulty could have been overcome, and the children not be exposed to suffer for many days from living in cold rooms.

At last I determined on falling entirely into the hands of God, who is very merciful and of tender compassion. I now asked the Lord for two things, viz.: "That He would be pleased to change the *north wind into a south wind,* and that he would give the workmen a mind to work.

Well, the memorable day came. The evening before, the bleak north wind blew still; but on the Wednesday the south wind blew *exactly as I had prayed.* The weather was so mild that no fire was needed

About half-past eight in the evening, the principal of the firm whence the boiler-makers came, arrived to see how the work was going on, and whether he could in any way speed the matter.

The principal went with me to see his men; to the foreman of whom he said : " The men will work late this evening, and come very early again to-morrow."

"*We would rather,*" said the leader, "*work all night.*"

Then remembered I the second part of my prayer, that God would give the men a mind to work. By morning the repair was accomplished, the leak was stopped, and in thirty hours the fire was again in the boiler ; *and all the time the south wind blew so mildly that there was not the least need of a fire.*

7. In the year 1865, the scarlet fever broke out in several of the Orphan Homes. In one of which were four hundred girls, and in the other four hundred and fifty. It appeared among the infants. The cases increased more and more. But we betook ourselves to God in prayer. Day by day we called upon Him regarding this trial, and generally two or three times a day. At last, when the infirmary rooms were filled, and some other rooms that could be spared for the occasion, to keep the sick children from the rest, and when we had no other rooms to spare, at least not without inconvenience, it pleased the Lord to answer our prayers, and in mercy stay the disease. The disease was very general in the town of Bristol, and many children died in consequence. *But not one in the Orphan Home died. All recovered.*

At another date, the whooping-cough also broke out among the four hundred and fifty girls of our Home, and though many were dying in the towns of the same disease, yet all in the Orphan Home recovered except one little girl who had very weak lungs, a constitutional tendency to consumption

8. In the early part of one Summer, it was found that we had several boys ready to be apprenticed, but there were no applications made by masters for apprentices. This was no small difficulty, as the master must be also willing to receive the apprentice into his own family. We again gave ourselves to *prayer,* instead of *advertising.* Some weeks passed, but the difficulty remained. We continued in prayer, and then one application was made for an apprentice, and from

the time we first began, we have been able to find places for eighteen boys."

The Consumptive's Home.

In the United States there is a Parallel Record to George Muller's Life of Faith and Trust, found in the history of the Consumptive's Home of Boston, Mass. It was established twelve years since by Doctor Cullis, who in the ardor of his faith and trust gave himself to the work of the Lord, by ministering in *Jesus' Name*, to the poor consumptives who were unable to provide for themselves. Doctor Cullis is a man of humility, and devoted to his life work, and has been most abundantly blessed by the Lord in his field. To the honor and glory of our Heavenly Father, he has never been forsaken by Him.

The Institution began twelve years ago, in small quarters Now it embraces a very large gathering of useful enterprises : *A Consumptive's Home, Children's Home, Grove Hall Church, Tract Repository*, a *Training College*, and a *Cancer Home*. The means provided have all been sent by the Lord, who has prompted the hearts of good people to send to it their voluntary contributions.

There is no financial fund, endowment, or pecuniary provision whatever existing for the support of the Home. No individuals have made any agreement for its support; there is no trade or occupation used or connected with it, whereby to obtain any remuneration. There has never been any appeal to man for assistance, no subscriptions ever taken, no contributions solicited, either publicly or privately; there are no agencies or connections to receive funds from any religious society for procuring charitable relief.

The supplies for the carrying on of this work, during these twelve years, have been wholly *in answer to believing prayer, to the Lord.*

They have fulfilled faithfully the Lord's commands, *" Cast all your cares on Him, for he careth for you."*   They have also pleaded in faith, without a doubt, *"Anything ye shall ask the Father in my name, I will do it."*   And they have asked and received, and the Provider has never yet failed them.

During the twelve years' time there has been sent to the Consumptive's Home, without any solicitation whatever, but in answer to believing prayer and faith and trust in God's providence, a sum no less than *three hundred and sixty thousand dollars, and over fifteen hundred patients have been gratuitously cared for.*   No one has been urged, asked, or even hinted to contribute to it.   Each morning, noon and night prayer has been offered to send means to provide for their daily wants, and the Great Shepherd has sent the supplies.

During these twelve years, the experiences of Doctor Cullis, the founder, have been most remarkable in the frequent answers to prayer in minute details of life, and especially in healing.   There are so many such cases, that there is no possible room to doubt.   There have often been moments, yes, days of distress and intense trial, when, with not a single penny on hand, it seemed as if failure had come; but faith could not let the promise go, neither was it possible for them to believe that He who could do so much, would forsake so good a work, which was undertaken only in obedience to the guidance and direction of the Lord; and God has always brought deliverance, and honored them and brought glory to his own name.

In the daily history of these struggles and trials and triumphs of faith, are found many surprising incidents, a few of which we relate.

A Bad Debt Paid.

"To-day a bill was paid of $31, which I had given up as good for nothing.   A long time ago I gave it to the Lord in prayer, and promised Him if it was ever canceled that it should be His."

Help in Need.

" The sums received for several days had been small. One day as the Doctor was in prayer for his needs, he received a note from a lady asking him to call at her house, naming the day and the hour. At the time appointed he called, and found the lady sick in consumption, near to death. She said she had some money which she wished to dispose of before her death. She placed in his hand a *five hundred dollar note*. It was her last gift. She had received it from the hand of the Lord, and she returned it to Him again."

Praying for Stoves.

" This afternoon, knowing the necessity of stoves for some of the upper rooms, as the weather is quite cool, I went to the Lord, in prayer, and told him of our need, praying Him in one way to supply us.

" I then went down town to a friend, to look at stoves and inquire the price, when he said, 'that's all right, I shall not charge anything,' and said he would see that they were put up. This man knew nothing of our great need; he had never visited the Home, knew but little about it, and not a word did he know of the state of my purse. "The Lord inclined the man's heart to give the stoves."

Praying for a Furnace.

"I am earnestly praying for the means to purchase a furnace, for we cannot receive patients into the new Home until it can be warmed. I am looking to the Lord, and He will help."

Seven days later. " A gentleman has this day ordered a furnace to be put in, with fourteen tons of coal at his expense. I will here say that his attention was not called to our need, but he asked how the house was to be warmed; he then learned of our want, and ordered as above.   Truly, 'Whoso-ever believeth in Him shall not be confounded.' "

The Lord's Return for Giving unto the Poor.

"This afternoon a poor woman, whose history I have known for some time, and who has a sick husband over eighty years of age, called on me, stating that she had only a ten-cent loaf of bread for herself and her husband to eat since Wednes-day, and to-day is Saturday.

"Notwithstanding my own need, I felt that I could not withhold from one in greater straits than myself, so in Christ's name, I gave her enough to procure necessary food for a few days.   The Lord did not forget it, but this evening has re-turned the amount with bountiful interest.   For the turn I gave Him, He has sent me $40.   '*There is that scattereth yet increaseth.*' "

A Watch given to the Lord—How the Lord returns a better one.

"Last year, during a season of great need, I sold my watch; yesterday, the Lord returned it by a gift of a much better one from a friend, who had purchased it abroad, knowing nothing of my need, thus proving, 'He that soweth bounti-fully, shall reap also bountifully.' "

The Lord Gave Double what was Asked for.

"This morning and noon I called upon the Lord in prayer for the means to pay a bill of $100.   By three, P. M., a check was sent me of $200."

Blessings amid Calamities.

"The roof of one of our houses having caught fire from a spark from a neighbor's chimney, it was mostly destroyed; some of the furniture, and the whole home badly damaged by water. All hearts thanked the Lord the circumstances were no worse. In the midst of our calamity, blessings surrounded us. An unknown donor sends in 20 tons of coal. For weeks I have been praying for the means to purchase our Winter fuel, and now the Lord has inclined the heart of an unknown friend to supply our need."

A Remarkable Promise.

At one period in the history of the Consumptive's Home, a sum of three thousand dollars placed in the safe, and reserved to be used for payment on the purchase of a new building was stolen, and there was not left a single dollar; every penny was gone.

Nothing daunted, again going to the Lord, and pleading the Lord's own promise, "*If ye abide in me, and my words abide in you, ye shall ask what ye will and it shall be done unto you.*" The request was made in prayer for the three thousand dollars, and the promise of the amount was definitely made to be paid out a certain day.

The day came. Before it had arrived, the Lord had sent the three thousand dollars with unusual contributions, and both the promises of the Lord and that of his children were kept.

The ordinary business man would have said it was foolishness for a poor man, with not a penny in the world, all his means stolen from him, to positively promise on a certain day the next month, to pay so large a sum, exactly the same as was stolen.

The skeptic would have said, " All foolish to plead before an unseen God, and ask for such a sum. You will never get it. Why didn't your God prevent your money from being stolen. If your Bible is true, he ought to have protected you from loss."

The answer to all these is thus: The Doctor did trust in the promise of an unseen God, whom he had tested in the past many hundred times, and who had always been faithful in keeping his promises, and his faith knew that his God would not suffer his own work to fail nor suffer reproach.

Still further to silence the skeptic, let it be said that after the robbery became known, the sympathy for the institution became so much greater, that the contributions voluntarily sent in consequence thereof replaced the three thousand dollars within thirty days, and produced far more in excess, to go towards other needs. Thus an adversity became a blessing   The Lord uses sorrow to produce good.

A Woman Delivered from the Habit of Drinking.

" I visited a family for whom I have felt a deep interest for weeks past. The father had been out of employment some time, and they have lacked food and clothing. Much of their trouble has been caused by the intemperance of the mother. Her husband has borne long and patiently with her, and although she would for a long time leave off drinking, it was only to fall again still lower. While furnishing them with clothing, and assisting them in other ways, I besought the mother to give her heart to Jesus, knowing that he could keep her from falling. She became a constant attendant at our meetings. Says *"Jesus has taken her love for drink all away."* One of her little ones, who is just beginning to talk, said the other day, "Mamma, you don't drink now." They are a happy family, and their home is greatly changed.

Prayer for Purchasers.

When removal to the new Home was determined upon, there still remained five of the old buildings on hand to be disposed of. This too was taken to the Lord in prayer that he might send purchasers.

One building was sold in October, and the remaining four in November. When it is considered that a portion was property usually very difficult of sale, and that no advertisement of it had been made, no other means than prayer resorted to, it must be convincing to all that there must be "one who knoweth all things," who hears and helps in financial as well as in spiritual necessities.

Asking for Large Gifts.

Upon the 26th of September the record of the Home was as follows: "There is due on the first of next month, $2,450 interest on our property, and we are now within four days of the time, with not a dollar towards it. For several days I have been asking that amount of the Lord."

Now here was a man depending wholly upon *chance gifts* for the livelihood of several hundred people, with a debt of over two thousand dollars to pay in four days. His occupation and work were such that no one could even possibly think of making any loans, as there was no security. Neither was it the principle or the practice of the Home ever to solicit a dollar. What was to be done? *It was taken to the Lord in prayer*, and all waited the result.

Was it at all probable that so large a sum of money could be sent in so short a time by any one or any number of persons?

That evening a letter from the probate office at Exeter, N. H., was received by Dr. Cullis, informing them of the death of a citizen of Portsmouth, with a bequest to the Home of *five thousand dollars*. The Lord answered their prayer the same day and sent *double what was asked for*.

A Severe Tumor Healed.

During the year 1872, there was under the professional care of Dr. Cullis, at the Consumptive's Home, a Christian lady with a tumor which confined her almost continuously to her bed in severe suffering. All remedies were unavailing, and the only human hope was the knife; but feeling in my own heart the power of the promise, I one morning sat down by her bedside, and taking up the Bible, I read aloud, God's promise to his believing children. *"And the prayer of faith shall save the sick, and the Lord shall raise him up . and if he have committed sins, they shall be forgiven him."*

I then asked her if she would trust the Lord to remove this tumor and restore her to health and to her missionary work. She replied, "I am willing to trust the Lord for it"

I then knelt and anointed her with oil in the name of the Lord, asking Him to fulfill his own word Soon after I left she got up and walked three miles. From that time the tumor rapidly lessened until all trace of it at length disappeared.

Faith Cured Her.

This incident was related by the lady herself in a public meeting in Boston, where it was heard by the sorrowing wife of an afflicted husband, whose statement is as follows:

" I was first confined to my house with a violent cold I lost my voice completely, suffered with pain in my lungs and expectorated almost constantly. I grew worse every day, and in a week called in a physician. On examination he found my lungs diseased. I also had fever. With all his care my cough grew worse, and night sweats set in; a few weeks later my wife was told by the Doctor that my lungs were badly ulcerated, and that my case being hopeless. it was not worth while for him to attend longer; also that she must not be surprised if I should pass away suddenly. I then tried some highly recommended medicine, which seemed only to increase my disease.

"When I became so weak as to be nearly helpless, Dr. Cullis was called in. He sounded my lungs and gave the same verdict, saying my only hope for recovery was in the Lord. Diarrhœa also set in, and my feet began to swell."

This statement will show his perfect helplessness.

After the return of his wife from the above meeting, he read over and over the precious promises of God, and became more and more convinced of the power of faith. Believing that "*He is faithful that promised*," he sent for Dr. Cullis to come and pray with him.

"Dr. C. prayed, anointed me with oil, and in the name of the Lord Jesus, commanded me to be healed. Instantly my whole being was thrilled with an unknown power, from the top of my head to the soles of my feet. From the moment I believed, the *work was done.* My lungs, so long diseased, breathed with new vigor, and I returned thanks to God for the results of faith. Since that memorable night I have taken no medicine, and my health has been constantly improving, so *that I am feeling better now than I did before my sickness.*"

Two years after he was seen by Dr. Cullis, and continued in perfect health, and engaged in active business.

Cured of Cancer.

A lady came to the Consumptive's Home with a cancer in the cheek, which had attained the size of a filbert. It had a very red and angry appearance. After prayer for her healing she went into the country, when some one remarked, 'E thinks that faith will cure her, but *that* is something that will have to be burned out or cut out.' Her friends tried to induce the use of various applications, all of which she firmly refused. She returned home in eight weeks, entirely cured. Her friends acknowledged, '*Faith did do good after all.*'

Cured of Neuralgia.

A lady of East Cambridge writes, "For nineteen years I have been afflicted with neuralgia; added to this, of late years a combination of diseases has rendered life an intolerable burden, and baffled the skill of every physician to whom I have applied. By the prayer of faith I have been healed, both body and soul, and made to rejoice continually. I can now say I am entirely well, and engaged in arduous work—often among the sick, losing whole nights of rest."

Cured of Spine Disease.

Dr. Cullis thus speaks of a signal answer to his prayer. "While at the home of L. R. in England, I was asked to pray with his daughter, who had spinal curvature. Subsequently L. R. writes, 'We are full of thankfulness and praise about E She is quite well and strong, and does everything like her sisters. She has such perfect faith that the Lord had healed her, that she at once put away the board and said she should never lie upon it again, and on the following Sunday she walked four miles in a hot sun, and sat for two hours on a bench without a back. As far as we can judge, she is quite well in every respect. For fifteen months before she had been a constant cause of anxiety to us—never walked or attended to study.'"

An Injured Leg Restored to Proper Length.

"Some months ago a young lady called, requesting to be prayed for. She simply told me that some years ago she was run over and her hip badly injured. I asked her if she could trust the Lord for healing. She replied, 'Yes.' I prayed with her, and she went home.

"I learned after a day or two, that she was perfectly cured, and obtained from her these facts: Some six years before, she was run over by a hack, and her hip so injured that she was confined to her bed for six months. She then got up with a permanent lameness, one limb being shorter than the other. In two or three instances since, she has been confined to her bed for three months at a time. She now walks perfectly, both limbs being of the same length. She says of herself, 'I can leap and run as well as any other person, and my heart overruns with praise and thanksgiving to God.'"

A Lost Voice Regained.

"Some nine months since a lady showed signs of indisposition, and soon was attacked by a cough. Change of air was prescribed, but after a lapse of some weeks she returned to her home, in no way improved. Physicians were consulted, her lungs found to be much irritated and pulse low. Soon all appetite left her, a hoarseness succeeded, resulting in entire loss of voice.

"There was little desire to eat, as everything taken into the stomach caused great distress. Months succeeded; nothing could be gained from medical treatment. I felt that I must trust all to God. I seemed to feel that God would heal me. I read in his Bible, 'The prayer of *faith shall save the sick.*' I accepted it at once, I felt sure that it was for me. I was led to visit Boston and see Doctor Cullis. I stated all the circumstances of my illness, and was asked if I could trust God to heal me? I replied, 'Yes, I am sure the Lord is able and willing.'

"'We knelt in prayer; *in a moment, as it were, my voice came to me, I was able to talk with ease,* and from that time nothing that I have eaten has given me any distress. The Lord's promises are sure, and He has filled my soul with joy and praise.'"

In speaking of the many cases of cures in answer to prayer, Doctor Cullis says: "I have noticed that in some cases the cure has been instantaneous; others I have prayed with two or three times, or even more. My explanation is, as far as I have been able to observe, that there has been oftentimes a question or lack of faith on the part of the patient; for some seem to come, not in faith, but as a matter of *experiment. God's word says it is the prayer of faith that shall save the sick.*"

From this it will be noticed that the *faith is that of the patient,* and the more strongly it is fixed on God and the promise, the surer the answer.

It is but justice to say, that in no case has there ever been the thought or the assumption, by Doctor Cullis himself, of having *any divinely conferred power* to heal all that come to him, or for whom he may pray. No such power would ever be given to any human creature by our Lord. It is the Lord himself who works the wonder—but solely because of the faith of sufferers who have sought the addition of the prayer of one who is stronger in faith and prayer than its own. Each must wait upon God, and must have faith without a doubt, and perfect willingness to trust all to Him, and continue to expect the blessing.

It should be noticed, also, that all who have come pleading the prayer of faith, and asking the Lord for relief, have either then, or before, *pledged themselves to the service of the Lord,* and have desired the good gifts they seek, that they may more efficiently work for His own honor and glory, and the good of others.

When such a desire for healing is united with the desire and the promise to work in future for the Lord, His own kingdom and glory, the Lord is pleased with it, and His promise is made sure to those who come in faith.

It is needless to say that those who come for prayer, with the desire only for *experiment,* and also those who are *withholding their lives or pledges of devotion to Him, need never expect an answer.*

Cured of St. Vitus' Dance.

"Very early in childhood, I was seized with a nervous trouble, something like St Vitus' Dance. As I grew older it did not pass off, but settled into a disease of the muscles. It became a terrible affliction It was usually under my control, but I could not endure protracted work of any kind, or unusual fatigue; I had consulted, in various cities, the best physicians, but they pronounced it incurable. All that could be done was to be careful of overwork and excitement. It must have been twenty-five years since I was first taken.

"Doctor Cullis asked me if I could give my body to the Lord to be healed; I felt that I could truly say 'Yes.' He then, in a simple manner, prayed that the Lord would restore strength of nerve and muscle I went home, touched and improved by the comforting words. At the end of the week I was startled at the recollection that I had felt hardly anything of my trouble. My nerves began to feel as if they were held with a grasp of iron. The muscles refused to move as before at every inclination. For two weeks this painful tension lasted Then I felt a gradual relaxation, and found that I was strong like other people. I tested myself in the severest way—walked, wrote and lifted—after each exertion I could enjoy perfect rest. The mystery of the miracles was explained to me. This power of God manifested in the past, is manifest to us still. Faith can grasp and use it. Close beside us stands a *living Christ.*"

Hip Disease Cured.

A lady from Brooklyn, N. Y., came to the Consumptive's Home for prayer cure.

"She had a diseased hip, and *had used crutches for twenty years.* Often the hip joint would slip from its socket, so that it was impossible for her to walk without crutches. She now writes, 'My lameness was incurable, and God interposed in my behalf, in answer to your prayer. I have been able to walk for five months without the crutches I have used for over twenty years.'"

A Bad Debt Paid.

A correspondent of Doctor Cullis, who was unable to collect a debt from a refractory and worthless debtor, promised to give it to the Lord, if it was ever paid. The following is his letter:

"Perhaps you remember that the writer, some months ago, asked you to pray that some money which had been due him a long time, and which to all human appearance was never to be paid, might by God's interposition be paid in full. Enclosed, find the full amount, $25, which was paid a few days since. All glory to Him, who *never, never fails.*"

Consumption Instantly Healed.

" At a meeting in the Chapel of the Consumptive's Home, held March 7, 1876, public prayer was offered for a young man in Florida, who was apparently gone in consumption; an interested friend had previously written him that prayer would be offered for him at that time.

"Not long after she received letters from him, stating that at *that same hour* he too had joined in supplication, and *was instantly healed.* He says that while before the Lord, pleading his promise, his voice and strength were taken away for a time. Then he began to praise the Lord, and to feel, 'tis done,' and it was done, and tells of the wonderful change, his ability to talk and sing, with no difficulty whatever."

Cured of Catarrh.

" I have been afflicted with catarrh for over twenty years. I had consulted many physicians and used many remedies—all failed to help me. In the Spring of 1874, I grew so much worse that life became a burden; I suffered from dizziness and great prostration; I was urged to go to you for faith cure. This was no new thing to me; I believed in it, yet found it difficult to exercise faith for myself

"My daughter went to see you, as I was then unable to go. I looked to God, and believed from that very moment. My whole soul and body seemed thrilled, and I began to gain strength immediately.

"In a few days I was able to go to your *Home.* You prayed simply that God would take all disease from me. I have been entirely well from that time; not only cured of catarrh, but tumors on my limbs were entirely removed. I desire to give God the praise; I bless him that He does forgive our transgressions and heal our diseases"

These instances are only a very few out of many, that have occurred, too numerous for repetition here. It must be admitted, that God has most signally blessed the faith of the inmates of the Consumptive's Home, answered their prayer for others. In nearly all the cases of healing which have occurred, the sufferers have failed in all other means, and in their extremity have depended wholly in faith in God.

In speaking of them, Doctor Cullis says: "We do not give these instances of the healing of the body, dear friends of Jesus, as in any degree paramount to the healing of the soul; but that as the dear children of God, we may claim all our privileges, and enjoy the knowledge of our fullness of possession in Him who declares "*all things are yours.*" Shall we in any manner, of smallest or largest import, limit the love and power of God, who deigneth out of the highest heaven to declare, "*The Lord thinketh upon me*" As an earthly parent separates no part of the well-being of his child from his watchful care, so doth our Heavenly Father not only "*forgive all our iniquities,*" but "*healeth all our diseases*" *Let us not confine faith operation to the saving of the soul, while God's word is full of previous promise for the saving, keeping, and healing of the body.*

"For I will restore health unto thee, and I will heal thee of thy wounds, saith the Lord."

A Mother's Faith—The Life of Beate Paulus.

In a sketch of the life of Beate Paulus, the wife of a German minister who lived on the borders of the Black Forest, are several incidents which illustrate the power of living faith, and the providence of a prayer-hearing God.

Though destitute of wealth, she much desired to educate her children, and five of her six boys were placed in school, while she struggled, and prayed, and toiled,—not only in the house, but out of doors,—to provide for their necessities

"On one occasion," writes one of her children, "shortly before harvest, the fields stood thick with corn, and our mother had already calculated that their produce would suffice to meet all claims for the year. She was standing at the window casting the matter over in her mind, with great satisfaction, when her attention was suddenly caught by some heavy, black clouds with white borders, drifting at a great rate across the Summer sky. 'It is a hail-storm!' she exclaimed in dismay, and quickly throwing up the window, she leaned out. Her eyes rested upon a frightful mass of wild storm-clouds, covering the western horizon, and approaching with rapid fury.

" 'O God!' she cried, 'there comes an awful tempest, and what *is* to become of my corn?' The black masses rolled nearer and nearer, while the ominous rushing movement that precedes a storm, began to rock the sultry air, and the dreaded hail-stones fell with violence. Half beside herself with anxiety about those fields lying at the eastern end of the valley, she now lifted her hands heavenward, and wringing them in terror, cried: 'Dear Father in heaven, what art thou doing? Thou knowest I cannot manage to pay for my boys at school, without the produce of those fields! Oh! turn

Thy hand, and do not let the hail blast my hopes!' Scarcely, however, had these words crossed her lips when she started, for it seemed to her as if a voice had whispered in her ear, 'Is my arm shortened that it cannot help thee in other ways?' Abashed, she shrank into a quiet corner, and there entreated God to forgive her want of faith. In the meantime the storm passed. And now various neighbors hurried in, proclaiming that the whole valley lay thickly covered with hail-stones, *down to the very edge of the parsonage fields, but the latter* had been quite spared. The storm had reached their border, and then suddenly taking another direction into the next valley. Moreover, that the whole village was in amazement, declaring that God had wrought a miracle for the sake of our mother, whom he loved. She listened, silently adoring the goodness of the Lord, and vowing that henceforth her confidence should be only in Him."

At another time she found herself unable to pay the expenses of the children's schooling, and the repeated demands for money were rendered more grievous by the reproaches of her husband, who charged her with attempting impossibilities, and told her that her self-will would involve them in disgrace. She, however, professed her unwavering confidence that the Lord would soon interpose for their relief, while his answer was: "We shall see; time will show."

In the midst of these trying circumstances, as her husband was one day sitting in his study, absorbed in meditation, the postman brought three letters from different towns where the boys were at school, each declaring that unless the dues were promptly settled, the lads would be dismissed. The father read the letters with growing excitement, and spreading them out upon the table before his wife as she entered the room, exclaimed: "There, look at them, and pay our debt with your faith! I have no money, nor can I tell where to go for any."

"Seizing the papers, she rapidly glanced through them, with a very grave face, but then answered firmly, 'It is all right; the business shall be settled. For He who says, "The

gold and silver is mine," will find it an easy thing to provide these sums.'   Saying which she hastily left the room.

"Our father readily supposed she intended making her way
to a certain rich friend who had helped us before.   He was
mistaken, for this time her steps turned in a different direction   We had in the parsonage an upper loft, shut off by a
trap-door from the lower one, and over this door it was that
she now knelt down, and began to deal with Him in whose
strength she had undertaken the work of her children's education.   She spread before Him those letters from the study
table, and told Him of her husband's half scoffing taunt.   She
also reminded Him how her life had been redeemed from the
very gates of death, for the children's sake, and then declared
that she could not believe that He meant to forsake her at this
juncture; she was willing to be the *second* whom He might
forsake, but she was determined not to be the *first*.

"In the meanwhile, her husband waited down stairs, and
night came on ; but she did not appear.   Supper was ready,
and yet she stayed in the loft.   Then the eldest girl, her
namesake Beate, ran up to call her; but the answer was,
'Take your supper without me, it is not time for me to eat.'
Late in the evening, the little messenger was again despatched,
but returned with the reply : 'Go to bed; the time has not
come for me to rest.'   A third time, at breakfast next morning, the girl called her mother.   'Leave me alone,' she said;
'I do not need breakfast; when I am ready I shall come.'
Thus the hours sped on, and down stairs her husband and
the children began to feel frightened, not daring, however, to
disturb her any more   At last the door opened, and she entered, her face beaming with a wonderful light.   The little
daughter thought that something extraordinary must have
happened; and running to her mother with open arms, asked
eagerly: 'What is it?   Did an angel from heaven bring the
money?'   'No, my child,' was the smiling answer, 'but now
I am sure that it will come.'   She had hardly spoken, when a
maid in peasant costume entered, saying : 'The master of the

Linden Inn sends to ask whether the Frau Pastorin can spare time to see him?' 'Ah, I know what he wants,' answered our mother. 'My best regards, and I will come at once.' Whereupon she started, and mine host, looking out of his window, saw her from afar, and came forward to welcome her with the words: 'O Madame, how glad I am you have come!' Then leading her into his back parlor he said; 'I cannot tell how it is, but the whole of this last night I could not sleep for thinking of you. For some time I have had several hundred *gulden* lying in that chest, and all night long I was haunted by the thought that you needed this money, and that I ought to give it to you. If that be the case, there it is— take it; and do not trouble about repaying me. Should you be able to make it up again, well and good—if not, never mind.' On this my mother said. 'Yes, I do most certainly need it, my kind friend; for all last night I too was awake, crying to God for help. Yesterday there came three letters, telling us that all our boys would be dismissed unless the money for their board is cleared at once.'

"'Is it really so?' exclaimed the innkeeper, who was a noble-hearted and spiritual Christian man. 'How strange and wonderful! Now I am doubly glad I asked you to come!' Then opening the chest, he produced three weighty packets, and handed them to her with a prayer that God's blessing might rest upon the gift. She accepted it with the simple words 'May God make good to you this service of Christian sympathy; for you have acted as the steward of One who has promised not even to leave the giving of a cup of cold water unrewarded.'

"Husband and children were eagerly awaiting her at home, and those three dismal letters still lay open on the table, when the mother, who had quitted that study in such deep emotion the day before, stepped up to her husband, radiant with joy. On each letter, she laid a roll of money and then cried · 'Look, there it is! And now believe that faith in God is no empty madness!'"

15

The Persecutor's Fate.

Dr. Eugenio Kincaid, the Burman missionary, states, that among the first converts in Ava were two men who had held respectable offices about the palace. Some time after they had been baptized, a neighbor determined to report them to government, and drew up a paper setting forth that these two men had forsaken the customs and religion of their fathers, were worshiping the foreigner's God, and went every Sunday to the teacher's house; with other similar charges. He presented the paper to the neighbors of the two disciples, taking their names as witnesses, and saying that he should go and present the accusation on the next day.

The two Christians heard of it, and went to Mr. Kincaid in great alarm, to consult as to what they should do. They said if they were accused to government, the mildest sentence they could expect would be imprisonment for life at hard labor, and perhaps they would be killed. Kincaid told them that they could not flee from Ava, if they would; that he saw nothing he could do for them, and all that they could do was to trust in God to protect them, and deliver them from the power of their enemies. They also prayed and soon left Kincaid, saying that they felt more calm, and could leave the matter with God.

That night the persecutor was attacked by a dreadful disease in the bowels, which so distressed him that he roared like a madman; and his friends, which is too often the case with the heathen, left him to suffer and die alone. The two Christians whom he would have ruined then went and took care of him till he died, two or three days after his attack. The whole affair was well known in the neighborhood, and from that time not a dog dared move his tongue against the Christians of Ava.

Is there no evidence in this of a special providence, and that God listens to the prayers of persecuted and distressed children?

The Captain and the Quadrant.

A godly man, the master of an American ship, during one voyage found his ship bemisted for days, and he became rather anxious respecting her safety. He went down to his cabin and prayed. The thought struck him, if he had with confidence committed his soul to God, he might certainly commit his ship to Him; and so, accordingly, he gave all into the hands of God, and felt at perfect peace; but still he prayed, that if He would be pleased to give a cloudless sky at twelve o'clock, he should like to take an observation to ascertain their real position, and whether they were on the right course

He came on deck at eleven o'clock, with the quadrant under his coat. As it was thick drizzling, the men looked at him with amazement. He went to his cabin, prayed, and came up. There seemed still to be no hope. Again he went down and prayed, and again he appeared on deck with his quadrant in his hand. It was now ten minutes to twelve o'clock, and still there was no appearance of a change; but he stood on the deck, waiting upon the Lord, when, in a few minutes, the mist seemed to be folded up and rolled away as by an omnipotent and invisible hand; the sun shown clearly from the blue vault of heaven, and there stood the man of prayer with the quadrant in his hand, but so awe-struck did he feel, and so "dreadful" was that place, that he could scarcely take advantage of the answer to his prayer. He, however, succeeded, although with trembling hands, and found, to his comfort, that all was well. But no sooner had he finished taking the observation than the mist rolled back over the heavens, and it began to drizzle as before.

This story of prayer was received from the lips of the good Captain Crossby, who was so useful in the Ardrossan awakening; and he himself was the man who prayed and waited upon his God with the quadrant in his hand.

The Faith of Dorothea Trudel.

The life of Dorothea Trudel has afforded some remarkable instances of answer to prayer; during the years 1850 to 1860, at the Swiss village of Mannedorf, near the Lake of Zurich, and that of Molltingen, were seen and witnessed, cases of cure in response to unyielding faith in the promises of the Lord.

Dorothea Trudel was a worker in flowers, and in time came to have many workers under her, and when she was about thirty-seven years of age, four or five of her workers fell sick. The sickness resisted all treatment, grew worse, appeared to be hopeless.   She was a deep, earnest Christian, and while diligent and unselfish as a nun, yet her anxiety for her work people drew her to earnest prayer and study of the Scriptures for relief.   Like a sudden light, she says, the well known prayer of the Epistle of James, 5 . 14, 15, flashed upon her.

"If medical skill was unavailing, was there not prayer ? And could not the same Lord who chose to heal through medicines, also heal without them ? Was he necessarily restricted to the one means ? There was a time when his healing power went forth directly; might it not be put forth directly still ? "

Agitated by these questions, she sought help in prayer, and then kneeling by the bedside of these sick people, she prayed for them.   They recovered; and the thought that at first had startled her, became now the settled conviction of her life.

Her reputation spread; others who were sick, came to her for relief, but she sought only the recovery of the patients by prayer alone.   Many recovered.   Her doors were besieged, and at last she consented to receive invalids at her home, from compassion.   By degrees her own house grew into three, and at last it became in fact a hospital.

She lived a life of humility, and perfect simplicity, yet strength of faith, and at her death her work was, and still is, carried on by Mr. Zeller, who also has had marvelous successes in answer to prayer.

Remarkable Cures.

There have been gathered together in her biography, well authenticated cases of answer to prayer, when the patient was considered wholly incapable of help from medical skill.

"There was one of a stiff knee, that had been treated in vain by the best physicians in France, Germany and Switzerland; one of an elderly man who could not walk, and had been given up by his physicians, but who soon dispensed with his crutches; a man came with a burned foot, and the surgeons said it was a case of '*either amputation or death,*' and he also was cured; one of the leading physicians of Wurtemburg, testifies to the cure of a hopeless patient of his own; another remained six weeks, and says he saw all kinds of sicknesses healed; cancers and fevers have been treated with success; epilepsy and insanity more frequently than any other form of disease

"Neither is the life and experience of Dorothea Trudel an exceptional one. Pastor Blumenhart of Wurtemberg, has had his home crowded for years with patients, and cures occur constantly.

"The mother of Dorothea Trudel was an eminently pious woman, and it was her custom, when any of her children were ill, to bring them in prayer before the feet of the Heavenly Physician, as Dorothea herself says: 'Our mother had no cure except prayer, and though at that time we did not understand, yet since then we have found it out, that it was the healing hand of the Saviour alone, that helped and restored us.'"

Cured of the Small-Pox.

"Even when I had the small-pox, and became blind, no doctor was sent for, and no one was told of it   Our father was not at home (he, father, most unfortunately, was not a religious person); and when our mother asked him to come, telling him how ill I was, he would not believe it, and preferred to remain with his friends. Our mother, however, was not in the least vexed or excited; she prayed for him, for all of us, especially for her sick child, and before my father came home, my eyes were re-opened."

Cured of Severe Fits.

"Once again, one of my brothers had a fit brought on through fright. It was a most violent and painful attack. and we were greatly alarmed. This time, also, our father was out; and our mother said to us, I know this fearful illness. my children; it is one of the heaviest trials which could have occurred, but Jesus, who cured that lunatic boy, can heal our child. Do not speak of the attack to any one; we will go only to Jesus about it; and then she prayed with us.

"Not long after, a second fit came on, and again our father was `taking his pleasure at the public house. This time mother told him what had happened in his absence; but he laughed at it, and said, 'I don't believe it; you were frightened at the child having bad dreams.'

"His wife replied, 'For the sake of your unbelief, I hope that the child will have another attack whilst you are at home, so that you may witness it yourself, then you will believe; I pray God, however, that this may be the last time.'

"It came to pass about a week after, that another most dreadful fit came on; the boy foamed violently, and threw himself about in fearful convulsions; on this occasion the father was present, and he was convinced of the nature of the attack, and alarmed at what he saw. *But the mother's prayer was heard; for the disease never showed itself again for thirty-four years, while both parents lived.*"

Buying a Cow.

"Our father going away abroad, he sold one of our two cows, and took the proceeds with him. (He, the father, was a reckless spendthrift, idle, and fond of the public inn) A rich neighbor directly offered to loan us money enough to buy another; this kind proposal we gratefully accepted. Although we did not understand much about bargains of this kind, yet the cow we purchased served us so remarkably, that we were obliged to acknowledge whence the blessing came. In Summer we could sell fourteen measures of milk; in Winter, twelve to the dairyman, so that the borrowed money was speedily paid.

"At the same time the cow performed the farm work required of it, with such strength and quickness, we were astonished. When our father, on his return, heard us speaking with pleasure of this animal, he became so enraged with the poor thing, that he was determined to sell it, and actually *offered it at half its value.*

"The faithless children were in a continual fright. When any one came near the house, we thought that we were assuredly going to lose our cow. But mother exhorted us not to be so fearful; for, said she, 'If your father could do always as he likes, none of you would be alive now; but God will never let him go any farther than he sees to be for our good. Believe me, God, who has given us this cow, will keep it for us as long as we need it.'

"And so it turned out, for the cow never left us whilst our mother was alive; and when we were all provided for, a purchaser came, who paid a high price for the creature, having heard of its wonderful powers from the man to whom we sold the milk for so many years; but no sooner was the animal taken to its new home, than the wonder ceased, and *this cow became no better than any other.*"

A Lady Cured, who had been rejected from an Asylum.

"Madam M——, the mother of twelve children, had been quite shattered in mind by the death of her husband, and had been actually sent away uncured from an asylum. She came to Dorothea's home, was blessed in remembrance in her prayers, *and after seven weeks went away perfectly cured.* She acknowledged the Lord was indeed her helper, and she has remained well to this day."

The Soul Cured as well as the Body.

On many occasions she experienced wonderful help from God, who, while performing marvels for the body, which is the least important part, accomplishes what is far greater, even the salvation of souls.

"Among others, one named B. T——, went to her, who had been suffering for six months from a disease of his bones, and had been for a lengthened period in a Swiss hospital, under medical treatment. At length he, by the advice of Christian friends, sought for relief from his malady at Dorothea's house His cure began in the first week of his visit, and in a few weeks he was completely recovered."

On one occasion a young artisan came, in whom cancer had made such progress as to render any approach to him almost unbearable.

"At the Bible lessons, this once frivolous man, now an earnest inquirer, learned where the improvement must begin; and from the day that he confessed his sins against God and man, the disease abated. Some time afterwards he acknowledged one sin he had hitherto concealed, and then he speedily recovered his bodily health, and returned to his home cured in spirit also."

"A lady in S—— had so injured her knee by a fall, that for weeks she lay in the greatest agony. The doctors declared that dropsy would supervene; but the Heavenly Physician fulfilled those promises which will abide until the end of the world; and by prayer, and the laying on of Dorothea's hand, the knee was cured in twenty-four hours, and the swelling vanished."

Prayer, Not Mesmerism.

"Several people have maintained that her work was one of mesmerism; and when once she was asked to visit an out patient, she earnestly implored the Lord *not* to heal this invalid through her means if she employed mesmerism; but if not, to permit recovery. The woman was cured in a short time, though Dorothea had never entered her house, and had, therefore, no opportunity of placing herself in a mesmeric relation to this patient."

Help in Pecuniary Affairs.

"In pecuniary affairs, also, the Lord was their helper. Many times something had to be paid, and they had no means wherewith to meet the claims. Once, God actually sent aid by means of an enemy, who offered money; another time, *three thousand francs* came from Holland, just as they were needed, and also unexpected on a third occasion they were about to borrow money to pay for bread, when two hundred and fifty francs arrived."

The Faith Life of Mr. Zeller.

After the death of Dorothea Trudel, the work at Mannedorf, instituted by her, has been furthered and carried on by Mr Samuel Zeller, who had been her associate. He has published two reports, which contain many instances of answers to prayer, showing that the Lord still gave blessed results, and rewarded their faithful trust.

"No disease is found to be more obstinate than epilepsy, yet several instances are recorded of patients being restored to perfect health. Persons afflicted with mental disorder and convulsions are frequently brought to Mannedorff, and many return cured or benefited.

"On one occasion, a lady who had been afflicted with constant headache for five years, found her disorder removed speedily under the influence of prayer. In other cases the passion for strong drink was taken away; fever more or less disappeared; and the subjects of various kinds of chronic diseases, even some apparently far gone in consumption, have found their strength return to them under the same influence.

" Unhappy victims of spiritualist delusions have found deliverance at the mercy-seat; and there, too, many in the bondage of sin have rejoiced in a present Saviour.

" One patient afflicted with convulsions, who came several years successively without being cured, at last confessed that she possessed a book of 'charms' in which she put some degree of faith, and she had recommended them to others. She was led to see the folly and sin of such things, and soon after the book was burned she was restored to health."

Many cases have occurred where the suffering patient was utterly unable to come to Mannedorff, but prayer has been offered there in their behalf, and the answers have been as frequent as with the cases which have come under the same roof.

" A brother living at R—— was seized with a violent fever, and appeared to be at death's door. Intelligence having been sent to Mannedorff, united prayer was made in his behalf, and very soon afterwards a telegraphic message announced that he was recovering On this occasion the promise was remembered with joy, ' Before they call I will answer.' "

" Perhaps one of the most striking cases of blessing recorded is that of a lady, who was subject to fits of insanity so violent that they threatened her life, and who was so far conscious of her miserable condition, that happening to go into a meeting where she heard God's word, she requested to be prayed for. A friend wrote to Mannedorf, describing the case, and asking prayer on her behalf; and only a fortnight later, the same friend communicated the happy news of her recovery. After a fit of unusual severity, she fell into a deep sleep, from which she awoke in her right mind; more than that, she learned to believe in the *Lord Jesus*, and rejoiced in His love."

" A patient in this institution, who arrived unconverted, and was thought to be in a dying state, heard the good news of Salvation, and was enabled to rejoice in the Lord, through simple trust in Him; and from that moment she began to rapidly recover from her disorder, and soon became strong enough to nurse another patient."

Another remarkable case was that of a young girl who, in consequence of the breaking off of a marriage engagement, manifested decided symptoms of insanity. She not only recovered from her malady, but found the Saviour.

The Blind Restored to Sight.

Prayer was asked for a young lady who was wholly blind. A letter received soon after brought this joyful news:

" In answer to your prayer for our niece, I must thankfully tell you, her eyes are so much better that the Doctor this morning told her to thank God for having saved her from the most dangerous kind of cataract.

" While examining her eyes, the Doctor, who is a Jew, took up a book lying near, and opening it told her to try and read, which she was able to do with ease. It was a hymn book, and the first words on which her eyes fell were these:

> ' Christ Jesus, glorious King of Light,
>   Great Conqueror, David's heir,
> Come now and give my blind eyes sight,
>   O Saviour, hear my prayer ''

" 'That will do,' said the Doctor, ' you are much better.'

" I for my part hastened to my chamber, and shutting the door fell on my knees with a cry of joyful praise."

Threats were made by many of the villagers that they would burn up the house for this institution, saying all manner of unreasonable things. " You can not prevent this by

prayer," said one writer, " we have taken an oath to do it."
Mr. Zeller remained quiet, taking no notice of these threats,
but quietly trusted in the Lord. Though other anonymous
letters came frequently, yet the threats were never carried
out.

It will be seen from this that, blessed as was the work of
faith, still the spirit of persecution was permitted by the
Lord only to make his own children rely more confidently on
Him, and that he might fulfill more positively his promise,
"No evil shall befall thee, no harm come nigh thy dwelling."

The Bank of Faith. God the Guardian of the Poor.

Perhaps the providence of God in supplying the wants of
the poor never was more closely watched and better described
than has been done by the late William Huntington, formerly
a minister in London, England, who, in a book with the quaint
title of the "Bank of Faith," tells how, in his course of life, day
by day the Lord guarded him, helped him, and provided for
every need, even the most trifling. It is a precious record
of faith and full of true encouragement. He answers as follows this question: *" Should we pray for temporal blessings?"*

" Some have affirmed that we have no warrant to pray for
temporal blessings, but, blessed be God, he has given us *'the
promise of the life that now is, and of that which is to come.'*
Yea, the promise of all things pertaining to life and Godli-
ness, and whatever God has promised we may warrantably
pray for.

"Those that came to our Saviour in the days of his flesh,
prayed chiefly for temporal mercies. The blind prayed for
sight, the lepers for a cure, the lame for the use of their
limbs, and the deaf for the use of their ears, and surely had
they prayed unwarrantably, their prayers would not have
been so miraculously answered.

"Elijah prayed for a temporal mercy when he prayed for rain, and it is clear that God answered him. Elisha works a miracle to produce a temporal mercy when he healed the barren plains of Jericho "

Is my reader a poor Christian? Take it patiently. God maketh the poor as well as the rich. Envy not the rich. Riches are often seen to be a canker-worm at the root of a good man's comfort, a snare in his life, an iron pillar at the back of his pride. Agar prayed to be fed with food convenient for him, and you may pray for the same, and what God gives you in answer to your prayer you will be thankful for.

That state is surely best which keeps you dependent on God and thankful to Him, and so you shall find it to the end. *Go on, poor Christian, trusting in the providence of God.*

The Life of his Child Saved.

"My eldest daughter now living fell sick at about five or six months old, and was wasted to a skeleton. She had a doctor to attend her, but she got worse and worse. It seemed as if God intended to bereave us of her, for he brought her even to death's door.

"My wife and I have sat up with her night after night, watching the cradle, expecting every breath to be her last, for two or three weeks together. At last I asked the Doctor if he thought there was any hope of her life. He answered, no, he would not flatter me. *She would surely die.*

" This distressed me beyond measure, and as he told me to do no more for her, I left my room, went to my garden in the evening, and, in my little tool house, wrestled hard with God in prayer for the life of the child.

"I went home satisfied that God had heard me; *and in three days the child was as well as she is now,* and ate as heartily. This effectually convinced me that all things were possible with God."

God Sent Supplies.

"When I had been three weeks out of employment, I found a new place, and after pawning all my best clothes to pay expenses, when the cart set us down at the new home on Monday morning, I had the total sum of *ten pence half-penny left*, to provide for myself, my wife and child, till the ensuing Saturday night.

"Though I was thus poor, yet I knew God had made me rich in faith. We went on our knees beseeching the Almighty to send relief, as he in his wisdom thought proper.

"The next evening my landlord's daughter, and son-in-law, came up to see their mother, and brought some baked meat, which they had just taken out of their oven, and brought for me and my wife to sup along with them.

"These poor people knew nothing of us, nor of our God. The next day in the evening they did the same, and kept sending victuals and garden stuff to us all the week long."

The God who Supplied Elijah by a Raven Supplied me with Fish.

One of the most beautiful instances ever known, which almost identically repeats the Bible over again, especially in the instance of Elijah as he was fed in an unseen way by the hand of God, is given in the life of Mr. Huntington He was wholly unable to provide for his family, and could depend only on God.

"As I went over a bridge, I cast my eye on the right-hand side, and there lay a *very large eel* on the mud by the river side, apparently dead. I caught hold of it and soon found it was only asleep. With difficulty I got it safe out of the mud upon the grass, and then carried it home. My little one was very fond of it, and it richly supplied all her wants that day. But at night I was informed the eel was all gone, so the next day afforded me the same distress and trouble as the preceding day had done.

"The next morning, as I entered the garden gate, I saw a *partridge* lie dead on the walk I took it up and found it warm; so I carried it home, and it richly supplied the table of our little one that day.

"Again the next day still found me unprovided, and brought forth fresh work for faith and prayer. However, the morrow took thought for the things of itself, for when I came to take the scythe in my hand to mow the short grass, I looked into the pond, and there I saw three very large carp lying on the water apparently sick When the master came I told him of it. He went and looked and said they were dead, and told me I might have them if I would, for they were not in season. However, they came in due season to me. *And I found, morning after morning, there lay two or three of these fish at a time, dead, just as I wanted them, till I believe there was not one live fish remaining, six inches long, in the pond, which was near three hundred feet in length.*

"I could not help weeping, admiring the goodness of God. As I studied the Bible, I clearly perceived that the most eminent saints of the Bible were brought into low circumstances, as Jacob, David, Moses, Joseph, Job and Jeremiah, and all the apostles, in order that the hand of providence might be watched."

God Takes away the Snow.

" In the Winter the Lord sent a very deep snow, which lay a considerable time on the ground We were brought into great straits, as our wheat was now of no use to us, and we could obtain no wood, the landlady saying that as the snow was likely to last some time, she must keep what little she had left, and could sell us no more.

"There was before us the fear of great suffering with the cold. I begged of God that he might *that night take away the snow*, and send us something to burn, that our little one might not perish with the cold, *and the next morning the snow was all gone.*"

Sight Restored.

" A violent humor came into my eyes, and for some months I was in danger of losing my sight. Both myself and my second daughter had it more or less for several years.

"In answer to prayer, God healed her eyes and mine too, so that our sight was perfectly recovered."

Praying for Tea.

" As the life of faith consists in bearing the cross of Christ, we must not expect to be long without trials. Providence soon frowned on me again, and I got behindhand, as usual.

" This happened at a time when my wife was about delivery of child, and we were destitute of those necessaries of life which are needful at such times. The nurse came; we told her there was no tea in the house. My wife replied, '*Set the kettle on, even if there is not.*'

"The nurse said, '*You have no tea, nor can you get any.*' My wife replied, '*Set on the kettle.*' She did so, and before it boiled, a woman (with whom at that time we had no acquaintance) came to the door, and told the nurse that she had brought some tea as a present for my wife."

The Lord Paid His Debt.

" It was the time of my returning from the north country. I observed that there were some small debts to be discharged. But the hand of God was fast closed; this continued for some time : and for all that time, I watched and observed narrowly.

" At this time there was a special debt due of twenty pounds. This sum hung long I looked different ways, and chalked out different roads for the Almighty to walk in; but his paths were in the deep waters, and his footsteps were not known; no raven came, neither in the morning, nor in the evening.

"There was a gentlewoman at my house on a visit, and I asked her if she had got the sum of twenty pounds in her pocket, telling her at the same time how much I wanted it. She told me she had not; if she had, I should have it. A few hours after, the same woman was coming into my study, but she found it locked, and knocked at the door; I let her in, and she said, 'I am sorry I disturbed you.' I replied, 'You do not disturb me; I have been begging a favor of God, and I had just done when you knocked; and that favor I have now got in faith, and shall shortly have in hand, and you will see it'"

"The afternoon of the same day, two gentlemen out of the city came to see me; and after a few hours of conversation, they left me, and to my great surprise, each of them at parting put a letter into my hand, which, when they were gone, *I opened, and found a ten pound note in each.* I immediately sent for the woman up-stairs, and let her read the letters, and then sent the money to pay the debt."

It is impossible to give in this page any large portion of the life of Mr. Huntington, who was rich in faith, and upon whom God showered abundant answers to prayer. But, like all of us, he, too, suffered extremely in all the necessities of life, yet ever looked to God above for help. Of his experience, he says in his own words, after having for years thoroughly tested the promises and faithfulness of God.

"*A succession of crosses was always followed with perpetual blessings, for as sure as adversity led the van, so sure prosperity brought up the rear.*

"*Never, no never, did the Holy Spirit withhold his prevalent intercession from me in times of trouble, nor did my God ever turn a deaf ear to my prayer, or fail to deliver me.*"

"*Many are the afflictions of the righteous, but the Lord delivereth him out of them all.*"

16

The Faith of Little Children.

God Keeps Hold of the Other Hand.

A little boy with his mother was returning from a visit; the night was very dark, and little could be seen ahead. She led her little boy, by the hand, who trustingly walked by her side. He had only just begun to learn and remember the stories of the Bible, and he believed and trusted everything he heard. After walking for sometime in the darkness, very silently, he burst out with,

"Mamma, I'm not afraid."

"Why, what makes you feel so."

"*Because, mamma, God keeps hold of the other hand.*"

This is the beautiful lesson older ones, too, must learn, the simple, childlike confidence in God, which gives no fear, no alarm.

The skeptic can never accuse little children of the same theories, philosophies, imaginations and beliefs which are characteristic of older heads. The child knows nothing of such books of reason, science or religion. Many a child who could not read has asked of God and his prayer has been answered; and when the whole world witnesses a little child, who in its innocence has been told that God lives, that God loves him, that God can do everything and will surely hear his prayer, and then in its care and grief, kneels before the God it trusts, offers its little prayer, *and the prayer is answered,* let none of maturer minds ever presume to doubt. The faith of little children is typical of the very simplest faith wherewith any human being must approach its Creator. The child never questions, never doubts; but in its simplicity asks, and God honors the trust. The following incident illustrates the point, *that not one thing is ere too small for God to consider, or a soul to bring to him in prayer.*

A Child whose Life was Saved in Answer to Prayer—by his own Prayer the Life of his Sister is Saved.

One of the most beautiful incidents ever known relating to the faith of children, and the reward of their trust, is contained in the following circumstance, personally known to the editor of this book, who was a participant in the facts.

The only child of a young married couple, living in this city, their pride, their hope and joy, and the darling of the whole family, was seized with severe sickness, grew rapidly worse. The grandfather, who was a skilled physician, was constantly present, ministering in every way, by every means, but nothing was of any avail. No medicine could cure, and the child seemed ready to die. No one could think of relief or knew where to find it. The grandfather, at last, proposed to lay the case before God, and ask the prayers of His people in the child's behalf. The mother was only too glad to ask other prayers with her own, to bring relief. The father, who had hitherto never seriously thought of religion, was in intense anxiety and despair. Here was his first, his only child about to be taken away from him, and then came the thought, is it possible his family life was not to be blessed; his child was in distress, no human effort was available. At last, he too joined in the prayer of his wife and father, and bowing

before the Great Unknown, unseen God, he poured out his
heart in prayer, saying, "*Lord, if thou wilt spare my child,
wilt give him life, and thus show to me thy power and will
to save, I will never doubt again, and will give thee my
heart*"

A request for prayer was written and sent to the pastor,
Dr. William Adams, of the Madison Square Church.   It
arrived after church service had begun; the sexton was unwilling to carry it to the pulpit, as it was against the rule,
but when told he *must, as a life was in great danger,* he consented, and delivered it to the pastor.

The messenger waited breathlessly, and when in silence
the doctor specifically mentioned the case before him, and
asked the Lord to heal and spare the little one, and comfort
the hearts of all, and make it a witness of his love and power,
the messenger accidentally looked at the clock, and it marked
just *quarter to eleven*, A. M.

When prayer was finished he returned home.   Arriving at
home, he was astonished to find the child better, its whole
condition had changed, the medicine had taken hold, and the
doctor now said everything was so hopeful the child would
surely recover, and it did.   But mark the unparalleled singularity of the scene.   The father asked the messenger the *time*
when the prayer was offered.   He replied, "At a *quarter to
eleven.*"   The father in astonishment said, "*At that very
moment* the disease changed, and the doctor said he was better."

The father, who had thus been proving the Lord with this
test of prayer and its identity of time in his answer, was so
overwhelmingly convinced of the real power of prayer, and
thereby of the real existence of God, and that a Christian life
was one of facts as well as beliefs, now finding that the Lord
had indeed kept His own promise, he, too, kept his promise
and gave his heart to the Lord, and became henceforth, a pro-
fessing Christian.

But there were more wonderful things yet to happen—a

period of five years passed. Other children were added to the family, and one day, the youngest, a sweet, beautiful girl, was taken suddenly ill with convulsions. The sickness for days tasked the strength of the mother, and the skill of the doctor, but no care, ingenuity, or knowledge could overcome the disease or subdue the pain. The little girl's fits were severe and distressing, and there were but short intervals between, just time to come out of one and with a gasp, pass into another still more terrible. In its occasional moments of reason, it would look piteously as if mutely appealing, and then the next convulsion would take it and seem to leave it just at death's door.

All attendants were worn with care, the doctor fairly lived in the house and forsook all his other business. The clergyman came and comforted the anxious hearts with words of sympathy and prayer; but her *little brother Merrill*, (whose own life we have just related,) tender-hearted, a mere child, scarce seven years of age, who had known of the Lord, and who believed that He was everywhere and could do everything, was intensely grieved at "Mamie's" distress, and came at last to his mother and asked if he could go and "*make a prayer to God for Sissy.*" The mother said, "Go." The little boy went back into his room, and kneeling humbly by the side of his bed, as he did at his night and morning prayers, uttered this request:

"*O God, please to bless little sister, she is very sick. Please stop her fits so she won't have any more. For Jesus' sake, amen.*"

He came back, told his mamma what he said, and added: "*Mamma, I don't think she will have any more.*"

Now mark how the Lord honored this simple faith of the little child. *From that very moment the fits left her. They never returned; and the child soon entirely recovered.*

Notice the full beauty and instruction of these two incidents: *Little Merrill's life was saved in answer to prayer; was the means of his father's salvation, and when he in turn had grown to an age when he could learn of God, his own prayer was the means of saving his own sister's life.*

Notice, too, that all earthly available means were used to save each child, but to no effect. Physicians and parents considered the case hopeless, and then committed it to the decision of God.

Notice, too, that when little Merrill was so sick, that the mother and doctor both prayed, yet it was not until his father had also prayed that the answer came. God meant to honor the faith of the first two, but was *waiting for the prayer of the third* ere he granted the request. That child's sickness was one of the purposes of God. Notice in the second case, that while father, mother, doctor, the clergyman, and others of the house were all trusting in prayer, yet the Lord *was waiting for the prayer of the little brother,* ere he sent the blessing of relief. Such an incident draws its own conclusion. *Never cease in prayer for anything which is to God's honor and glory. Use all the possible means to help God   Where human means are of no avail, commit it to God and wait in humble resignation.   Ask others to pray, too, for the same object,* that when the answer comes, God may be glorified before the sight of others as well as your own. When so many are waiting to see if *God* will honor his promises, depend upon it, *God will be found faithful to all his word*

Trusting in God's Promises.

"It was a fierce, wild night in March, and the blustering wind was blowing, accompanied by the sharp, sleety snow. It was very desolate without, but still more desolate within the home I am going to describe to you. The room was large and almost bare, and the wind whistled through the cracks in the most dismal manner. In one corner of the room stood an old-fashioned bedstead upon which a woman lay, her emaciated form showing her to be in the last stage of consumption. A low fire burned in the large fire-place, and before it a little girl was kneeling. She had a small testament, and was trying by the dim fire-light to read a chapter, as was her custom, before going to bed. A faint voice called to her from the bed, 'Nellie, my daughter, read the 14th chapter of St. John for your Mother.' 'Yes, Mother,' was the reply, and after turning the leaves a few moments, the child began. All that long Winter day that poor mother had been tortured with pain and remorse. She was poor, very poor, and she knew she must die and leave her child to the mercies of the world. Her husband had died several years before. Since then she had struggled on, as best she could, till now she had almost grown to doubt God's promises to the helpless. 'In my Father's house are many mansions.' 'I go to prepare a place for you.' Here the little reader paused, and crept to her mother's side. She lay motionless, with closed eyes, while great hot tears were stealing down her wasted cheeks. 'Mother, He has a place almost ready for you, hasn't He.' 'Yes, my child, and I am going very soon, but *He* will watch over you, Nellie, when Mother has gone to her last home.'

"The weeks went slowly by to the suffering invalid; but when the violets were blooming, they made a grave upon the hillside, and laid the weary body down to rest, but the spirit had gone to the home which Christ himself had gone to prepare.

"Years passed away. It was sunny May. The little church of Grenville was crowded. I noticed in one of the seats a lady plainly but neatly attired. There was nothing remarkable in the face with its mournful brown eyes, and decided looking mouth and chin. I ransacked my memory to find who the lady was. Suddenly a vision of the poor widow came. This, then, was the little girl, little Nellie Mason. 'We will read a part of the 14th chapter of St. John,' the minister said. 'In my Father's house are many mansions; I go to prepare a place for you.' The slow, deliberate tones recalled me from my reverie, and I looked at Nellie. Her head was bowed, but I could see the tears flowing like rain "

The Faith of a Little Child.

An incident most beautiful was told in the Fulton Street prayer meeting by a converted Jew.

"Journeying in the cars, I was attracted by two little girls, Jewesses. I asked them if they loved Jesus. To my surprise, they said they did. I found that their mother was in a seat near by. She had attended some of the gospel meetings for Jews, and was interested in them. She said her husband had not been to church or synagogue for eleven years, and she did not know his views on religion. Her two little girls had attended a Methodist Sunday school, and there learned of Jesus. A day or so after, the mother was taken very sick, and remedies failing, the eldest child, a little over eight years old, said: 'O Mamma, if you will let me pray to Jesus for you, He can take away your pains and give you sleep.' She knelt with her sister and prayed in simple words to Jesus to heal her mother, telling Him that He had so promised to hear prayer. Shortly after, the mother, after long hours of restlessness and suffering, fell into a deep sleep and awoke relieved of pain and much refreshed. She heard from her daughter's lips the story of her faith in Jesus and love for Him, and then sent for me, begging me to pray for her. I am glad to tell you that she is now a converted woman, a believer in the Lord Jesus Christ."

The Wanderer Found.

A mother sent a request for prayer to the Fulton Street prayer-meeting, that she might hear from him who had long ago left home, and wandered far away. She had been praying very earnestly for him, and soon she wrote that she had just heard from him, and heard too that he had become a Christian and learned to trust in Him.

Are You There.

A mother, one morning, gave her two little ones books and toys to amuse them while she went up-stairs to attend to something. A half hour passed quietly away, and then one of the little ones went to the foot of the stairs, and in a timid voice called out, "Mamma, are you there?"

"Yes, darling."

"All right," said the little one, and went on with her play. By-and-by the question was repeated, "Mamma, are you there?"

"Yes, darling."

"All right," said the child again, and once more went on with her play. And this is just the way we should feel towards Jesus. He has gone up-stairs, to the right hand of God, to attend to some things for us. He has left us down in this lower room of this world to be occupied here for a while. But to keep us from being worried by fear or care, He speaks to us from His word, as that mother spoke to her little ones. He says to us, "Fear not; I am with thee. I will never leave thee, nor forsake thee." "The Lord will provide."

And so we see how certain it is that God does provide relief in trouble for those who love and serve Him.

God Knows the Bottom of the Barrel.

"Mother, I think God always hears when we scrape the bottom of the barrel," said a little boy to his mother one day. His mother was poor. They often used up their last stick of wood and their last bit of bread before they could tell where the next supply was to come from. But they had so often been provided for in unexpected ways, just when they were most in need, that the little boy thought *God always heard when they scraped the bottom of the barrel*. This was only that little fellow's way of saying what Abraham said when he called the name of the place where God had delivered him, "Jehovah-Jireh."

God's Care for Little Children in Little Wants.

" I was early taught that God cares for His children, even to regard their *little* daily wants. An illustration of my implicit confidence, which I do not remember ever to have been betrayed, occurred when I was about ten years of age. I was accustomed to give five cents each Sabbath at the Sunday School collection for foreign missions. This money was not given me directly by my parents; but I was allowed to go on an errand, or to do some little piece of work for a neighbor and thus earn it, outside of the performance of the duties that naturally fell to my·lot at home. At one time, when I was attending school about a mile from home, my time out of school was taken up by my walk to and from it and the chores which necessarily fall to a farmer's boy, so that for some months I had no opportunity of earning anything. One Sabbath morning, I dropped my last silver piece into the collection, with a prayer—which I always offered at such a time— that God would bless it to the heathen, that some one might be led to Him by it.

" I went home that day with a child's anxiety, feeling that I could not bear the thought of giving nothing for the heathen on next Sabbath, and yet not seeing how I could possibly obtain it. That night I asked my Heavenly Father to provide the money for me. The anxiety was all gone; for I felt that God would answer. Next morning, when almost at the school-house, I found a handkerchief in the road, in the corner of which was securely tied a silver quarter and a silver dime. Instantly my thoughts flew to the next Sabbath, and to the prayer I had offered. O, yes! I thought, God has more than answered my prayer; instead of giving me just enough for next Sabbath, He has given me enough for seven Sabbaths.

Then the thought came, somebody lost it; yes, it was my duty to find the owner, which I did not expect would be difficult, although it was in town. So I cheerfully gave it up, thinking that 'the Lord will provide' in some other way. I took it directly to my teacher, and asked her to find the owner. She made faithful inquiry, but no one was found to claim it. Who can question this being an answer to prayer, when we think of the numerous *chances* against its occurring just as it did."

A Child's Prayer for Papa.

A drunkard, who had run through his property, returned one night to his unfurnished house. He entered his empty hall Anguish was gnawing at his heart-strings, and language was inadequate to express his agony as he entered his wife's apartment, and there beheld the victims of his appetite, his loving wife and a darling child. Morose and sullen, he seated himself without saying a word; he could not speak; he could not look up then. The mother said to the little angel at her side, "Come, my child, it is time to go to bed;'" and that little baby, as she was wont, knelt by her mother's lap and gazing wistfully into the face of her suffering parent, like a piece of chiseled statuary, slowly repeated her nightly orison. When she had finished, the child (but four years of age) said to her mother, " Dear Mother, may I not offer up one more prayer ? " " Yes, yes, my sweet pet, pray ; " and she lifted up her tiny hands, closed her eyes, and prayed: " O God ! spare, oh! spare my dear papa ! " That prayer was lifted with electric rapidity to the throne of God. It was heard on high—it was heard on earth. The responsive " Amen ! " burst from the father's lips, and his heart of stone became a heart of flesh. Wife and child were both clasped to his bosom, and in penitence he said " My child, you have saved your father from the grave of a drunkard. I'll sign the pledge ! "

A Little Quaker Boy's Prayer right out in Meeting.

A little Quaker boy, about six years old, after sitting, like the rest of the congregation, in silence, all being afraid to speak first, as he thought, got up on the seat, and, folding his arms over his breast, murmured in a clear, sweet voice, just loud enough to be distinctly heard on the front seat, " I do wish the Lord would make us all gooder, and gooder, and gooder, till there is no bad left."

What the Little Children may Do.

At family prayer, little Mary, one evening when all was silent, looked anxiously in the face of her backsliding father, who had ceased to pray in his family, and said to him with quivering lips, " Pa, is God dead ? "

" No, my child—why do you ask that ? "

" Why, Pa, you never talk to him now as you used to do," she replied.

These words haunted the father until he was mercifully reclaimed.

The Unbelieving Father led to go to Church.

An unbelieving father came home one evening and asked where his little girl was. " She has gone to bed," said his wife. " I'll just go and give her one kiss," said the father, for he loved his little daughter dearly As he stood at the door of her bedroom, he heard some one praying. It was his little Jane, and he heard her say, " Do, God Almighty, please lead daddy to hear Mr. Stowell preach."

She had often asked him to go, and he had always said, " No, no, my child." After listening to her prayer, he determined, the next time she asked him, to accompany her, which he did, and heard a sermon which took his attention and pricked his conscience. On leaving the church, he clasped the hand of his little girl in his, and said, " Jane, thy God shall be my God, and thy minister shall be my minister." And the man became a true follower of the Lord.

A Child's Prayer for Relief.

An interesting little daughter of a professor in Danville, Kentucky, in the Summer of 1876, in eating a watermelon, got one of the seeds lodged in her windpipe. The effort was made to remove it, but proved ineffectual, and it was thought that the child would have to be taken to one of the large cities to have an operation performed by a skillful surgeon. To this she was decidedly opposed, and pleaded with her mamma to tell her if there was no other way of relief. Finally, in order to quiet her childish fears, her Christian mother told her to ask God to help her.

The little one went into an adjoining room and offered her prayer to God to help her. Shortly thereafter she came running to her mamma with the seed in her hand, and her beautiful and intelligent face lighted up with joy. In response to the eager inquiry of the mother, the little one said that she had asked God to help her, and while she was praying she was taken with a severe cough, in which she threw up the seed.

God's Care over His People—The Praying Widow.

A young widow with two children was living in the city of Berlin. She was a Christian woman, and trusted in Jehovah-Jireh to take care of her. One evening she had to be away for a while. During her absence a man entered her house for the purpose of robbing her. But " the Lord who provides " protected her from this danger in a very singular way.

254 ANSWERS TO PRAYER.

On returning to her home she found a note lying on her table, which read as follows:

"Madam, I came here with the intention of robbing you, but the sight of this little room, with the religious pictures hanging around in it, and those two sweet-looking children quietly sleeping in their little bed, have touched my heart. I cannot take anything of yours. The small amount of money lying on your desk I leave untouched, and I take the liberty of adding fifty dollars besides." The Bible tells us that "the hearts of men are in the hands of God, and he turneth them as the rivers of waters are turned." He turned the heart of this robber from his wicked purpose, and in this way he protected the widow who trusted in him.

God Saved a Family Mercifully.

One morning a Christian farmer, in Rhode Island, put two bushels of rye in his wagon and started to the mill to get it ground. On his way to the mill he had to drive over a bridge that had no railings to the sides of it. When he reached the middle of this bridge his horse, a quiet, gentle creature, began all at once to back. In spite of all the farmer could do, he kept on backing till the hinder wheels went over the side of the bridge, and the bag of grain was tipped out and fell into the stream. Then the horse stood still. Some men came to help the farmer. The wagon was lifted back and the bag of grain was fished up from the water. Of course it could not be taken to the mill in that state. So the farmer had to take it home and dry it. He had prayed that morning that God would protect and help him through the day, and he wondered what this accident had happened for. He found out, however, before long. On spreading out the grain to dry he noticed a great many small pieces of glass mixed up with it. If this had been ground up with the grain into the flour it would have caused the death of himself and his family. But Jehovah-Jireh was on that bridge. He made the horse back and throw the grain into the water to save the family from the danger that threatened them.

A Child's Faith in the Lord's Prayer.

About the 30th of July, 1864, the beautiful village of Chambersburgh was invaded and pillaged by the Confederate army. A superintendent of a Sabbath school, formerly resident in the South, but who had been obliged to flee to the North because of his known faithfulness to the national government, was residing there, knowing that if discovered by the Confederate soldiers, he would be in great peril of life, property and every indignity,—in the gray dawn of that memorable day, with his wife and two little girls, again on foot, he fled to the chain of mountains lying north-west of the doomed village.

After remaining out for some days and nights, with no shelter but such as was afforded by the friendly boughs of large forest trees, and without food, they became nearly famished. At last, the head of the family, unable to endure the agony of beholding his wife and children starving to death before his face, and he not able to render the needed relief, withdrew to a place by himself, that he might not witness the sad death of his loved ones. With his back against a large oak, he had been seated only a short time, when his eldest little daughter, not quite ten years old, came to him and exclaimed:

"*Father, father, I have found such a precious text in my little Testament, which I brought to the mountain with me, for very joy I could not stop to read it to mother, but hastened to you with it. Please listen while I read.*" To which he said:

"Yes, my child, read it. There is comfort to be found in the Scriptures. We will not long be together on earth, and there could be no better way of spending our last mortal hours." To which she replied:

"O, father, I believe that we will not die at this time; that we will not be permitted to starve; that God will surely send us relief; but do let me read." Then opening her dear little volume, at the ninth verse of the sixth chapter of Matthew, she read as follows :

" ' *Our Father, which art in heaven, hallowed be Thy name, Thy kingdom come; Thy will be done on earth as it is in heaven; give us this day our daily bread.' O, father, to think that our dear Saviour Himself taught His disciples to pray for their daily bread. These are His own words. It is not possible, therefore, that He will allow any person to starve, who, in His own appointed language, asks Him for food. Will He not, dear father, hear our prayers for bread?* "

At once and forever the scales fell from the eyes of that parent. With tears streaming down his cheeks, he clasped his child to his bosom, and earnestly repeated the Lord's Prayer. *He had scarcely finished it when a small dog ran to where he and his daughter were upon their knees, and barked so fiercely as to attract to the spot its owner, a wealthy Pennsylvania farmer,* who was upon the mountain in search of cattle that he had lost for several days The kind-hearted tiller of the soil immediately piloted the suffering family to his own comfortable home, and properly provided for their wants.

A Child Preserved from Wolves.

A little girl only nine years old, named Sutherland, living at Platteville, Col., was recently saved from death by ferocious forest wolves as follows : The child went with her father on a cold afternoon to the woods to find the cattle, and was told to follow the calves home, while the father continued his search for the cows. She did so, but the calves misled her, and very soon she became conscious that she was lost. Night came on, and with it the cold of November and the dreaded wolves. With a strange calmness she continued on her uncertain way. The next day, Sunday, at 10 A. M., she reached, in her wanderings, the house of John Beebe, near a place called Evans, having traveled constantly eighteen hours, and a distance of not less than twenty-five miles. *All night the wolves growled around her, but harmed her not;* neither was she in the least frightened by them. All know that in ordinary cases fierce packs of bloodthirsty wolves would devour a man, and even a horse. But this little one was invincible in her trusting, simple faith. The narrative states: "She said that the wolves kept close to her heels and snapped at her feet; but her mother told her that if she was *good* the Lord would *always* take care of her; so she asked the Lord to take care of her, and she knew the wolves would not hurt her, *because God wouldn't let them!*" The child was hunted for by a great number of people, and being found was restored shortly to her parents in perfect health and soundness.

Jesus Cured Me.

In the family of a missionary pastor in Kansas, was a daughter of twelve years of age, seriously afflicted with chronic rheumatism. For three years she suffered, until the leg was shrunken, stiff at the knee, shorter by some two inches than the other, and the hip joint was being gradually drawn from its socket. The child read of Mrs. Miller's cure by prayer, originally published in *The Advance,* and wondered why she could not also be cured by the same means. She repeated to her mother some of the promised answers to prayer, and asked: "Don't Jesus mean what he says, and isn't it just as true now as then?" The mother endeavored to divert her attention by representing the affliction as a blessing. The physician also called and left another prescription, and encouraged the child to hope for benefit from it. The child could not, however, be diverted from the thought that Jesus could and would heal her. After the doctor's departure she said: "*Mamma, I cannot have that plaster put on.*"

"Why, dear."

17

"*Because, mother, Jesus is going to cure me, and he must have all the glory. Dr. —— doesn't believe in God; if we put the plaster on, he will say it was that which helped me; and it must be all Jesus.*" So earnest was she, that her mother at length placed the package, just as she had received it, on a shelf, and said no more about it.

The little girl and her mother were alone that day, the father being absent from home. When the household duties were done she called her mother to her.

"*Mother, will you pray now to Jesus to cure me? I have got the faith; I know he will if you will ask him.*" The mother, overcome, yielded to her daughter's request, and commenced praying. She was blest with unusual consciousness of the presence of God, and became insensible of all outward surroundings, pleading for the child. She remained in this state of intercession for more than an hour, when she was aroused by her daughter, who with her hand on the mother's shoulder was joyfully exclaiming, "*Mother, dear mother, wake up! Don't you see Jesus has cured me? O, I am well! I am all well!*" and she danced about the room, literally healed.

One week from that day, the girl was seen by the writer in the "*Advance,*" who says she was *out sliding on the ice with her companions.* From that day to this she has had no further trouble; *the limb is full, round and perfect;* there is *no difference between it and the other*

To every question asked she replies, with the overflowing gratitude of a loving heart, "Jesus cured me!"

The Little Boy who Wanted His Sister to Read the Bible.

Rev. Mr. Spurgeon, of London, tells of the excellent faith of a little boy in one of the schools of Edinburgh, who had attended a prayer-meeting, and at the last said to his teacher who conducted it:

"Teacher, I wish my sister could be got to read the Bible; she never reads it."

"Why, Johnny, should your sister read the Bible?"

"Because if she once read it I am sure it would do her good, and she would be converted and saved."

"Do you think so, Johnny?"

"Yes, I do, sir; and I wish the next time there was a prayer-meeting you would ask the people to pray for my sister, that she may begin to read the Bible."

"Well, well, it shall be done, John."

So the teacher gave out that a little boy was anxious that prayer should be offered that his sister might read the Bible. John was observed to get up and go out. The teacher thought it very rude of the boy to disturb the people in a crowded room, and so the next day, when the lad came, he said:

"John, I thought it very rude of you to get up in the prayer-meeting and go out. You ought not to have done so."

"O, sir," said the boy, "I did not mean to be rude; *but I thought I should like to go home and see my sister reading her Bible for the first time.*"

True to his faith, when he reached his home, he found the little girl reading her Bible.

Nettie's Daily Bread.

A little girl in a wretched attic, whose sick mother had no bread, knelt down by the bedside, and said slowly: "Give us this day our daily bread." Then she went into the street and began to wonder where God kept his bread. She turned around the corner and saw a large, well-filled baker's shop.

"This," thought Nettie, "is the place." So she entered confidently, and said to the big baker, "I've come for it."

"Come for what?"

"My daily bread," she said, pointing to the tempting

loaves. "I'll take two, if you please—one for mother and one for me."

"All right," said the baker, putting them into a bag, and giving them to his little customer, who started at once into the street.

"Stop, you little rogue!" he said, roughly; "where is your money?"

"I haven't any," she said simply

"Haven't any!" he repeated, angrily; "you little thief, what brought you here, then?"   .

The hard words frightened the little girl, who, bursting into tears, said: "Mother is sick, and I am so hungry. In my prayers I said, 'Give us this day our daily bread,' and then I thought *God meant me to fetch it, and so I came.*"

The rough, but kind-hearted baker was softened by the child's simple tale, and instead of chiding her or visiting threats of punishment, as is usually the case, he said: "*You poor, dear girl, here, take this to your mother,*" and he filled a large basketful and gave it to her.

The Brother's Prayer.

A physician, who for many years practiced his profession in the State of California, was called once to see the child of Mr. Doak, of Calveras County, living on the road between San Andreas and Stockton, and not far from the mining town of Campo Seco, or Dry Camp. He says: The patient was a little girl about ten years of age, bright and intelligent and one of twins, the other being a boy, equally bright and well-disposed. The primary symptoms had indicated inflammation of the stomach, which the attending physician had hopelessly combated, and finally, when by metastasis it attacked the brain, with other unfavorable symptoms, he was inclined to abandon the case in despair.

It was at this juncture I was called in. The symptoms were exceedingly unfavorable, and my own opinion coincided with my professional brother's. However, we determined to go to work. A day and night of incessant watching, and the state of the patient caused us both to feel the case hopeless, and we only continued our attendance at the earnest solicitation of the child's mother. The anxious, care-worn and restless sorrow of the little brother, his deep grief as he saw his sister given over to the power of the King of Terrors, had attracted our attention. He would creep up to the bedside of his sister silently, with pale and tearful face, controlling his emotion with great effort, and then steal away again and weep bitterly. With a vague, indefinite idea of comforting the little fellow, I took him to my knee, and was about to utter some platitude, when the little fellow, looking me in the face, his own the very picture of grief, burst out with—

"Oh, Doctor, must sister die ?"

" Yes," I replied, "but,"—

Before I could go farther he again interrupted me :

" Oh, Doctor, is there nothing, nothing that will save her ? Can nobody, nobody save my sister ?"

For an instant the teachings of a tender and pious mother flashed over my mind. They had been long neglected, were almost forgotten. California, in those days, was not well calculated to fasten more deeply on the mind home teachings. There were very few whose religious training survived the ordeal, and for a long time I had hardly thought of prayer. But the question brought out with the vividness of a flash of lightning, and as suddenly, all that had been obscured by my course of life, and, hardly knowing what I did, I spoke to him of the power that might reside in prayer. I said, God had promised to answer prayer. I dared not allow the skeptical doubt, that came to my own mind, meet the ear of that innocent boy, and told him, more as my mother had often told me than with any thought of impressing a serious subject on his mind, " *That the prayers of little boys, even, God would hear.*" I left that night with some simple directions, that were given more to satisfy the mother than from having the slightest hope of eventual recovery, promising to return next day.

In the morning, as I rode to the door, the little boy was playing round with a bright and cheerful countenance, and looked so happy that involuntarily I asked:

"Is your sister better?"

"Oh, no, Doctor," he replied, "but she is going to get well."

"How do you know," I asked.

"*Because I prayed to God,*" said he, "and *he told me she would.*"

"How did he tell you?"

The little fellow looked at me for an instant, and reverently placing his hand on the region of his heart, said:

"*He told me in my heart.*"

Going to the room where my patient was lying, I found no change whatever, but in spite of my own convictions there had sprung up a hope within me. The medical gentleman with whom I was in consultation came to the room, and as he did, *a thought of a very simple remedy* I had seen used by an old negro woman, in a very dissimilar case, *occurred to my mind.* It became *so persistently present* that I mentioned it to my brother practitioner. He looked surprised, but merely remarked, "It can do no harm." I applied it. In two hours we both felt the case was out of danger.

The second day after that, as we rode from the house, my friend asked me how I came to think of so simple a remedy

"*I think it was that boy's prayer,*" I replied

"Why, Doctor! you are not so superstitious as to connect that boy's prayers with his sister's recovery," said he.

"Yes, I do," I replied; for the life of me I cannot help thinking his prayers were more powerful than our remedies."

Light Given to a Blind Child.

"A missionary visiting one of the mission schools of Brooklyn, was introduced to a remarkable child. He was brought into the school from the highways and hedges, and young as he was, he had been taught of God. One day he was playing with powder, and putting his mouth to the match to blow it, it exploded, and the whole charge went into his face and eyes. He became totally blind, and the physician gave but little hope of recovery. But the little sufferer was patient and calm, and even hopeful; sitting through the dark days meditating on what he had learned at the mission Sabbath-school, and repeating passages of Scripture and many a beautiful hymn.

"One evening after the physician had spoken discouragingly, and his parents, as he perceived, were in deep distress, he was absorbed on his knees in a corner of the room in earnest prayer. His voice, though subdued almost to a whisper, was indicative of intense feeling. His parents inquired what he had been praying so earnestly for. Why, said he, that *Jesus Christ would open my eyes. The doctor says he can't, and so I thought I would ask the Savior to do it for me. God honored his faith. In a few days his sight came to him; and the prayer was answered. He can now see clearly.*"

Asking The Lord to Help Him in his Lessons.

"A little boy was at school, he was diligent, and determined to succeed, but found that parsing was rather hard.

"One day he went to his mamma for a little help in analyzing some sentences. She told him the proper manner of doing it, and he followed her directions; but he was much troubled that he could not understand the whys and wherefores himself.

"His mamma told him it was rather hard for him then, but that after he had studied a little longer, it would be quite easy,

"Johnnie went into another room to study alone, but after a little came back, his face perfectly radiant with joy. He said : 'O mamma, I want to begin again. I asked Jesus to help me, and now I think I see just how it is. He always helps us when we ask him ;' and with unspeakable delight he with his mamma went over his lesson again."

Give us this day our Daily Bread.

"The *American Messenger* tells the story of Johnny Hall, a poor boy. His mother worked hard for their daily bread. 'Please give me something to eat; I am very hungry,' he said one evening. His mother let the work upon which she was sewing fall from her knee, and drew Johnny toward her. Her tears fell fast as she said : 'Mamma is very poor, and cannot give you any supper to-night.' 'Never mind, mamma; I shall soon be asleep, and then I sha'n't feel hungry. But you will sit and sew, and be so hungry and cold. Poor mamma,' he said, and kissed her many times to comfort her.

"'Now, Johnny, you may say your prayers ;' for dearly as his mother loved him, she could ill afford to lose a moment from her work. He repeated 'Our Father' with her until they came to the petition, 'Give us this day our daily bread.' The earnestness, almost agony, with which the mother uttered these words, impressed Johnny strongly. He said them over again : '*Give us this day our daily bread.*' Then opening his blue eyes, he fixed them on his mother, and said: 'We shall never be hungry any more. God is *our Father*, and he *will* hear us.' The prayer was finished and Johnny laid to rest The mother sewed with renewed energy. Her heart was sustained by the simple faith of her child. Many were the gracious promises which came to her remembrance. Although tired and hungry, still it was with a light heart she sank to rest.

"Early in the morning a gentleman called on his way to

business. He wished Johnny's mother to come to his home to take charge of his two motherless boys. She immediately accepted the offer. They were thus provided with all the comforts of a good home. Johnny is a man now, but he has never forgotten the time when he prayed so earnestly for his daily bread.

"*God will hear prayer* is his firm belief. In many ways has he had the faith of his childhood confirmed. He looks to God as his Father with the same trust now as then.

God will Take Care of Me.

"When the yellow fever raged in New Orleans, the pestilence visited a Christian household, and the father died. Then the mother was suddenly seized, and knowing that she must die, she gathered the four children around her bed, the oldest being only about ten years of age, and said to them that God was about to take her home to heaven. She urged them to have no fears, and assured them that the kind, heavenly Father who had so long provided for them would surely come and take care of them. The children, with almost breaking hearts, believed what the dying mother had told them.

"She was buried. The three youngest soon followed her, although they received every necessary attention from friends during their sickness. The oldest, a boy, was also seized by the pestilence, and in an unguarded moment, under the influence of delirium, wandered from his sick-bed out into the suburbs of the city, and lying down in the tall grass by the roadside, looked steadfastly up, murmuring, incoherently at times, 'Mother said God would come and take care of me— would come and take care of me!' A gentleman happening to pass at the time, and hearing the unusual sounds, went where the lad was lying, and rousing him, asked him what he was doing there   Said the little fellow in reply · '*Father died ; mother died ; little brother and sisters died. But just before mother went away into heaven, she told us to have no fear, for God would come and take care of us, and I am now waiting for him to come down and take me. I know he will come, for mother said so, and she always told us the truth.'*

" 'Well,' said the gentleman, whose kindliest sympathies were stirred by the little fellow's sad condition and his implicit confidence in his sainted mother's pious instructions, *'God has sent me, my son, to take care of you.'* So he had him carried to his home, and kindly nursed and cared for by his own family. He recovered, and to-day is one of the most useful Christian young men in the far West, where he has fixed his home."

Laura Healed.

"A Christian teacher, connected with a Southern Orphan Asylum, writes *The Christian*, that often when the children were sick, and most of them came to me more or less diseased, I cried to the Lord for help, and He who ' bore our infirmities, and carried our sicknesses,' healed them. Oh it is so good to trust in the Lord ! How much better to rely on Him 'in whom we live, and move, and have our being,' than to put confidence in man, even in the most skillful physician To confirm and strengthen the faith of the doubting, I send you the following account of the healing of one of our orphans.

"Laura was one of a large orphan family, living on Port Royal Island, S. C. When her mother died, she went to live with a colored woman who made her work very hard, 'tote' wood and water, hoe cotton and corn, do all manner of drudgery, rise at daybreak, and live on scanty food. Laura suffered from want, exposure and abuse. The freed-women of the plantation looked with pity into her eyes, and desired her to run away. But she replied, 'Aunt Dora will run after me, and when she done cotch me, she'll stripe me well with the lash ; she done tell so already.'

"One morning, however, when Laura went to the creek for crabs, a good aunty followed her, and throwing a shawl over the poor child's rags, said, 'Now, Laura, put foot for Beau-fort fast as ever you can, and when you get there, inquire where Mrs. Mather lives: go straight to her; she has a good home for jes sich poor creeters as you be.' Laura obeyed, hastened to Beaufort, seven miles distant, found my home, was made welcome, and her miserable rags exchanged for good clean clothes. In the morning, I said, 'Laura, did you sleep well last night?' She replied, 'O, missis, my heart too full of joy to sleep. Me lay awake all night, thinking how happy me is in dis nice, clean bed, all to myself. Me never sleep in a bed before, missis'

"Laura, then about thirteen years old, came to me with a hard cough, and pain in her side. I put on flannels, gave her a generous diet, and hoped, that with rest and cheerful surroundings, she would soon rally as other children had, who came to me in a similar broken-down condition. Still the cough and pain continued. I dosed her with various re-storatives, such as flax-seed, and slippery elm, etc., but all were of no avail She steadily grew worse. Every week I could see she declined. Her appetite failed; night sweats came on; and she was so weak that most of the day she lay in bed. The children, all of whom loved Laura, she was so patient and gentle, whispered one to another, 'Laura is gwine to die; dere is def in her eye"

"One evening in midwinter, the poor child's short breath, fluttering pulse, and cold, clammy sweat alarmed me, and I felt sure that unless the dear Lord interposed in her behalf, her time with us was very short. I lingered by her bed till near midnight in prayer for her recovery. I could not give her up. Again in my own room I poured out my soul in prayer for the child, and then slept. About two o'clock, I suddenly awoke, and heard what seemed a voice saying to me, *'Go to Laura; I can heal her now, the conditions are right; you are both calm and trustful.'*

"I arose quickly, hastened to her room and said to her, 'Laura, do you want to get well?' 'O, yes, missis, me

wants to get well.' 'Do you believe Jesus can cure you?'
She replied, "I know he can if he will.' 'Well, Laura,' I
said, ' Jesus has just waked me out of a sound sleep, and told
me to go and tell you that he *will cure you now.* Do you
believe he will, Laura?' 'Yes, missis, me *do believe,*' she
replied earnestly. She then repeated this prayer. 'O, Jesus,
do please to make me well; let me live a long time, and be a
good and useful woman.'

"The burden had rolled off my heart; I returned to my
room and slept sweetly. In the morning, Tamar, Laura's
attendant, met me at the door, exclaiming joyfully, 'O, I'se
so glad! Laura is a heap better, Missis. She wake me up
long time before day and begged me to get her something to
eat, she so hungry.'

"From that night Laura rapidly recovered. Her cough
abated, her appetite was restored, her night sweats ceased,
and in less than a month she was strong and well."

A Little Slave's Faith.

A missionary in India, passing one day through the school
room, observed a little boy engaged in prayer, and overheard
him say, " O, Lord Jesus, I thank thee for sending big ship
into my country and wicked men to steal me and bring me
here, that I might hear about Thee and love Thee. And
now, Lord Jesus, I have one great favor to ask Thee. Please
to send wicked men with another big ship, and let them
catch my father and my mother, and bring them to this country, that they may hear the missionaries preach and love
Thee."

The missionary in a few days after saw him standing on
the sea-shore, looking very intently as the ships came in.
"What are you looking at, Tom?" "I am looking to see if
Jesus Christ answers prayer."

For two years he was to be seen day after day watching
the arrival of every ship. One day, as the missionary was

viewing him, he observed him capering about and exhibiting the liveliest joy.

"Well, Tom, what gives you so much joy?" "O, Jesus Christ answer prayer. Father and mother come in that ship," which was actually the case.

A Good Reason for Praying.

A little girl about four years of age being asked, "Why do you pray to God?" replied. "Because I know He hears me, and I love to pray to Him."

"But how do you know He hears you?"

Putting her little hand to her heart, she said, "I know He does, because there is something *here* that tells me so."

My Heart Talked.

A child six years old, in a Sunday school, said: "When we kneel down in the school-room to pray, it seems as if my heart talked."

Why, Sir, I Begged.

A little boy, one of the Sunday school children in Jamaica, called upon the missionary and stated that he had lately been very ill, and in his sickness often wished his minister had been present to pray with him.

"But, Thomas," said the missionary, "I hope you prayed." "Oh, yes, sir." "Did you repeat the collect I taught you?" "I prayed." "Well, but how did you pray?" "Why, sir, I begged."

A Little Child's Prayer for Healing.

A very little child, who had but recently learned to talk, and the daughter of a Home missionary, had been for weeks troubled with a severe cough, which was very severe in its weakness upon her.   At last her father said to her, " Daughter, ask Jesus, the good Lord, to heal you."

Putting up her little hands as she lay in bed, she said, *"Dear Jesus, will oo please to cure me, and do please tell papa what to give me."*

The father, who was listening, thought several times of *" syrup of ipecac,"* but did not connect it immediately with the prayer.   At last the thought came so often before him, that he felt, " Well, it will do no harm, perhaps this is what the Lord wants me to give her."   He procured it, administered it, and in three hours the little child's cough had wholly ceased, and she was playing on the floor with the other children.   A most singular feature is the fact that the same medicine was administered at other times and had no effect in relief.

The Blessedness of Giving.

———— • • ————

" *Blessed is he that considereth the poor; the Lord will deliver him in time of trouble.*"

" *Honor the Lord with thy substance, and with the first fruits of all thine increase, so shall thy barns be filled with plenty.*"

" *There is that scattereth and yet increaseth; and there is that withholdeth more than is meet, but it lendeth to poverty.*"

" *The liberal soul shall be made fat, and he that watereth shall be watered also himself.*"

" *He that hath pity upon the poor lendeth unto the Lord; and that which he hath given will He pay him again.*"

" *Whoso stoppeth his ears at the cry of the poor, he also shall cry himself, but shall not be heard.*"

" *He that hath a bountiful eye shall be blessed, for he giveth of his bread to the poor.*"

" *He that putteth his trust in the Lord shall be made fat.*"

" *He that giveth unto the poor shall not lack; but he that hideth his eye shall have many a curse.*"

" *Cast thy bread upon the waters, for thou shalt find it after many days.*"

" *If thou draw out thy soul to the hungry, and satisfy the afflicted soul, the Lord shall guide thee continually, and satisfy thy soul in drought, and make fat thy bones. And thou shalt be like a watered garden, and like a spring of water, whose waters fail not.*"

" *He which soweth bountifully, shall reap also bountifully.*"

" *Every man according as he purposeth in his heart, so let him give; not grudgingly, nor of necessity, for*

God Loveth a Cheerful Giver.

How the Lord Blesses Those Who Give Liberally to His Cause.

A disciple of the Lord Jesus, poor in this world's goods, but rich in faith, became greatly perplexed in regard to the meaning of the forty-second verse of the fifth chapter of Matthew. The words are: "Give to him that asketh thee; and from him that would borrow of thee turn not thou away." After a season of prolonged mental inquiry, as to whether the language was to be regarded as literal or not, she suddenly paused and exclaimed : "It is easy enough to find out; test it and see."

It was Saturday. Her money, all but two dollars, had been expended in providing for the Sabbath. The amount left, which was absolutely needed for the following Monday, she put in her pocket, and went out.

On the street, a friend, whose husband had been for some time out of business, met her and stated their distresses, and asked if she could lend them *two dollars to last over the Sabbath.*

She was surprised. The test had come sooner than she expected, but, without hesitation, the money was "*lent to the Lord,*" and the now penniless believer went home to wait and see.

Now mark the result. Monday came, and with it the needs to be supplied. While pondering what course to pursue, a knock was heard, and, on opening the door, a lady, with a bundle in her hand, inquired if she could do a little work for her. Replying in the affirmative, and naming the price, the lady took from her pocket-book two dollars, and handed it to her, saying : "It is more than you ask, but you might as well have it." "I was never more astonished," said this true disciple, "and literally shouted for joy. I had tested and proved that the promises of God are yea and amen in Christ Jesus. Glory to God. I have never doubted since; and though often in straits, I have always been delivered."

Would it not be well for Christians to "test" where they cannot understand? "Ye are my friends," said the blessed Lord, "if ye do whatsoever I command you." Obedience will solve difficulties that reasoning cannot unravel. Try and see.

Dividing with God.

A merchant, in answer to inquiries, refers back to a period when, he says, "In consecrating my life anew to God, aware of the ensnaring influences of riches, and the necessity of deciding on a plan of charity before wealth should bias my judgment, I adopted the following system:

"I decided to balance my accounts as nearly as I could, every month; and reserving such a portion of profits as might appear adequate to cover probable losses, to lay aside, by entry on a benevolent account, one-tenth of the remaining profits, great or small, as a fund for benevolent expenditure, supporting myself and family on the remaining nine-tenths. I further determined, that when at any time my net profits, that is, profits from which clerk-hire and store expenses had been deducted, should exceed $500 in a month, I would give twelve and a half per cent; if over $700, fifteen per cent.; if over $900, seventeen and a half per cent.; if over $1,100, twenty per cent.; if over $1,300, twenty-two and a half per cent.; thus increasing the proportion of the whole as God should prosper, until at $1,500, I should give twenty-five per cent., or $375 a month. As capital was of the utmost importance to my success in business, I decided not to increase the foregoing scale until I had acquired a certain capital, after which I would give one-quarter of all net profits, great or small; and on the acquisition of another certain amount of capital, I decided to give half; and on acquiring what I determined would be a full sufficiency of capital, then to give the whole of my net profits.

"It is now several years since I adopted this plan, and under it I have acquired a handsome capital, and have been prospered beyond my most sanguine expectations. Although constantly giving, I have never yet touched the bottom of my fund, and have been repeatedly astonished to find what large drafts it would bear. True, during some months I have encountered a salutary trial of faith, when this rule has led me to lay by the tenth, while the remainder proved inadequate to my support; but the tide has soon turned, and with gratitude I have recognized a heavenly hand more than making good all past deficiencies."

Prosperity and Liberality.

A London correspondent of the *Western Christian Advocate*, writing some years ago of raising a fund for the extinction of debts on chapels, gives the following incident:

"A gentleman named Wilkes, who was promised a subscription of one thousand guineas to this fund, has a history so remarkable as to be worth relating across the Atlantic Seven years ago he was a journeyman mechanic. Having invented and patented some kind of a crank or spindle used in the cotton manufacture, and needing capital to start himself in the business of making them, he made it a matter of earnest prayer that he might be directed to some one able and willing to assist him. In a singular and unexpected manner he fell in with an elderly Quaker, a perfect stranger, who accosted him with the strange inquiry: 'Friend, I should like to know if a little money would be of any service to thee.' Having satisfied himself as to Wilkes' genius and honesty, the Quaker at once advanced him the required amount. The praying mechanic started in business on his own account, and everything he has touched of late appeared to prosper.

"Hearing of a field in Ireland offered for sale, in which was a deserted mine, he went over to see it; bought the field for a small sum, recommenced working the mine, and it now turns out to yield abundance of excellent copper. For the year 1852, he promised to give the Missionary Society a *guinea a day;* but such abundance has poured in upon him during the year, that he felt that to be below his duty, and has, therefore, enlarged his subscription for the present year seven-fold. He is actually giving to that noble cause seven guineas daily, or upwards of $10,500 a year, during this year, 1853; in addition to which he has just given one thousand guineas to the fund above referred to." "It is pleasing to add," says the writer, "that this remarkable man retains the utmost simplicity."

Would that liberality and prosperity might ever go hand in hand Often, as wealth increases liberality is starved out, and the rich give far less than the poor in proportion to their means and ability.

The Deacon's Singing School.

"I am going out to see if I can start a singing school," said a good man, as he stood buttoning up his overcoat, and muffling up his ears, one bitterly cold Winter night.

"A singing school," said his wife, "how will you do that?"

"I have heard of a widow around the corner a block or two who is in suffering circumstances. She has five little children, and two of them down sick, and has neither fire nor food. So Bennie Hope, the office boy tells me. I thought I would just step around and look into the case."

"Go, by all means," said his wife, "and lose no time. If they are in such need we can give some relief. But I cannot see what all this has to do with starting a singing school. But never mind, you need not stop to tell me now; go quickly and do all you can for the poor woman."

So out into the piercing cold of the wintry night went the husband, while the wife turned to the fireside and her sleeping babes, who, in their warm cribs, with the glow of health upon their cheeks, showed that they knew nothing of cold or pinching want. With a thankful spirit she thought of her blessings, as she sat down to her little pile of mending. Very busily and quietly she worked, puzzling all the time over what her husband could have meant by starting a singing school. A singing school and the widow—how queer! What possible connection could they have?

At last she grew tired of the puzzling thought, and said to herself, "I won't bother myself thinking about it any more. He will tell me all about it when he comes home. I only hope we may be able to help the poor widow and make her 'poor heart sing for joy.' There," she exclaimed, "can that be what he meant? The widow's heart singing for joy! Wouldn't that be a singing school? It must be; it is just like John How funny that I should find it out!" and she laughed merrily at her lucky guess. Taking up her work again, she stitched away with a happy smile on her face, as she thought over again her husband's words, and followed him in imagination in his kind ministrations. By-and-by two shining tears dropped down, tears of pure joy, drawn from the deep wells of her love for her husband, of whom she thought she never felt so fond before. At the first sound of footsteps she sprang to open the door.

"Oh, John! did you start the singing school?"

"I reckon I did," said the husband, as soon as he could loose his wrappings; "but I want you to hunt up some flannels and things to help to keep it up."

"Oh, yes! I will; I know now what you mean. I have thought it all out. Making the widow's 'heart sing for joy' is your singing school. (Job. xxix : 13.) What a precious work, John! 'Pure religion and undefiled is to visit the fatherless and widows in their affliction.' My own heart has been singing for joy all the evening because of your work, and I do not mean to let you do it alone. I want to draw out some of this wonderful music."

It Pays to Give to The Lord.

"A clergyman states, that soon after he dedicated himself to the service of Christ, he resolved, as Jacob did, 'Of all that thou shalt give me, I will surely give a tenth unto thee.' Of the first $500 he earned, he gave $130, and in such a way that it incited a wealthy friend to give several hundreds more, including a donation of $100 to this clergyman himself. For four years, the clergyman says, 'My expenses were small, my habits economical, and the only *luxury* in which I indulged was the luxury of giving. In the two first of these years I was permitted to give $500' 'On a review of my ministry of about sixteen years,' he adds, 'I find God has graciously permitted me to give to the cause of my Redeemer nearly $1,200, by which amount about forty life memberships have been created in various evangelical societies. During all these years God has prospered me; has given me almost uninterrupted health; has surrounded me with sweet domestic ties; and my congregation, by means in part perhaps of a steady example, have given *more in these sixteen years* than in all their long previous history."

Another Example of Beneficence.

"A liberal donor, in enclosing $100 to a sister institution, but strictly withholding his name, says, 'When I began business, it was with the intention and hope to become rich. A year afterward I became, as I trust, a Christian, and about the same time met with 'Cobb's Resolutions,' which I adopted. Some four or five years later, I read 'Normand Smith's Memoir,' and also Wesley's 'Sermon on the use of Money,' which led me to devote all my gains to benevolent uses, reserving to myself $5,000 while I remained unmarried, part of which I have bequeathed to relatives, and the remainder to benevolent societies. Up to this time—about sixteen years—by the grace of God—nothing else—I have given about $24,500 to benevolent purposes, and lent about $500 to those in need, which has not been returned; making in all about $25,000."

Commendable Examples.

The Methodist Missionary Society mention one of their donors who, for twenty years, has used the power given him of getting wealth, for his Lord, in which time he has been enabled to appropriate to benevolent purposes *more than thirty thousand dollars*, while operating with a capital of but five thousand dollars. Another business man of that denomination in Boston, during fifteen years, has appropriated *thirty-nine thousand dollars*.

System in Giving.

A correspondent of the American Tract Society says, "It was their publications which induced me to appropriate statedly one-tenth of my income to the cause of the Lord. After acting upon that scale nearly two years, and finding that although *my donations greatly exceeded those of former years*, my affairs were not thereby involved in any embarrassment; but that, on the contrary, with increasing contributions to the leading objects of Christian benevolence and to general charity, came an *increased store and enlarging resources*, I concluded, with a heart throbbing with grateful emotions to my Creator, in view of his great love and kindness toward me, that I would increase the proportion."

Lending to The Lord.

"A poor man, some of whose family were sick, lived near Deacon Murray, (referred to in the tract, 'Worth of a Dollar,') and occasionally called at his house for a supply of milk. One morning he came while the family were at breakfast.

Mrs. Murray rose to wait upon him, but the deacon said to her, 'Wait till after breakfast.' She did so, and meanwhile the deacon made some inquiries of the man about his family and circumstances.

"After family worship the deacon invited him to go out to the barn with him. When they got into the yard, the deacon, pointing to one of the cows, exclaimed, 'There, take that cow, and drive her home.' The man thanked him heartily for the cow, and started for home; but the deacon was observed to stand in the attitude of deep thought until the man had gone some rods. He then looked up, and called out, 'Hey, bring that cow back.' The man looked around, and the deacon added, 'Let that cow come back, and you come back too.' He did so; and when he came into the yard again, the deacon said, 'There, now, take your pick out of the cows, *I a'n't going to lend to the Lord the poorest cow I've got.*'"

A Steward of his Lord's Bounty.

An aged benevolent friend in a western city, states some interesting facts respecting his own experience in giving systematically as the Lord prospered him. He says, "Our country and professors of religion in it have become 'rich and increased in goods,' but I fear that a due proportion is not returned to the Giver of every good.

"I commenced business in 1809 with $600, and united with the 'Northern Missionary Society No. 2,' which met monthly for prayer, and required the payment of two dollars a year from each member. That year I married, and the next united with the Christian church. No definite system of giving 'as the Lord had prospered' me, was fully made until the close of the year 1841. The previous fourteen years had been assiduously devoted to the interests of Sabbath-schools and the temperance enterprise, when I found both my physical and pecuniary energies diminished, the latter being less than $30,000.

"After days and nights of close examination into my affairs, with meditation and prayer, I promised the Lord of all, I would try at the close of every year to see what was the value of my property, and the one-quarter of the increase I would return to him in such way as my judgment, aided by his word and providence, might direct.

"For more than fifteen years I have lived up to this resolve, and though most of the time I have been unable to attend to active business, the investments I have made have more than quadrupled the value of my property, and in that time enabled me to return to Him 'from whom all blessings flow,' $11,739.61."

The Five-Dollar Gold Piece.

"'A friend,' says a venerable clergyman, Rev. Mr. H——, 'at a time when gold was scarce, made me a present of a five-dollar gold piece. I resolved not to spend it, and for a long time carried it in my pocket as a token of friendship. In riding about the country, I one day fell in with an acquaintance, who presented a subscription-book for the erection of a church in a destitute place.

"'I can do nothing for you, Mr B——,' said I; 'my heart is in this good undertaking, but my pocket is entirely empty; having no money, you must excuse me.'

"'Oh, certainly,' said he, 'all right, sir. We know you always give when it is in your power.'

"We parted; and after I had proceeded some distance, I bethought me of the piece of gold in my vest pocket. 'What,' said I to myself, 'I told that man I had no money, when I had by me all the time this gold pocket-piece. This was an untruth, and I have done wrong.' I kept reproaching myself in this way until I stopped, and took from my pocket the five-dollar piece.

"'Of what use,' said I, 'is this piece of money, stowed away so nicely in my pocket?' I made up my mind to turn

back, and rode as fast as I could until I overtook Mr. B——,
to whom I gave the coin, and resumed my journey

"A few days after, I stopped at the house of a lady, who
treated me very hospitably, for which I could make no return.
except in thanks and Christian counsel. When I took leave,
she slipped into my vest pocket a little folded paper, which
she told me to give to my wife. I supposed it was some trifle
for the children, and thought no more of it until I reached
home. I handed it to my wife, who opened it, and to my astonishment *it was a five-dollar gold piece, the identical
pocket-piece I had parted with but a few days before.* I
knew it was the same, for I had made a mark upon it; how
this had been brought about was a mystery, but that the
hand of the Lord was in it I could not doubt. 'See,' said I
to my wife; 'I thought I *gave* that money, but I only *lent*
it; how soon has the Lord returned it! Never again will I
doubt his word.'

"I afterward learned that Mr B—— had paid over the coin
to the husband of the lady at whose house I staid, along with
some other money, in payment for lumber, and he had given
it to his wife.

"Take my advice, and when appealed to for aid, fear not
to give of your poverty; depend upon it the Lord will not let
you lose by it, if you wish to do good If you wish to prosper, 'Give, and it shall be given unto you; for with the same
measure that ye mete, it shall be measured to you again'
'Trust in the Lord, and do good, so shalt thou dwell in the
land, and verily thou shalt be fed.' "

A New Year's Incident.

"One New Year's day I was going out to visit some of my
poorer neighbors, and thought I would take a sovereign to a
certain widow who had seen days of competence and comfort.
I went to look in my drawer, and was so sorry to find I had but
one sovereign left in my bank for the poor, and my allowance

would not be due for two or three weeks. I had nearly closed the drawer upon the solitary sovereign, when this passage of Scripture flashed so vividly into my mind, 'The Lord is able to give thee much more than this,' (2 Chron. xxv : 9.) that I again opened the drawer, took the money, and entered the carriage which was waiting for me. When I arrived at Mrs. A.'s, and with many good wishes for the New Year, offered her the sovereign, I shall never forget her face of surprised joy. The tears ran down her cheeks while she took my hands and said, 'May the God of the widow and fatherless bless you; we had not one penny in the house, nor a morsel of bread; it is he who has heard my prayers, and sent you again and again to supply my need.' You who pray for and visit the poor, and enjoy the blessedness of relieving their temporal wants and of speaking to them of Jesus, you will understand the gladness of heart with which I returned home.

"In the country we had only one post daily; so when evening came on, and it was nearly ten o'clock, I was not a little surprised at receiving a letter. When I opened it, how my heart beat for joy when I read these words from a comparative stranger: 'You will have many poor just now to claim your pity and your help, may I beg you to dispense the enclosed five pounds as you see fit? and I have ordered a box of soap to be sent to you for the same purpose.' These boxes of soap are worth four pounds. Thus did our gracious God send nine times as much as I gave for his sake, before that day had closed."

Feneberg's Loan to the Lord.

"A poor man with an empty purse came one day to Michael Feneberg, the godly pastor of Seeg, in Bavaria, and begged three crowns, that he might finish his journey. It was all the money Feneberg had, but as he besought him so earnestly in the name of Jesus, in the name of Jesus he gave it.

Immediately after, he found himself in great outward need, and seeing no way of relief he prayed, saying, 'Lord, I lent Thee three crowns; Thou hast not yet returned them, and Thou knowest how I need them. Lord, I pray Thee, give them back.' The same day a messenger brought a money-letter, which Gossner, his assistant, reached over to Feneberg, saying, 'Here, father, is what you expended.' The letter contained two hundred thalers, or about one hundred and fifty dollars, which the poor traveler had begged from a rich man for the vicar; and the childlike old man, in joyful amazement, cried out, 'Ah, dear Lord, one dare ask nothing of Thee, for straightway Thou makest one feel so much ashamed!'"

Compound Interest.

The Christian tells of a minister in Ohio, who in 1860 was engaged to statedly supply a congregation who were in arrears for a whole year's salary to their former pastor, and were only able to promise their 'supply' five dollars a Sunday till the old debt should be paid. At the close of the year, only about two-thirds of this amount had been paid. So it was not strange that their 'supply' soon found himself in arrears for many things. That year the cost of his periodicals alone had amounted to sixteen dollars. This he could not pay, and as none of them could be stopped without payment of arrearages, the debt must continue to increase.

On New Year's day the minister was called to marry a couple, and gave the fee, five dollars, to his wife saying, "I want you to get yourself a dress with this." There was a kind of material much worn then, which she had very much admired, a dress of which would cost four dollars. So she went to the Mission periodical to find the address of the Mission Secretary, thinking to send the extra dollar there. But as she glanced over its pages and noticed the trials and straits of the missionaries, and the embarrassment of the Board that year, her heart was touched and she felt that they

needed the money more than she did the dress, and instead
of the one she concluded to send the five dollars.

She went to her husband and read her letter to him. "O,"
said he, "I'm afraid we are too poor to give so much" With a
little feeling of disappointment she said, " Well, give me the
change and I will send what I had intended at first." "No,"
said he, ' you have given it, and I dare not take it back."

And so with a prayer that God would accept and bless the
gift she signed her letter, " A Friend of Missions," thinking,
as no one would know the author, that was the last she would
hear about it in this world.

The ladies of that congregation were accustomed to meet
weekly at the parsonage to sew for those in need. The next
week a lady who was visiting in the place came with her
friends, and as she entered the parlor she tossed a bundle into the lap of the minister's wife, saying, " Mrs. ——, here is
a present for you "

The present was a dress pattern of the same kind of material she had intended to purchase. And as she thought to herself, " God has given me this in place of what I have given,"
she was reminded of the words, " Give, and it shall be given
to you." But that was not the end.

A short time afterwards she received a letter from the
Secretary of the Board of Missions, enclosing a printed copy
of her own letter, and asking if she were the author of it;
and added, " If so, a large-hearted man in New York has
authorized me to send you twenty-five dollars, with a special
request that you purchase a dress worth five dollars, and give
the rest to your husband and children." There was her five
dollars back, with four times as much more added to it.

The Brown Towel.

The editor of *The Christian Woman* tells the story of a
poor woman who, in her anxiety to give to the Lord, could
find nothing but a poor brown towel.

"They must be very poor who have *nothing* to give," said Mrs. Jarvis, as she deposited a pair of beautiful English blankets in a box that was being filled by the ladies of the church to be sent to the poor.

"And now, ladies, as you are nearly through, I would like to tell you an incident in my history: I was once very poor."

"You once very poor?" said a lady.

"Yes; I was once *very poor*. There came to our village a missionary to deliver a lecture. I felt very desirous to go; but having no decent apparel to wear, I was often deprived of going to church, although I was a member.

"I waited until it was late, and then slipped in and took a seat behind the door.

"I listened with streaming eyes to the missionary's acount of the destitution and darkness in heathen lands. Poor as I was, I felt it to be a great privilege to live in a Christian land and to be able to read my Bible.

"It was proposed by our pastor that the congregation should fill a box and send it out with the missionary on his return.

"O," thought I, "how I would like to send something" "When I returned home my poor children were still sleeping soundly, and my disconsolate husband waiting my return, for he had been out of employment some time. After he had gone to bed I went to looking over my clothes, but I could find nothing that was suitable that I could possibly spare; then I began looking over the children's things, but could find nothing that the poor dears could be deprived of, so I went to bed with a heavy heart, and lay a long time thinking of the destitution of the poor heathen, and how much better off I was.

"I got to thinking over my little stock again. There was nothing I could put into the box except two brown towels.

"Next day I got my towels, pieced out the best one, and when it was almost dark, put on my bonnet, went to the

church, slipped my towel into the box, and came away thinking that the Lord knew I had done what I could.

"And now, ladies, let me tell you it was not long after that
till my husband got into a good situation; and prosperity has
followed us ever since.   So I date back my prosperity to this
incident of the brown towel."

Her story was done, and, as her carriage was waiting at the
door, she took her departure, leaving us all mute with surprise that one so rich and generous had been trained to give
amid poverty.

Giving Blessed.

A merchant of St. Petersburg, at his own cost, supported
several native missionaries in India, and gave liberally to the
cause of Christ at home.   On being asked how he could
afford to do it, he replied :

"Before my conversion, when I served the world and self,
I did it on a grand scale, and at the most lavish expense.
And when God by his grace called me out of darkness, I
resolved that Christ and his cause should have more than I
had ever spent for the world.   And as to giving *so much*, it
is God who enables me to do it; for, at my conversion, I solemnly promised that I would give to his cause a fixed proportion of all that my business brought in to me; and every
year since I made that promise, it has brought me in about
double what it did the year before, so that I easily can, as I do,
double my gifts for his service "

And so good old John Bunyan tells us,

> "A man there was, some called him mad,
>   The more he gave, the more he had."

And there are truth and instruction in the inscription on the
Italian tombstone, "What I gave away, I saved; what I
spent, I used; what I kept, I lost."   "Giving to the Lord,"
says another, " is but transporting our goods to a higher floor."
And, says Dr. Barrow, "In defiance of all the torture and

malice and might of the world, the *liberal* man will ever be rich; for God's providence is his estate; God's wisdom and power, his defence; God's love and favor, his reward; and God's word, his security."

Richard Baxter says, " I never prospered more in my small estate than when I gave most. My rule has been, *first*, to continue to need, myself, as little as may be, to lay out none on *need-nots*, but to live frugally on a little; *second*, to serve God in any place, upon that competency which he allowed me to myself, that what I had myself might be as good a work for common good, as that which I gave to others; and *third*, to do all the good I could with all the rest, preferring the most public and durable object, and the nearest. And the more I have practiced this, the more I have had to do it with; and when I gave almost all, more came in, I scarce knew how, at least unexpected. But when by improvidence I have cast myself into necessities of using more upon myself or upon things in themselves of less importance, I have prospered much less than when I did otherwise. And when I had contented myself to devote a stock I had gotten to charitable uses *after my death*, instead of laying it out at present, in all probability, *that* is like to be lost; whereas, when I took the present opportunity, and trusted God for the time to come, I wanted nothing and lost nothing."

These are a few of many evidences, that where we give from right motives, we are never the poorer, but the richer for doing it. " The liberal soul shall be made fat, and he that watereth, shall be watered also, himself."

Lending to the Lord.

As a series of religious meetings was held in a Baptist church in ——, and the hearts of God's people were greatly encouraged, the church was consumed by fire. It was proposed to continue the meetings in the Congregational church, but the workmen were coming the next morning to demolish

and rebuild it.   It was then proposed to hire the workmen to
delay, that the people might assemble for three days more,
but nothing was done; when the Congregational pastor walking his study, and thinking that some souls might be gathered
in, went to the workmen, and handed them $10 from his own
pocket, which he could ill afford; the meetings were con
tinued, and a number of souls hopefully converted to God.
The day following, as he passed the house, the man to whom
he paid the $10 called to him, and constrained him to receive
back the whole amount, saying it was of no value compared
with the saving of a soul.

The Liberal Farmer.

A farmer in one of the retired mountain towns of Massachusetts, began business in 1818, with six hundred dollars in
debt.   He began with the determination to pay the debt in
six years, in equal installments, and to give all his net income
if any remained above those installments.   The income of the
first year, however, was expended in purchasing stock and
other necessaries for his farm.

In the six next years he paid off the debt, and having abandoned the intention of ever being any richer, he has ever
since given his entire income, after supporting his family and
thoroughly educating his six children

During all this period he has lived with the strictest economy, and everything pertaining to his house, table, dress and
equipage has been in the most simple style, and though he
has twice been a member of the State Senate, he conscien-
tiously retains this simplicity in his mode of life.   The farm
is rocky and remote from the village, and his whole property, real and personal, would not exceed in value three thousand dollars.   Yet sometimes he has been enabled to give
from $200 to $300 a year.

Experience of a Saddler.

Normand Smith, a saddler of Hartford, Conn., after practicing for years an elevated system of benevolence, bequeathed in charity the sum of $30,000.

An anonymous writer says of himself, that he commenced business and prosecuted it in the usual way till he lost $900, which was all he was worth, and found himself in debt $1,100.

Being led by his trials to take God's word as his guide in business as well as in heart and religion, he determined to give his earnings liberally unto the Lord.

The first year he gave $12. For eighteen years the amount increased by about 25 per cent., and the last year he gave $850, and he says he did it easier than during the first year he paid the $12. Besides, though with nothing but his hands to depend on when he began this course, he paid the whole debt of $1,100 with interest, though it took him nine years to do it.

Jacob not Blessed until He Became a Liberal Giver.

Jacob went out from his father's house "with his staff," a poor man. But at Bethel he vowed to give to God the *tenth* of all that God should bestow on him. Commencing thus, God blessed him, and in twenty years he returned with great riches.

The Lord's Insurance Money.

A tradesman in New York had pledged to give to the Lord a certain portion of his business receipts as fast as they were collected. He called this *The Lord's insurance money*, for, said he, " so long as I give so long will the Lord help me and bless me, and in some way he will give me the means to give, so it is no money lost. Rather it is a blessing to my heart to keep it open in gratitude, a blessing to dispose of it to

19

gladden other hearts, and the surest way to keep the Lord's favor with me."

The results of his experience were blessed indeed, as he said, "I never realized before how closely the Lord is connected with all my interests, and how he helps me in all my business plans. Things happen constantly which show me constantly that some one who knows more than I is benefiting me—protecting me. Bad debts have been paid which I did not expect. Errand boys, just getting into sly and bad habits, have been discovered ere their thefts had proceeded far. As I needed competent help in my business, it has come just as it was wanted. When customers were failing, somehow their debts to me were paid, although they failed to pay others. A severe fire came to my office and apparently seemed to have swept all my valuables away. But it was stopped at just the right moment, and not one thing valuable was lost. The insurance companies paid me enough to replace every damage, and the office was renewed better than before. The Lord sends me business enough to pay for my debts, yet others are dull. *I cannot tell why it is, except that I always pray for my business, and ask the Lord to bless it for the good of others,* and that the means which come from it may be used for his cause. When I stop giving, business stops coming. When I stop praying specially for it, perplexities arise. As long as I pray for it, it all moves easily, and I have no care or trouble. The Lord is my Banker, my Helper, my Insurer, my Deliverer, my Patron, and my Blessed Savior of temporal things as well as spiritual."

Give and it Shall be Given.

" 'Cheerful giving,' writes an aged minister, 'is what enriches the giver and brings down a blessing from above. A poor clergyman attended one of Zion's festivals in a distant city. The railroad company supplied him with a return ticket, and though many of his brethren would secure treasures from the book-stores, but a solitary twenty-five cent scrip was in his possession, and he would need that to pay for refreshment on his way home. It was the last day of the feast. Mention, again and again, was made of the widow's mite, or poor men's gifts, and, as the boxes were passed, he felt sad that, in his deep poverty, he could not cast in a single penny. As the assembly was dismissed, it was announced that collectors would stand at the door to gather up the *fragments* which ought to be in the Lord's treasury. With slow steps this good man passed down and put that last money he possessed into the waiting box.

"In a few moments, a gentleman of the city invited him to his table to dine, with quite a number of the dignitaries of the church. During the repast, the host was called from the table for a little time. At the conclusion of a pleasant entertainment, the poor minister was taken one side and an envelope put into his hands, with this remark : 'I was called from the table by a man who has long owed me a small debt, which I thought was lost a long time since, and I cannot think what it was paid to-day for, except that I might give it to you.' The envelope contained twenty-five dollars. When the books are opened, that rich steward will see how his money was used, and thank God, who put it into his heart to dispose of it thus."

"Lending to the Lord."

" A physician who is not a professor of religion, in a neighboring city, has for many years exhibited an unshaken faith in that declaration. He told me that he has made many experiments on it, and the Lord has fulfilled his words, ' That which he hath given will He pay him again,' in every case. One of his 'experiments' came under my observation.

"It was a bleak and chilling day in the Winter of 1847–8. The doctor was going his rounds and met a poor colored boy in the street. He was nearly frozen to death. He accosted the doctor, and asked him most piteously for a little money, stating, at the same time, that his master, an old Quaker, had excluded him from the house, and compelled him to remain in the barn; he could stand it no longer, and desired to go home—twenty miles up the river. The doctor now had the materials for another test of the promise. 'You shall not suffer if I can help you,' was his cheering reply to the boy. He requested him to call at his office, and went to a neighboring hotel and told the landlord to keep the boy until farther orders Late in the evening the boy again appeared at the office, and stated that the landlord had said, 'We don't keep darkies over night.' The doctor immediately started out in search of new quarters, and, after some difficulty, found a colored woman who was willing to keep the boy for a few days. In a short time the river, which had been closed with ice, was open. The doctor paid the bills, gave the boy a dollar, and bade him God speed. That is what he calls lending to the Lord. Now for the payment When he called at the house of the colored person to pay the bill, he 'accidentally' met an old lady, who scrutinized him closely, and at length said, ' A'n't you Doctor B—— ?' ' Yes,' was the reply; ' but who are you ?' 'No matter about my name; I owe you four dollars, which you have long since forgotten, and which I did not intend to pay you till I saw what you have done to that poor boy. The Lord bless you for your kindness. Next week you shall have your money.' She came according to her promise and offered the money, but the doctor was unwilling to take it, as he had no charge on his books. She forced it on him. He afterwards simply remarked, ' My meeting that woman was not a mere *accident*, the Lord always fulfills his promise. I generally get my capital back, with compound interest.' "

The Praying Shoe-maker.

A shoe-maker being asked how he contrived to give so much, replied that it was easily done by obeying St. Paul's precept in 1 Cor. 16:2: "Upon the first day of the week let every

one of you lay by him in store, as God hath prospered him."
"I earn," said he, "one day with another, about a dollar a
day, and I can without inconvenience to myself or family lay
by five cents of this sum for charitable purposes ; the amount
is thirty cents a week. My wife takes in sewing and washing, and earns something like two dollars a week, and she lays
by ten cents of that. My children each of them earn a shil-
ling or two, and are glad to contribute their penny ; so that
altogether we *lay by us in store* forty cents a week. And if
we have been unusually prospered, we contribute something
more. The weekly amount is deposited every Sunday morning in a box kept for that purpose, and reserved for future
use Thus, by these small earnings, we have learned that it
is more blessed to give than to receive. The yearly amount
saved in this way is about *twenty-five dollars ;* and I distrib-
ute this among the various benevolent societies, according to
the best of my judgment."

The History and Business Successes of Liberal Givers.

Mr. Nathaniel R. Cobb, a merchant connected with the
Baptist church in Boston, in 1821, at the age of twenty-three,
drew up and subscribed the following covenant, to which he
faithfully adhered till on his death-bed he praised God that
by acting according to it he had given in charity more than
$40,000.

"By the grace of God, I will never be worth more than
$50,000.

"By the grace of God, I will give one-fourth of the net
profits of my business to charitable and religious uses.

"If I am ever worth $20,000, I will give one-half of my
net profits ; and if I am ever worth $30,000, I will give three-
fourths ; and the whole, after $50,000. So help me God, or
give to a more faithful steward, and set me aside.

"N. R. COBB."

Faith in God's Liberality.

A clergyman, himself an exponent of God's bountiful dealings with men, was called upon in test of his own principles of giving to the Lord.

Preaching, in the morning, a sermon on Foreign Missions, an unusually large contribution was taken up   In the afternoon, he listened to another sermon, by a brother, on Home Missions, and the subject became so important that he was led closely to agitate the question how much he should himself give to the cause.   " I was, indeed, in a great strait between charity and necessity.   I felt desirous to contribute ; but, there I was, on a journey, and I had given so much in the morning that I really feared I had no more money than would bear my expenses.

" The collection was taken ; I gave my last dollar, and trusted in the Lord to provide   I proceeded on my journey, stopping to see a friend for whom I had collected forty dollars. I was now one hundred and forty miles from home, and how my expenses were to be met, I could not imagine   But, judge my surprise, when, on presenting the money to my friend, he took a hundred dollars, and, adding it to the forty, placed the whole of it in my hand, saying he would make me a present of it.

" Gratitude and joy swelled my bosom ; my mind at once remembered my sacrifice of the day before, and now I had realized the literal fulfillment of the promise, ' Give, and it shall be given unto you ; good measure, pressed down and running over, shall men give into your bosom.' "

He Gave His Last $5 to the Lord.

A missionary agent thus relates this incident in the life of a poor physician :

" I preached a missionary sermon in the town of ——, and a physician subscribed and paid five dollars. A gentleman standing by told me that the five dollars was all he had, or was worth; that he had lost his property and paid up his debts, and moved into town to commence practicing, with no other resources than that five-dollar bill. He and his wife were obliged to board out, as he was not able to keep house.

"I resolved, at once, that I would keep watch of that man, and see what the Lord would do with him. About a year after this interview, I visited the place again, and found the physician keeping house in good style.

"During the Summer, while the cholera raged in the country, by a series of events, guided, as he believes, by the providence of God, most of the practice was thrown into his hands, and he had taken more than $2,500."

Believe

Nothing of Your God

But what is

Most Noble and Generous.

—Pres. Edwards.

More Things

Are Wrought by Prayer

Than the World

Dreams of.

—Tennyson.

PRAYERS ANSWERED

In Business and Social Anxieties.

––––•••––––

Help In Paying a Mortgage.

A BUSINESS man in New York had several large amounts due for payment. An unprecedented series of calls from tradesmen wishing their bills paid sooner than customary, drained his means, and he was satisfied from the situation that his means would not be sufficient to pay them all. His business receipts, at this juncture, fell to one-half what they had usually been. A loan was due at the bank; a mortgage on his property, as well as large notes. He could do no more than ask the Lord constantly in prayer, to either send supplies of business, or open ways of relief. Committing his cares all to the Lord, he endeavored to throw off his burden and with diligence in trade do what was possible for protection.

He was greatly surprised when the bank loan fell due to learn that a trifling payment would be acceptable, and the rest extended at his convenience. This was remarkable, as the security had depreciated somewhat, and the loan had been then extended longer than usual.

The holder of the mortgage did not call as usual for his interest. In great surprise the tradesman dropped a note, saying he would meet his demand, but if not all the mortgage was needed, its extension would benefit the use of the capital in his business.   To his surprise, he received a reply that the mortgage would be extended one-half until the next interest day, and the rest might be paid now if it could be spared. *This was just the money which the tradesman could spare*, and was intending to propose, but refrained from mentioning it.

A sudden opportunity in business arose which enabled him to see how to use the rest of the money he had on hand, as capital, whereby he could clear within three months the remainder of the mortgage before it became due.

Thus the Lord in answer to prayer, relieved his necessities, eased his creditors, gave him knowledge and intelligence of profitable ways of trade, and helped him freely according to his faith.

Thus business needs prayer, as well as the interests of the home, the church and the soul.   When the means derived in business is used to bless the Lord's poor, " *The Lord will deliver him in time of trouble.*"

A Remarkable Prayer and Its Answer.

A lady, who had led for many years a life of faith, caring for orphans and invalids, was led one day in thought to wish that she might devote all her money to the work of the Lord, and use it specially for one branch of his service which few had ever entered.   She possessed only a thousand dollars ; and not knowing whether the thought was her own and therefore rash, or whether it came from the Lord, she asked the Lord in prayer, that if the thought was from *Him* "it might be continually before me ; if it were not, that I might cease to think of the matter."

" It was kept before me as a privilege, to help me realize a greater personal nearness to God as my Father.   It was a very important matter, and fearing a mistake, I requested a sign.   I asked God, if he wished me to give the money, (which we held at His disposal,) that *He* would send me *one dollar*, (no more, no less,) from some individual with whom I had no acquaintance. About three weeks after my request, I attended a prayer-meeting, where about a dozen ladies were gathered. After the meeting, an elderly lady I had never seen before, put something in my hand saying, ' *You will not be offended, dear, will you?* ' When I looked at the money, I found that it *was just one dollar*, my token. I exclaimed, mentally, dear Lord, do not let me ever doubt thee again. I afterwards asked the lady why she gave me the dollar. She said, 'Before I went to the prayer-meeting, I felt that I ought to take a dollar with me, and when I saw you, I felt that you were the one I should give it to.' "

" Nearly five years have passed since then, when I gave all, and my purse has never been empty. I have been constantly occupied in work of love, and my Father has sweetly cared for me in every respect."

This lady in her faith work has had under her constant care as many as twenty-two helpless invalids, of utter poverty, yet prayer has always brought them needed supplies, and the Lord has kept them.

Recovery from Insanity.

A most remarkable case of recovery from insanity is given by President William M. Brooks, of Tabor College, Iowa.

" A young lady of my acquaintance, of a finished education, lost her reason in the Winter of 1871–2, and in August, 1872, was placed in the institution for the insane, at Mt. Pleasant, Ia. No encouragement was given of her recovery, and a year later, when her father visited her, in June, 1873, she appeared so badly, that he said it would be a relief to know that she was dead. Soon after, Mrs H., the wife of a Baptist minister, who had long known and loved her, being shut up for days in a dark room, because of inflamed eyes, felt drawn out in special prayer in her behalf, and finally sent for the father and told him of her exercises, and of the assurance gained that his daughter would be fully restored.

"In a few days, came news of a sudden change for the better, and in a little over two months she returned home well, and is now teaching with all her powers in full vigor.

"The acting superintendent of the hospital, who is not a professed Christian, and who knew nothing of the prayers referred to, said that when the change occurred there was not a case among the five hundred inmates of which he had less hope, and that it was the most remarkable case of recovery which he had known during the eight years of his connection with the hospital."

Seeking Direction in Business.

A lady clerk employed in an apparently successful business was offered an opportunity in a new business, which, though much smaller and less successful than the first, yet had rich promise in it for the future. The salary promised was the same in either case. In doubt, she often waited upon the Lord, and asked to be guided,—a whisper in her heart kept saying, "Go," "Go." Constant praying kept it growing stronger and stronger,—at last she decided to go, feeling it was the decision of the Lord. She accepted the new position, was pleased, and often declared she never desired to return. The old business in less than three years decreased so that half of the employes were discharged; the rest had their salaries reduced. The new business doubled in its extent, and her salary was increased one-fifth.

Seeking Guidance of the Lord.

A school teacher, without family or a special home, in New York City, asked the Lord for direction in finding a home, and prayed often that the way might be made so plain, she might acknowledge His hand, and understand His direction.

Soon it transpired, in taking lunch at a restaurant kept by a man and his wife, that they advised her to choose a certain family hotel. She did so, and found in time more friends and acquaintances, and a pleasanter home than she ever possessed before.

She also gained new scholars to her school. Sufficient to pay for her living.

Was she not fully answered? *"They that seek the Lord shall not want any good thing."*

Saved from Cholera.

The Rev. J. B. Waterbury relates several incidents which prove the power of Prayer.

"In the year 1832 he was compelled by pulmonary symptoms, to leave his field of ministerial labor in one of the eastern cities, and travel south, hoping that a milder climate might be favorable.

" He had not proceeded far, before the cholera, that fearful scourge, made its appearance in the States, and obliged him to rejoin his family in the city of Brooklyn.

"Whilst many were dying around him, *his health* continued to improve; so that with the disappearance of the epidemic he found himself sufficiently restored to venture, if Providence should open the door, to resume his ministerial work

" But where should he go? The future, to human view, was shrouded in uncertainty. In so important a matter, affecting his usefulness and happiness, there was nothing left, but to give himself to prayer His faith in that promise, 'In all thy ways acknowledge Him, and He will direct thy Paths,' led him to pray without ceasing, 'Lord, what wilt thou have me to do.'"

On a certain day, when the burden lay heavily upon his heart, he retired as usual, to implore light and guidance. He read on that occasion, the chapter of Acts where, by divine direction, Cornelius the Centurion sent messengers to Peter at Joppa, to come to him with the Gospel. The apostle, meanwhile, is instructed by a vision to go to Cornelius.

The case was so applicable to the circumstances that the writer was led to cry mightily to God for light to be shed also upon *his* path.

While thus praying the door-bell rang, and the servant announced two men who wished to see me.

This was somewhat startling. After introducing themselves, they remarked that they had come on a very important errand, viz: to ask my services for a vacant church in which they were officers

"But how is this," I inquired, "How did you know of *me?*"

They did not until that very day. But inquiring at the Bible House in Nassau street if any of the officers of that Society knew of a minister who could be recommended to fill their pulpit, now vacant for some months.

Dr. B., the Secretary, answered, "Yes, I know a young minister in Brooklyn, whom I can recommend, provided his health, which has been delicate, is adequate."

So the messenger came inadvertently over to B——, and I was called from my knees to receive their invitation. I promptly responded, "Yes, I will go? for what was I that I could withstand God. A successful and happy ministry of fourteen years, attests the good results of that decision.

The Aid of the Lord in Business and Social Prosperity. The Wonderful Deliverance of Daniel Loest.

John Daniel Loest, a celebrated German tradesman of Berlin, Germany, was, by the aid of the Lord, so prospered in his worldly circumstances, that by steady industry, he raised himself to rank with the most respectable tradesmen of Berlin, where he kept a well-frequented fringe and trimming shop.

He was always benevolent, willing to help others, and both fervent in spirit and constant in prayer, asking the help of the Lord in the minutest details of his business.

Yet there once occurred in his experience a season of severest trial, which demanded his utmost trust and unflinching confidence in God. He seemed almost forsaken, and circumstances almost impossible to overcome. But his deliverance so astonished him that he was lost in wonder at the mysterious way in which the Lord helped his business and sent him all that he needed.

By means of acquaintances of high social character, whom he fully trusted as good Christians, never supposing there could be any degree of hypocrisy, he became security for a Christian lady of good property to the amount of *six hundred thalers.* The attorney assured him that there was not a shadow of a risk in going security for her, as her property would be more than ample to cover any claim

Months elapsed, and the circumstance forgotten, when Mr. Loest was most unpleasantly reminded by receiving an order from the Court to pay in on the following Tuesday the *six hundred thalers* for which he had become security, under the penalty of execution.

He now discovered that he had been designedly mystified, and there was no escape. The six hundred thalers must be paid before the next Tuesday. He had just accepted a bill for *three hundred thalers*, to be paid for on the ensuing Saturday. And in his first thoughts of his perplexity, he hoped to get out of his dilemma by hurrying to a rich friend to obtain a loan. On his way to his friend's home, he stumbled on another acquaintance who had lent him *four hundred* thalers on a mere note of hand, and he saluted him with the news that he must try for repayment of that sum on the following Friday, as he required it to pay for a parcel of goods which would arrive that day.

"You shall have it," said Loest, as he hurried on to his friend The friend was at home, but before Loest could speak his errand, he is addressed thus: "It is lucky you came, my friend, for I was just going to send for you, to request you to make provision to pay me back the *five hun-*

dred thalers you owe me, for I must needs have it on Wednesday to pay off a mortgage on my house, which has just been called up." "*You shall have it,*" replied Loest, calmly, yet his heart became heavier every moment.

Suddenly it occurred to him that the widow of a friend just dead was possessed of large means, and she might be inclined to help him.   But alas, disappointment thickened fast upon him.   Loest owed the deceased friend five hundred thalers for note, and three hundred thalers for goods just delivered. As he entered the room of the widow, she handed him an order from the court of trustees, under which he was bound to pay up *the five hundred thalers on Thursday,* and, continued the lady, before the poor man had time to utter a word, "I would earnestly entreat you to pay the other three hundred thalers early on Saturday to me, for there are accounts constantly pouring in on me, and the funeral expenses," here her voice faltered.   "It shall be cared for," said Loest, and he withdrew, not having had opportunity to utter one word as to the business that took him thither.   He had failed at every turn; not one thing was for him, all seemed against him.   But though the waves surged, and rose, and oppressed, yet they did not overwhelm his hope; the more the discouragements, the greater became his faith that all things were appointed for his good, and thought he could not guess, yet even the trial would result by God's own working hand, to the honor and glory of his great name.

Yet here was his situation.   *Six hundred thalers to be paid on Tuesday, five hundred on Wednesday, five hundred on Thursday, four hundred on Friday, three hundred Saturday morning, and three hundred on Saturday afternoon; in all, two thousand six hundred thalers.*   It was already the Saturday just previous, and his purse contained only *four thalers.* There was only one prospect left, and he went to a rich money lender, and in response to his request for relief in money difficulties, was met with this reply of irony and sarcasm from one who loved to indulge his enmity to the Christian faith.   "*You in money difficulties, or any difficulties, Mr. Loest! I cannot believe it; it is altogether impossible! you are at all times and in all places boasting that you have such a rich and loving Master! Why don't you apply to him now."* And the unseen face could not conceal his pleasure at this opportunity of testing a Christian.

Loest turned away; hard as the random taunt and remark of his opponent was, yet it recalled him to a sense of his duty, and his forgetfulness of the fact that he had not hitherto asked of God for special help in this circumstance. With cheerful steps he hurried home, and in long and imploring prayer, asked for help and forgiveness in this, his neglect of trust in one so rich and generous. He was refreshed and comforted, and the Sunday was one of peace and sweetness. He knew and felt assured, *"That the Lord would provide."*

The eventful week opened, and on Monday he arose with a cheerful thought in his heart; ere he had had full time to dress, he noticed with great surprise, that both his sister and the assistant in the store, seemed, notwithstanding the earliness of the hour, to have full as much as they could do in serving customers and making up parcels, and he at once hastened into the shop to give them assistance, and thus it continued all day. *Never, in all his experience,* could Loest remember such a ceaseless stream of customers as poured, on that memorable Monday, into his rather out-of-the-way shop. Cooking dinner was out of the question; neither masters nor maid had time for that; coffee and bread, taken by each in turn, served instead of the accustomed meal, and still the customers came and went; still three pairs of hands were in requisition to satisfy their wants.

Nor was it for new purchasers alone, that money came in. More than one long outstanding account, accompanied by excuses for delayed payment, and assurances that it had not been possible to settle it sooner, enlarged the contents of the till; and the honest-hearted debtor, on whom this unwonted

20

stream of money flowed in, was tempted every minute to call
out, "*It is the Lord.*"

At length night came, when Loest and his literally worn
out assistants, after having poured out their hearts in thankful adoration in family prayer, sat down to the first meal they
had that day enjoyed in common. When it was over, the
brother and sister set themselves to count over the money
which had that day been taken. Each hundred thalers was
set by itself, and the result showed *six hundred and three
thalers, fourteen silver groschen.*

This was sufficient to pay the first debt due the next day,
and leave but ten shillings and eight pence over, a trifle less
than they commenced the day with. Loest was lost in wonder and grateful emotion at this gracious testimony of how
faithfully his Lord could minister to him in his earthly
necessities.

"How countless must be the host of his ministering servants, seen or unseen, since He can employ some hundreds
of them, and send them to buy of Daniel Loest to-day, or pay
him that bill which thou owest. What a wondrous God is
ours, who in the government of this great universe, does not
overlook my mean affairs, nor forget His gracious promise,
'Call upon me in the day of trouble, and I will deliver thee.'"

Tuesday was a repetition of Monday's splendid business,
and brought in the five hundred thalers which he needed the
next morning to pay off the mortgage of his friend's house,
due that day.

Wednesday's sales gave him five hundred more thalers,
which he was obliged to have ready to pay on Thursday morning into the court of trustees.

Thursday's sales brought him four hundred thalers, just
the amount he had given promise to pay the next day for
goods delivered.

And Friday's sales gave him just three hundred thalers
with which to honor the widow's demand on Saturday, to pay
funeral and contingent expenses.

During these days of wonderful business and deliverances, after each indebtedness was discharged, there still was not left cash in hand a sum exceeding three to five dollars.

On Saturday morning, after he had sent the three hundred thalers to the widow, he had left precisely two thalers and twenty silver groschen (six shillings eight pence sterling), the smallest balance he had yet had; and what seemed most alarming, the rush to the shop seemed to be entirely over; for while during the five days past, he had had scarcely time to draw his breath from hurry and bustle, he was now left in undisturbed possession of his place. Not a single customer appeared. The wants of the vicinity seemed to have come to an end, for not a child even entered to fetch a pennyworth of thread, or a few ells of tape. This utter cessation of trade was as unusual and out of the accustomed shop business, as the extra rush had been.

At five o'clock on Saturday, was due the debt of three hundred thalers to his scoffing and tantalizing money lender. Three o'clock came, and still there was but six shillings eight pence in the till. Where was his money to come from? But Loest sat still, and "*possessed his soul in patience*," for he knew the Lord would choose the best time, and he desired to be found waiting and watching for the Lord's coming. The trial was severe. It seemed hopeless, and if it should happen that the creditor came and went away unsatisfied, his commercial character would be injured, his credit shaken, and his reputation severely suffer. That last hour ran slowly on. At a *quarter to four*, almost the last few moments of painful suspense, a little old woman came in, and asking for Mr. Loest, said to him half in a whisper, "I live here close by, quite alone, in a cellar, and I have had a few thalers paid me, and now I want to beg of you to be so good as to keep them for me. I have not slept over night since I had them; it is a great charge for a lone woman like me."

Loest was only too glad to accept the money, and offered interest, which she declined. She hurried back, brought in her money, counted it out on his table, and there *were just three hunderd thalers*, six rouleaux of fifty thalers each.

She had scarcely left the house, with her receipt in her pocket, ere the clerk of the creditor with his demand in his hand, rushed into Loest's presence. He received his three hundred thalers, and both parted speechless with amazement.

Loest was lost in wonder at the marvellous way and exactness of time in which the Lord delivered him, while the creditor was astonished thus to find Loest's Mighty Friend had not failed him in his hour of need.

Thus in one short week, from a beginning of less than five thalers, God had so exactly supplied his business needs that he had paid all his obligations of two thousand six hundred thalers, saved him from failure, saved his honor and good name, and now all was peace.

The history of Loest and other providences which helped him in his business, are still further given more at length in a little book, " *The Believing Tradesman,*" from the records of the Religious Tract Society of Berlin

This sketch illustrates the necessity of looking to God daily for help, and strength, and success, and deliverance in our business occupations as well as the concerns of our soul, and must effectively prove that those who use their business and the means from it to honor the good works of the Lord on earth, will be blessed on earth with the favor of the Lord. It teaches the sublime lesson that *money and prosperity are gifts from the Lord,* and must be considered as such, acknowledged with thankfulness, and used to please the Giver.

Whenever the Christian learns to love the gift more than the Giver, the Lord takes it often away to remind him of his need of dependence upon *Him.* But whenever the Christian loves the *Giver* because of His gifts, and spends his means again to please his Heavenly Father, he becomes the Father's steward, and his lap is filled with bountiful blessings, such as one finds by true experience, " *The Lord is my Shepherd, I shall not want.*"

Spurgeon's Prayer for Money.

Charles Spurgeon relates this incident connected with his ministry: "When the college, of which I am President, had been commenced, for a year or so all my means stayed; my purse was dried up, and I had no other means of carrying it on. In this very house, one Sunday evening, I had paid away all I had for the support of my young men for the ministry. There is a dear friend now sitting behind me who knows the truth of what I am saying. I said to him, *'There is nothing left, whatever.'* He said, 'You *have a good banker, sir.'* 'Yes,' I said, 'and I should like to draw upon him now, for I have nothing.' 'Well,' said he, 'how do you know, have you prayed about it?' 'Yes, I have.' 'Well, then leave it with Him; have you opened your letters?' 'No, I do not open my letters on Sundays.' 'Well,' said he, 'open them for once.' I did so, and in the first one I opened there was a banker's letter to this effect: 'Dear Sir, we beg to inform you that a lady, totally unknown to us, has left with us two hundred pounds for you to use in the education of young men.' Such a sum has never come since, and it never came before; and I have no more idea than the dead in their graves how it came then, nor from whom it came, but to me it seemed that it came directly from God."

The Prayer of Latimer.

The prayers of the martyr, Latimer, were very remarkable for their faith. There were three principal matters for which he prayed:

1. That God would give him grace to stand to his doctrine until death.

2 That God would of His mercy restore His gospel to England once again, repeating and insisting on these words "once again," as though he had seen God before him, and spoken to Him face to face.

3. That God would preserve Elizabeth; with many tears, desiring God to make her a comfort to this comfortless realm of England. All these requests were most fully and graciously answered.

A Mother's Prayers Answered.

A Christian evangelist, whose work has been most singularly blessed, related this incident, how once in the days of his folly and sin, while as yet his course of life ran counter to the fondest wishes and prayers of his mother's heart, he one day asked her the strange question, whether she really believed that he ever would be converted to God. And her answer, inexpressibly touching and instructive, as being the answer of *assured faith*, which could see as yet no signs of the coming of what it so anxiously sought, was,

"Yes, I believe that you will one day be as eminent as a Christian, and an instrument for good, as you have been eminent in sin, and an instrument for evil."

In later years the evangelist looked back with admiration to the faith of his mother, and thanked the Lord for His gracious answer to her prayers.

How the Lord Rescued Him.

A wonderful incident is told by Dr. S. I. Prime among his many facts relating to prayer, as published in *The Observer* and "*The Power of Prayer.*"

" A young man held a good position in a large publishing house in this city. He was about thirty years old, a married man, and happy in all the relations of life. The missionary of the church knew him through years of comfort and prosperity. Years passed away, and there came a dark place in his life. Intemperance, of the most depraved kind, made his career most dreadful. He disappeared, and was not heard from for some time. He separated himself from his family, and from all good.

"He was met in Boston one day by an old friend, after long years, who noticed a marked difference in his appearance. He approached him, grasped him by the hand and said:

"'I am a changed man. I one day got up in the morning, after a night of wakefulness, and thinking over what a wretch I had become, and how wretched I had made my poor wife and children, I resolved to go to the barn, and there all alone, to pray that God would take away utterly forever my accursed thirst for rum, and to pray till I felt answered that my prayer was heard. I went down on my knees, and on them I stayed until I had asked God many times to take away all my appetite for rum and tobacco, and everything else which was displeasing to Him, and make me a new creature in Christ Jesus—a holy, devoted Christian man, for the sake of Him who died for sinners. I told God that I could not be denied; I could not get up from my knees till I was forgiven and the curse was forever removed. I was in earnest in my prayer.

"'I was on my knees two hours, short hours, as they seemed to me; two blessed hours, for I arose from my knees assured that all of the dreadful past was forgiven, and my sins blotted out forever. Oh! I tell you, God hears prayer. God has made me a happy man. I left all my appetite in the old barn. In that old barn, I was born again. Not one twinge of the old appetite has ever been felt since then.'"

Jesus Keeps Me from Drinking.

A young man arose in the Fulton Street prayer-meeting one day, and detailed his struggles and triumphs with his appetites. He was a perfect drunkard, helpless, poor; his friends' best efforts to reclaim him were of no avail. The most solemn vows that he had ever taken, still were unable to hold him up. At last he gave himself up for lost. There seemed no hope for him, and in his despair he wandered away to the ocean shore. He met a young man who showed him a good many favors, and to whom he offered a drink from his flask of liquor.

" 'No,' said he, 'I never drink intoxicating drink, and I ask the Lord Jesus to help me never to touch it.'

" I looked at him with surprise, and inquired, 'Are you a Christian ? '

" ' Yes, I trust I am,' he answered.

" '*And does Jesus keep you from drinking intoxicating liquor ?* '

" '*He does, and I never wish to touch it.*'

" That short answer set me to thinking. In it was revealed a new power. I went home that night and said to myself, as I went, '*How do I know but Christ would keep me from drinking if I would ask him?*'

" When I got to my room, I thought over my whole case, and then I knelt down and told Jesus what a poor, miserable wretch I was ; how I had struggled against my appetite, and had always been overcome by it. I told Him if he would take the appetite away I would give myself up to Him to be his forever, and I would forever love and serve Him. I told Him that I felt assured that He could help me, and that He would.

" Now I stand here, and I tell you all most solemnly, *that Jesus took me at my word.* He did take away my appetite then and there, so that, from that sacred moment of casting myself on his help, I have not tasted a drop of liquor, nor *desired* to taste it. *The old appetite is gone.*

" The last two weeks have been rich experience of Divine goodness and grace."

Mr. Moody's Faith in Prayer. A Remarkable Answer.

Mr. Moody, on his return from England, while conducting a prayer-meeting in Northfield, Mass., gave this illustration of the power of prayer to subdue the most unlikely cases of sin and unbelief :

"There is not a heart so hard that God cannot touch it. While in Edinburgh, a man was pointed out to me by a friend who said, 'Moody, that man is chairman of the Edinburgh infidel club.' So I went and sat down beside him, and said, 'Well, my friend, I am glad to see you at this meeting. Are you not concerned about your welfare?' He said that he did not believe in a hereafter. I said, 'Well, you just get down on your knees and let me pray for you.'

"*'I don't believe in prayer.'*

"I tried unsuccessfully to get the man down on his knees, and finally knelt down beside him and prayed for him. Well, he made a good deal of sport over it, and I met him again many times in Edinburgh after that. A year ago last month, while in the north of Scotland, I met the man again. Placing my hand on his shoulder, I asked, '*Hasn't God answered the prayer?*'

"He replied, 'There is no God. I am just the same as I always have been. If you believe in a God, and in answer to prayer, do as I told you. Try your hand on me.'

"'Well,' I said, 'God's time will come; there are a great many praying for you; and I have faith to believe you are going to be blessed.'

"Six months ago I was in Liverpool, and there I got a letter from the leading barrister of Edinburgh, telling me that my friend, the infidel, had come to Christ, and that of his club of thirty men *seventeen* had followed his example.

"How it happened he could not say, but whereas he was once blind, now he could see. God has answered the prayer. '*I didn't know how it was to be answered,*' said Mr. Moody, '*but I believed it would be and it was done. What we want to do is to come boldly to God.*'"

The Wonders of a Single Prayer.

The Rev. Dr. Edwin F. Hatfield, of New York City, well known and eminent among the clergymen of the Presbyterian church, is personally acquainted with the following instance of a remarkable case in answer to prayer. From the mother of the daughter he obtained this statement, which has been published by Dr. Patton, of Chicago, in his volume, "On Prayer."

"My daughter was for fourteen months afflicted with hip disease. It was brought on by a fall, and a consequent dislocation, when she was eight years of age.

"Her right side was paralyzed, and she had an abscess. I placed her in a hospital, under the care of good nurses, and the very best medical advice.

"Everything possible was done for her, but all to no avail; she grew worse instead of better, and the doctors directed me, as there was no hope for her, to take her home to die.

"But I did not cease to hope. I did as the doctors directed, but continued to pray the prayer of faith for her recovery for two weeks. One morning, at the end of this period, we were conversing together about the wonderful cures wrought by the Savior, when on earth, and particularly that of the man at the pool of Bethesda.

"In the midst of our conversation, my daughter rose to obtain a drink of water, when she exclaimed, '*Mother, I can walk.*' 'Thanks be to God!' said I, 'Come, and let me see you!'

"Her crutches, the only means by which she could move about, before, were now useless. Upon examination, I found that the abscess had entirely disappeared, and that the paralyzed limb was restored whole, like the other.

"She was again dangerously ill, five months afterward. I prayed for her recovery one night, before retiring, and the next morning she arose, perfectly cured."

She is now twenty-one years of age, and during all this

intervening time has been free from any trouble of this kind. To-day she is as well as any one, working and running about' without the slightest trouble."

The Tavern Keeper Overcome.

Rev. Charles G. Finney relates, in his "Spirit of Prayer," of an acquaintance of his whose faith and importunity in prayer and the answer were very remarkable:

"In a town in the northern part of the State of New York, where there was a revival, there was a certain individual, who was a most violent and outrageous opposer. He kept a tavern, and used to delight in swearing at a desperate rate, whenever there were Christians within hearing, on purpose to hurt their feelings. He was so bad, that one man said he believed he should have to sell his place or give it away, and move out of town, for he could not live near a man that swore so.

"This good man of faith and prayer that I have spoken of, was passing through the town and heard the case, and was very much grieved and distressed for the individual. He took him on his praying list. The case weighed on his mind when he was asleep, and when he was awake. He kept thinking about him, and praying for him, for days; and the first we knew of it, this ungodly man came into a meeting, and got up and confessed his sins, and poured out his soul His bar-room immediately became the place where they held prayer-meetings."

Victories over Bad Habits, Tobacco, Opium, etc.

The Rev. W. H. Boole, a city missionary in New York City, has been witness in his ministries, of many cases of complete deliverance from bad habits, and appetites, solely by believing prayer. Many are contained in a little tract

written by him, " The Wonder of Grace." He gives a few
of these incidents :

" One is an officer in a church in New York, who had used
tobacco for forty years, making during that time many efforts
to abandon the practice, but always failing because of the
resultant inward growing. But he was brought to an act of
specific faith in Jesus, to save him from the appetite, and now,
after several years, he testifies, 'From that hour all desire
left me, and I have ever since hated, what I once so fondly
loved.' "

" Another is of a prominent church member in Brooklyn,
N Y., who had used tobacco for thirty years, and could not
endure to be without a cigar in his mouth, and sometimes
even rose and smoked in the night; after many failures to
overcome the habit, one night when alone, he cast himself
on his Savior for just this victory; and from that hour was
delivered from the desire as well as from the outward act, and
now wonders that he ever loved the filthy practice."

" A certain old lady, who lived near Westbrook, Conn,
aged seventy, was a confirmed opium eater, and used daily,
an amount sufficient to kill twenty persons. She was led to
see that the habit was a *sin ;* and as such, she abandoned it,
with specific application to Christ to save her from it. She
was heard, and lived for two years afterward, free from any
desire for that drug. '

" A similar case was that of a carpenter, in Brooklyn,
N. Y , who, from taking morphine to allay the pain of a fractured leg, fell into its habitual use, till he almost lived upon
it for several years after his recovery. He once swallowed, in
the presence of several physicians, a dose which it was calculated would destroy the lives of two hundred ordinary men.
Not long since, he was made to look at this as a sin, and tried
to break off the habit, abstaining, with an alarming reaction,
till five physicians declared that death would ensue, if he did
not resume it. This he did for a year ; but then on a certain
Sunday evening, broke off again, casting himself by faith on

Christ, from which moment the desire left him, and has never returned, and he has experienced no reaction or other ill effect, but has greatly improved in health."

Mrs. Whitney's Cure in Answer to Prayer.

Mrs. C. S. Whitney of Hartford, Conn., a lady well known for her Christian work among the poor, thus gives in a letter to Dr. Patton, her personal testimony of the efficacy of prayer.

"Three years ago, I was healed of a bodily disease. I had been troubled from my birth with canker, and at times suffered greatly I had consulted some of the best physicians in the land, and had been treated by the most skillful. My case was said to be incurable. When I learned to trust Christ for everything, I applied to Him for healing. My husband joined with me in this prayer for three weeks; but all the time I was growing worse. I then prayed for entire submission. About the first of October, 1872, my stomach, throat and mouth were so cankered, I could scarcely eat anything. One day, I took up the little book entitled, 'Dorothea Trudel;' and while reading, I seemed to hear a voice saying unto me, *'All things are possible unto him that believeth.'* *'According to thy faith be it unto thee.'* I claimed the faith, and immediately asked God to heal me, and in His own way. While yet on my knees, it seemed very clear to me that I should go to Boston, and ask Doctor Cullis to pray with me. I obeyed that leading, and made preparations to go the day following Just as I was ready to start for the depot, I realized that I was cured. An entire change was wrought in my system, and my soul was filled with joy and gratitude."

President Finney's Prayer for Rain.

The following incident of the prayer of President Finney for rain, and its immediate answer, is furnished by Professor Cowles, the intimate friend of President Finney:

"Somewhat more than twenty years ago, the village of Oberlin and its adjacent country along the lake shore, suffered severely through the hot season from a total failure of rain, for nearly three months. Clouds that seemed to promise rain were repelled from the heated dry atmosphere over the land, and attracted by the more moist atmosphere over the lake, to pour out their waters there. On one such occasion, the clouds had gathered dark, low, and heavy over the lakes, and lay there with no particular indication of rising. President Finney walked out with his eye on these clouds. I give the sequel in his own words, as they fell from his lips, less than three months since.

"'In this walk I met Ralph, who turned sharply upon me. 'Mr. Finney, I should like to know what you mean in preaching that God is always wise and always good, when you see him pouring out that great rain upon the lake, where it can do no good, and leaving us to suffer so terribly for the want of that wasted water?'

"'His words cut me to the heart; I turned, and ran home to my closet, fell on my knees, and told the Lord what Ralph had been saying about Him; and besought Him, for the honor of His great name, to confound this caviler, and show forth the glory of His power and the greatness of His love. I pleaded with Him that He had encouraged His people to pray for rain, and that now the time seemed to have come for Him to show His power in this thing, and His faithfulness as a hearer of prayer.

"'Before I rose from my knees, there was a sound of a rushing, mighty wind. I looked out, and lo! the heavens were black; that cloud was rolling up, and soon the rain fell in torrents, two full hours'

"The writer, (Professor Cowles,) himself remembers how that cloud lay over the lake; how it drove him, also, to his closet; and that soon and signally the prayers of that hour came back to us in mighty rain."

Luther's Mighty Prayer and Prophecy.

At one time in the life of Luther, there was a critical moment in the affairs of the Reformation. Bitter persecution prevailed with extraordinary power, and threatened every one They were the dark days when faith could only cling. There were but few friends to the reformers, and these were of little strength. Their enemies were every where strong, proud, arrogant. But Luther relied on his God, and at this moment, with his favorite hymn in his heart, *"A strong fortress is our God,"* he went to the Lord in prayer, and prayed that omnipotence would come to the help of their weakness. Long he wrestled alone with God in his closet, till like Jacob he prevailed. Then he went into the room, where his family had assembled, with joyous heart and shining face, and raising both hands, and lifting his eyes heavenward, exclaimed, *"We have overcome, we have overcome."*

This was astonishing, as there was not the slightest of news which had yet been heard to give them hope of relief. But immediately after that, the welcome tidings came that *the Emperor, Charles V., had issued his Proclamation of "Religious Toleration in Germany."* In Luther's prayer was fulfilled the remarkable promise of Proverbs, 21: 1. *"The king's heart is in the hand of the Lord, as the rivers of water ; he turneth it whithersoever he will."*

John Knox and his Prophetical Prayer.

"John Knox was famous for his earnest prayers. Queen Mary said that she feared his prayers more than she did all the armies of Europe. One night, in the days of his bitterest persecution, while he and his friends were praying together, Knox spoke out, and declared *that deliverance has come.* He could not tell how. *Immediately the* news came that *Queen Mary was dead.*"

Melancthon's Life saved from Death in Answer to Luther's Prayer.

The most powerful tribute to the efficacy of prayer, was the answer to Luther's prayer which the Lord sent. A messenger was sent to Luther that Melancthon was dying. He found him presenting the usual premonitory symptoms of death. Melancthon roused, looked in the face of Luther, and said, "O Luther, is this you? Why don't you let me depart in peace." "*We can't spare you yet, Philip,*" was the reply, and turning around, he threw himself upon his knees, and wrestled with God for his recovery for upwards of an hour. He went from his knees to the bed, and took his friend by the hand, again he said, "Dear Luther, why don't you let me depart in peace?" "No, no, Philip; we can not spare you yet," was the reply. He then ordered some soup, and when pressed to take it, Melancthon declined, again saying, "Dear Luther, why will you not let me go home and be at rest." "We can not spare you yet, Philip," was the reply. He then added, "Philip, take this soup, or I will excommunicate you." He took the soup, regained his wonted health, and labored for years afterwards in the cause of the Reformation; and when Luther returned home he said to his wife with joy, "God gave me my brother Melancthon back in direct answer to prayer"

In this incident is given this extraordinary statement that while death has really seized a man, who too wished to die, and did not want to live longer on the earth, yet his life was given back to him again in answer to the prayer of faith of another.

The Wonderful Power of Faith and Trust in the Lord to deliver wholly from Bad Habits.

A victim of licentiousness and sensuousness, who often, amid his sinful pleasures, had the memory of Christian parents before him, felt his was indeed a life of shame. But the downward steps had destroyed his will, his self-control, his manliness, his virtue. He had no power to resist, all was wickedness, irresolution, constant yielding. In vain he hung back, and tried to save himself from the cursed appetite, at last he realized that in a few weeks' time he must go to the grave; strength could not stand such a waste of life. "What a miserable life. What wicked ways, what wicked thoughts; how I wish I was pure; O, that I might get free; I do not love this sin any more, I don't want it, but I can't stop it. O, I wish I could be a Christian, and wholly free."

Such were his constant thoughts. In mercy, the Lord who had been reading his thoughts, sent him a great reverse in business, and in agony of heart, he knew not where to turn but to the Lord, and pray for relief. His prayer, too, asked to be emancipated from his wickedness, and his strength and health restored. *"Lord, save me and I will* be thine forever. I am lost unless thou wilt come and save."

By gradual degrees, in the absorption of his thoughts over other distresses, his mind was diverted from his usual ways and thoughts of sinful living; gradually the habits of lust grew less and less strong, and finally ceased altogether. But the body still remained under excessive weakness But faith that the Lord who had saved others, could save him too, led him to pray, not only for the destruction of the habit, but entire recovery from its evil effects. His perseverance was persistent, and met with a *triumphant reward*. After a long time, he felt himself wholly healed. New strength, new life, came back to him. "It seems as if my life had been put back again ten years, and I was young again." "I never have any more wicked thoughts or imaginations, while I was once full of them.　Since I learned to seek the Lord and love his Bible, I have never had such peace, or purity.　I love the name and tender mercies of my God."　If in a few months, prayer saved that man's life, and so wholly changed it from a foul blot to a thing of purity, what can it not do again.　*No sin can ever be conquered until in humility either saint or sinner* gets down upon his knees, and implores the love and power of the Lord in *never ceasing prayer*, to wholly emancipate him from the control of the evil habit.　*The Lord will surely hear it.*　He can as truly deliver the body from the most persistent and enchaining habit, as he can wholly convert the mind and heart.　The result is not always instantaneous; more often gradual, but *always sure* if the sufferer *always prays.*

It is simple enough for the sinning one to believe that the *Lord can*, and seeking the Bible *for the Lord's own promis? that he will ; to cling to it and never surrender*

The sin may be repeated when you can not resist it, ar? do not desire for it, but take all pains to avoid; still pray though you often fail; still try, still trust the Lord to loose your chains and remove your desire, and deliverance is sure to come at last.

Recovery from Paralysis.

"Between two and three years ago, the writer was struck down by paralysis, disabling entirely the limbs of the left side.　In this apparently helpless state, I employed a man to take care of me, and felt that unless God should interpose, I must be a continuous burden on my friends.　My kind physician gave me no hope of *entire recovery.*

"In this state I made my prayer to God continually, that he would so far restore my strength as to enable me to take care of myself

"This prayer he was pleased to answer, for in eight weeks

I dismissed my attendant, finding myself able to take care of myself. I now walk more than half a mile each day, and attend to all the associations of home life. I record with thankfulness this restoration of my disabled frame in answer to prayer."

The Stolen Bonds Returned.

The *New York Observer* relates a remarkable instance of the return of stolen property, which in its extraordinary way can be accounted for only by the control of a Supreme Will, and all in answer to prayer

"On February 16, 1877, United States and railroad bonds and mortgages to the amount of $160,000, belonging to Edgar H. Richards, were stolen from the banking house of James G. King's Sons, of this city. No clue whatever to the robbers could be obtained. Several parties were arrested on suspicion, but nothing could be proved, and the mystery remained unsolved.

"Mr. Richards, being a member of one of our most prominent churches, made it a subject of constant prayer, that the Lord would wholly prevent the thieves from any use of the property and cause it to be returned to him. When asked if he was ever incredulous, he said, ' No, I have never lost my faith in recovering this property. I believe in prayer, and I have made it from the first a subject of prayer, and it will be answered.'

" Meanwhile some curious influences must have been at work among the thieves, for they acted in an extraordinary manner as follows :

" One day last week a stranger, well dressed, modest looking, gentlemanly, walked into the office of Elliott F. Shepard, Esq., one of Messrs. King's counsel, and tendered his services for the recovery of the property, asserting he knew nothing about the robbery, nor the thieves, but that he could get the treasure He was told that a reward would be paid for the

capture of the thieves, but he earnestly protested that it was
entirely out of his power to obtain any clue to the person or
whereabouts of the thief; and no inquiries ever disclosed that
this was not a perfectly true statement.   Indeed, it proved
that he had been selected as an agent to do this work, and
that there were at least five or six connecting intermediaries
between him and the robbers, each exercising that virtue
which is called honor among thieves, and which on this occasion proved a wall of adamant to every attempt to pierce it or
break it down.

"True to his word the stranger caused the delivery at Mr.
Shepard's office, at the appointed hour to a second, of an ordinary pasteboard bandbox, wrapped in newspaper, by the
hands of a little boy.   He had come in a pelting rain-storm,
and part of the newspaper had become torn, and disclosed the
blue, unsuspected hat box.   The boy knew nothing about it,
except that a gentleman had given him a dime in the street
to bring the box.

"Mr. Richards being present, opened the bandbox, examined and checked off the contents with one of Messrs. King's
head clerks, and found every single item of his missing secu-
rities, stocks, bonds, mortgages, accounts, bank books, wills,
everything.   A most remarkable thing!   The parties could
hardly believe their eyes."

Mr. Moody's Answers to Prayers.

Mr. D. L. Moody, the Evangelist, when a boy, was possessed of an unusual amount of muscular strength and animal spirits, and a strong will that knew little of impossibility
or submission.   When only six years old, being wistful to do
something to help his mother, he was set to drive the cows
of a neighboring farmer to and from their mountain pasture.
On one occasion, a heavy fence fell upon him from which he
could not extricate himself.   After trying his utmost and
crying as loud as he could for help, but in vain, the thought

struck him that God would help him if he asked him. In his own simple language he prayed to his mother's God for help, and made another effort, and succeeded in getting free.

This, his first answer to prayer, made a vivid impression on his heart, which gave a decided turn to his opening life.

No Flour in the House—In the days of Famine, his Soul shall be Satisfied.

Mr. Moody's domestic life has always been a happy one, but in the early days of his marriage, he was very poor, and his faith was often put to the severest tests.

One day, on leaving home in his missionary work and labors of love, he remarked to his wife, "I have no money, and the house is without supplies. It looks dark; is it possible that the Lord has had enough of me in this mission work, and is going to send me back again to sell boots and shoes." But he prayed In a day or two, a stranger sent him two checks of $50 each—one for himself, and one for his school.

On another occasion his wife informed him that they had no flour for the day's use, and asked him to order some on his way. Having no money in his possession, he was perplexed how to proceed to raise the required amount; but meeting a person in whose spiritual welfare he was concerned, he forgot all about such sublunary considerations as money and flour, and went heart and soul into the Lord's work before him.

On his return home at night, he felt somewhat nervous about his reception on account of his not having sent the flour, but to his joyful surprise, he found that on his arrival the table was spread with a bountiful repast.

It seems that a friend of his was powerfully impressed that morning, and without seeing the family or knowing anything about their need, had packed up a barrel of flour and sent it.

Others of his friends, who were interested in his work, and felt confidence in his work, *unknown to him*, selected a new house, and furnished it throughout with every facility for convenience and comfort, and when all was completed invited him and his family to it, and made him a present of the loan of his house, and all its contents.

Thus the *Great Helper* remembered him and answered his daily prayer, "Give us this day our daily bread."

Persevering Prayer.

At one of the prayer-meetings at the Brooklyn tabernacle, Mr. Moody closed by narrating an instance of persevering prayer by a Christian wife for an infidel husband. She resolved to pray for him at noon for eighteen months, and at the expiration of that time, her knocking not having been responded to, she exclaimed, "*Lord, I will pray for him every day, and at all hours, as long as life lasts.*"

That day the Lord heard her knock, and gave her the desire of her heart, in the conversion of her husband. When the Lord saw her faith would not give up, he sent the answer immediately.

Noah's Prayer.—He Did not get Discouraged.

The life of faith and the necessity of uncompromising hold on the promises, expecting their fulfillment, is admirably explained in the illustration of Noah's prayer. One day Mr. Moody was much discouraged, and it was as dark a Sabbath as ever he had, and a friend suggested to him to study the life of Noah.

"I got out my Bible, and the thought came over me, 'Here is a man who labored and talked a hundred years, and didn't succeed; didn't get a convert notwithstanding all his efforts, all his prayers, but he didn't get discouraged'

"But he took God at his word; he worked right on; he prayed right on; and he waited God's time. And, my friends, from that time, I have never been discouraged. Whenever I think of him, it lifts me up out of the darkness into the light. Don't get discouraged."

The lesson of Noah's life is briefly this: He never converted a soul outside of his own family. That was the work God gave him to do, and he prayed and waited and worked, and never gave up, and he was saved and all his family with him.

So every Christian must recognize that his field is not far off, but right around him, in his house, among his friends, working, praying, waiting, but never getting discouraged. The Lord will never fail those who *"abide in Him."*

Samuel Hick's Prayer for Rain.

Samuel Hick was one of the men of *"mighty faith"* in the Lord, and as a preacher among the Methodists of England. He was of great eminence for his happy spirit, remarkable trust, powerful and practical preaching, and unbounded liberality. Among the many incidents connected with his life of faith, we quote a few to illustrate with what simplicity he expected always an answer to his prayer, and was not satisfied until he got it:

In the course of a Summer of excessive drought a few years back, when the grain suffered greatly, and many of the cattle, especially in Lincolnshire, died. Samuel Hick was much affected. He visited Knaresborough, at which place he preached on the Lord's day.

Remaining in the town and neighborhood over the Sabbath, he appeared extremely restless in the house in which he resided, during the whole of Monday. He spoke but little—was full of thought, now praying, now walking about the room, next sitting in a crouching posture—then suddenly starting up and going to the door, turning his eyes toward heaven, as if looking for some celestial phenomenon, when he would return again, groan in spirit, and resume his seat. The family, being impressed with his movements, asked him whether there was anything the matter with him or whether he expected any person, as the occasion of his going to the door so frequently.

"Bless you Bairns," was his reply, "do you not recollect that I was praying for rain last night in the pulpit, and what will the infidel at Knaresborough think if it do not come; if my Lord should fail me, and not stand by me." But it must have time; it can not be here yet; it has to come from the sea. Neither can it be seen at first. The prophet only saw a bit of cloud like a man's hand. By and by it spread along the sky. I am looking for an answer to my prayer, but it must have time.

He continued in the same unsettled state, occasionally going out, and looking with intensity on the pure azure over his head; for *a more unclouded sky was rarely ever seen.* Contrary to all external signs of rain, and contrary to the expectations of all, except himself, the sky became overcast toward evening, and the clouds dropped the fullness of a shower upon the earth. His very soul seemed to drink in the falling drops. The family grouped around him, like children around their father, while he gave out his favorite hymn, *"I'll praise my Maker while I've breath;"* "and after singing it with a countenance all a-glow, through the sunshine of heaven upon his soul, he knelt down and prayed. All were overpowered; it was a season of refreshing from the presence of the Lord.

His biographer says of him: "Samuel had no weather-glass upon which to look except the Bible, in which he was taught to believe, and expect *that* for which he prayed; nothing on which he could depend but God, and *his faith* was set in God for *rain.*"

Praying for the Wind to Come.

A remarkable incident, showing how God makes the winds to obey him in obedience to the prayer of his righteous ones, and the expectations of their faith, occurred also in Samuel Hick's life, which is really an astonishing proof of God's supernatural power.

A church gathering was to take place at Micklefield, and Samuel had promised two loads of corn for their use. " The day fixed drew near, but there was no flour in the house, and the wind-mills, in consequence of a long calm, stretched out their arms in vain to catch the rising breezes. In the midst of this death-like quiet, Samuel carried his corn to the mill nearest his own residence, and requested the miller to unfurl his sails. The miller objected, stating that there was "no wind." Samuel, on the other hand, continued to urge his request, saying, "*I will go and pray while you spread the cloth.*" More with a view of gratifying the applicant than of any faith he had, the man stretched his canvas. *No sooner had he done this than, to his utter astonishment, a fine breeze sprung up, the fans whirled around, the corn was converted into meal, and Samuel returned with his burden rejoicing,* and had everything in readiness for the festival.

In the mean time, a neighbor who had seen the fan in vigorous motion, took also some corn to be ground; but the wind had dropped, and the miller remarked to him, " You must send for Sammy Hick to pray for the wind to blow again."

Snails in the Ark.

To many who with despondency protest that they have not faith enough, get along so slow, are too weak, &c., the following sharp retort of Hick will prove a bright lining to their dark cloud of failing, and lead them to plod on in prayer.

"To a gentleman laboring under great nervous depression,

whom he had visited, and who was moving along the streets as though he was apprehensive that every step would shake his system in pieces, he was rendered singularly useful. They met, and Samuel, having a deeper interest in the soul than the body, asked: 'Well, how are you getting on your way to Heaven.' "

The poor invalid, in a dejected, half desponding tone, replied, "But slowly I fear," intimating that he was creeping along only at a poor pace.

"Why bless you Bairn," returned Samuel, "*there were snails in the ark.*"

The reply was so earnest, so unexpected, and met the dispirited man so immediately on his own ground, that the temptation broke away, and he was out of his depression.

It was a resurrection to his feelings, inferring that if the snail reached the ark and was saved, he too, "faint yet pursuing," might gain admission into heaven.

"He Gave All the Money He Had.

At one time he attended a missionary meeting near Harrowgate. "We had a blessed meeting," said Samuel, "I was very happy and gave all the money I had in my pocket." After the meeting was concluded, he mounted his horse to return home. No one had offered to pay his expenses—he had not a farthing in his pocket. Advanced in life—a slow rider, and not a very sprightly horse—in the night—alone—twenty miles from home. Think of the lonesomeness, the time for the tempter to come and lead him to distrust in his Lord. But he struggled; the trial was short and the victory complete, for, said he, "Devil, I never stuck fast yet."

Just as he entered Harewood, a gentleman took his horse by the bridle, asked him where he had been, talked with him long, and to whom Samuel's talk was a wonderful consolation. Said Sammy:

"I have not wanted for any good thing, and could always .

pray with Job, 'The Lord gave and the Lord taketh away, blessed be the name of the Lord.'"

The gentleman asked, "Can you read?"

"Yes," returned Samuel.

"Then," replied the gentleman, holding a piece of paper in his hand, which was rendered visible by the glimmering light of the stars,

"There is a five pound note for you. You love God and his cause, and I believe you will never want."

And Sammy said, "I cried for joy. This was a fair salvation from the Lord. When I got home, I told my wife. She burst into tears, and we praised the Lord together,'' and he added· "You see, we never give to the Lord but He gives in return."

"The Lord Will Provide."

A poor but pious widow in Boston, in her eighty-seventh year, said to a friend, "When I was left a widow with three little children, I was brought into such extremity that they were crying for bread, and I had nothing for them to eat. As I arose on a Sabbath morning, I knew not what to do but to ask my heavenly Father to feed my little ones, and commit myself and them to his care.

"I then went out to the well to get a pail of water, and saw on the ground a six cent piece, which I took up; and learning that it did not belong to any of those who lived in the same house with me, I thought I might take it to feed my famishing children. Though it was a Sabbath morning, I felt that it would be right to go to a baker who lived in the neighborhood, tell him our circumstances, and buy bread with the money Providence had thus cast in my way. The baker not only did this, but the Lord opened his heart to add a bountiful supply; and from that hour to the present, which is nearly fifty years, I have never doubted that *God would take care of his children.*"

Abraham Lincoln's Faith in Prayer.

When President Lincoln left his home in Springfield, Ill., February 11, 1861, on his way to Washington, he made the following farewell address to his friends and neighbors: "My friends, no one not in my position can appreciate the sadness I feel at this parting. To this people I owe all I am. Here I have lived more than a quarter of a century; here my children were born, and here one of them lies buried. I know not how soon I shall see you again. A duty devolves upon me which is perhaps greater than that which has devolved upon any other man since the days of Washington. He would never have succeeded except for the aid of Divine Providence, upon which he at all times relied. I feel that I cannot succeed without the same Divine aid which sustained him, and on the same Almighty Being I place my reliance for support; and I hope you, my friends, will all pray that I may receive that Divine assistance, without which I cannot succeed, but with which success is certain Again, I bid you all an affectionate farewell." That simple but earnest request sent an electric thrill through every Christian heart, and without doubt, in response to it, more prayer was offered for him throughout his administration, than for any one who ever before occupied the Presidential chair.

At a Sabbath-school convention in Massachusetts, a speaker stated that a friend of his, during an interview with Mr. Lincoln, asked him if he loved Jesus. The President buried his face in his handkerchief and wept. He then said, "When I left home to take this chair of state, I requested my countrymen to pray for me. I was not then a Christian. When my son died—the severest trial of my life—I was not a Christian. But when I went to Gettysburg, and looked upon the graves of our dead heroes who had fallen in defence of their country, I then and there consecrated myself to Christ. *I do love Jesus.*" Rev. Mr. Adams, of Philadelphia, stated in his Thanksgiving sermon that, having an appointment to meet the President at 5 o'clock in the morning, he went a quarter of an hour before the time. While waiting for the hour, he heard a voice in the next room as if in grave conversation, and asked the servant, " Who is talking in the next room ? " " It is the President, sir." " Is anybody with him ? " " No, sir ; he is reading the Bible." " Is that his habit so early in the morning ? " " Yes, sir. He spends every morning, from 4 o'clock to 5, in reading the Scriptures and praying."

It was the Lord who Guided the mind of Mr. Lincoln in his extraordinary act of the Emancipation of the Slaves of America. The Lord had prepared it, and chose him as the means whereby to accomplish it.

Were not his Prayers and efforts specially blessed by the Lord in wisdom, for the guidance of our Nation?

Extraordinary Care of the Lord in Answer to Prayer.

" The scenes of the riots in New York, at the time of our civil war, are of national celebrity ; but few, however, know that one of the most atrocious acts of cruelty attempted to be perpetrated by the malefactors, and which utterly failed of its purpose, *came solely in answer to prayer.* On the first day of the mob, however, several thousand men, *women and children*, armed with clubs and brickbats, suddenly appeared at the door of the Colored Orphan Asylum, and effected an entrance by breaking down the front door with an axe. The building was soon fired in ten or fifteen places, and the work of destruction was accomplished in twenty minutes

" There were at the time two hundred and twenty-three children in the building with their attendants and teachers. The matron having assembled all the children after the first alarm, one of the teachers thus addressed them : 'Children, do you believe that Almighty God can deliver you from a mob ?' The reply was promptly made in the affirmative. 'Then,' said she, 'I wish you now to pray silently to God to protect

you from this mob. I believe that he is able and will do it
Pray earnestly to him, and when I give the signal, go in
order, without noise, to the dining-room' At this every head
was instantly bowed in prayer, such prayer as is not frequently offered, the silent, earnest supplication of terrified
and persecuted little children. When, at the sound of the
bell, their heads were raised, the teacher said the tears were
streaming, but not a sound, not even a sob, was to be heard.
They then quietly went down stairs and through the halls, and
she remarked that 'to her dying day she should never forget
the scene;' the few moments of eloquent silence, the streaming noiseless tears, the funereal march through the halls, the
yells and the horrible sounds which were nearer and nearer
approaching. *Not one of these helpless innocents was injured in the least*; but in spite of the threats and the blood-
thirstiness of the rioters, through whom they were obliged to
pass, all were removed unmolested to a place of safety."

A Remarkable Decision by a Jury.

"In one of our northern cities, a trial at law took place between a Christian and an infidel. The latter had sued the
former for a heavy sum, falsely alleging his promise to pay it
for some stocks which he claimed to have sold him. The
Christian admitted AN OFFER of the stock, but protested that
so far from promising the sum demanded, he had steadily refused to make any trade whatever with the plaintiff. Each of
the parties to the suit had a friend who fully corroborated their
assertions. Thus the case went before the jury for decision.

"The charge of the judge was stern and significant. 'It
was a grave and most painful task which devolved upon him
to instruct the jurors that one of the parties before them must
be guilty of deliberate and willful perjury. Their statements
were wholly irreconcilable with each other; nay more, were
diametrically opposite; and that either were innocently mistaken in their assertions was impossible.

" ' Your verdict, gentlemen,' he said in conclusion, ' must decide upon which side this awful and heaven-daring iniquity belongs. The God of truth help you to find the truth, that the innocent suffer not.'

" It was late in the day when the judge's charge was given, and the finding of the jury was to be rendered in the morning. The plaintiff went carelessly from the court arm in arm with the wicked associate whom he had bribed to swear falsely on his behalf. The defendant and his friend walked away together in painful silence. When the Christian reached his home, he told his family of the judge's solemn charge and of the grave responsibility which rested upon the jurors. ' They are to decide which of us has perjured ourselves on this trial,' he said; ' and how terrible a thing for me if they should be mistaken in their judgment. There is so little of any thing tangible for their decision to rest upon, that it seems to me as if a breath might blow it either way. They cannot see our hearts, and I feel as if only God could enable them to discern the truth. Let us spend the evening in prayer that he may give them a clear vision.' "

The twelve jurymen ate their supper in perplexed silence, and were shut in their room for deliberation and consultation. "I never sat in such a case before," said the foreman. "The plaintiff and defendant have sworn point-blank against each other; and how we are to tell which speaks the truth, I can not see. I should not like to make a mistake in the matter; it would be a sad affair to convict an innocent man of perjury " Again there was silence among them, as if each were weighing the case in his own mind. "*For myself* I feel as if the truth must be with the defendant; I am constrained to think that he is an honest man. What say you, gentlemen ? " *Every hand was raised in affirmation of this opinion.* They were fully persuaded of its truth, and *gave a unanimous verdict accordingly.*

Thus the Christian man was rightfully acquitted, and gave thanks to God, with a new and stronger confidence in the power of prayer. "Call upon me in the day of trouble; I will deliver thee, and thou shalt glorify me," saith the Lord.

That Wonderful $25. Another Evidence of the Ever-Present Spirit of God.

The following incident is marvelous, as at the time of its occurrence neither party had ever been known to each other:

In *New Haven, Conn.*, lives a little invalid widow, almost helpless, with no one upon whom to rely for support, and only indebted to friendly acquaintances for a temporary home. With no money, no acquaintances, she had nowhere else to turn to but to the Father of all good. She had prayed often, and often had answers, but this time, though needing money, still she received none. The answer was long delayed; she was almost discouraged. "*Was God at last to fail and forget her? No, it could not be. Let God be true even if I perish, I shall still cling to Him. I can not give Him up.*"

Just at that time a business man in New York, who had been absent on a long journey for the Summer and had just returned, happened to pick up a note among many hundred lying on his desk, and noticed that the writer asked for some trifling favor, saying she was poor, had no means.

Her circumstances were unknown; he knew nothing but her name. He was eager to *minister to the little ones of the Lord,* and felt deeply impressed in prayer that morning, in asking a blessing on his day's labors, that he might be able to help the need of some of " his children " who might then be in want. In his business hours the thought came over him with the depth of emotion, "WHAT CAN I DO? LORD, THY SERVANT IS READY." Just at that moment he picked up this note of the little invalid, who asked the trivial favor, saying it would be such a comfort. (*No money whatever was asked for in this note.*)

Suddenly the thought came to him, "*Perhaps this is my very opportunity. This may be the Lord's little one in need.*" But there was nothing in the letter to indicate she was a Christian. She solicited no money or pecuniary help.

Immediately there came to his mind, amid floods of tears, "*Inasmuch as ye have done it unto the least of these, my children, ye have done it unto me.*" Instantly he understood it as a message from the Lord, and the intimation of the Holy Spirit. He immediately sat down and wrote a check for $25, and enclosed it to her, saying, "*I know not your need ; you have not asked me for help, but I send you something which may be useful. I trust you are a Christian. I shall be happy to learn if it has done good, and made you happy. Give me no thanks. The Lord's blessing is enough for me.*"

The letter was sent and forgotten, but a strange presentiment came over the mind of the writer. "*I am afraid I did not direct that letter right.*" He sent a second postal card, asking if a letter had been received at her home ; if not, to go to her post office and inquire.

Now notice the wonderful singularity of incident. Here is a man sending money, *never asked for, to an unknown person, about whom he knew nothing , then misdirecting his letter,* and then remembering and *sending another message to go and find where the first had gone to. But notice the marvelous result.* The little invalid received the postal card, but not the letter. She sent to the post office, and sure enough there was the first letter with its misdirection. She was *just in time* to save it from being sent to *another woman of the same name living in another part of the same city.*

She opened her letter, and with tears of thankfulness perused this wonderful reply, a marvelous witness to the power of an overruling Spirit, who had directed everything.

"My heart is full, that God should so answer my simple prayer. I first asked him for $10, then $15, *and then for* $25. I asked him for $25 several times, and was astonished at my boldness, but the amount was so fixed in my mind, I

22

could not ask for anything else, and then I humbly trusted it
to Him, and from that time I thought, I will not name any
sum ; let it be as He knows my need.   And how He has honored my simple faith and trust in these dark days.   *Your letter contained exactly the $25 I prayed for.*   I have not had
$1.50 to spend this Summer.   I have suffered for everything.
But through it all I have felt such perfect faith in the Lord,
that his hand was leading me, even when I could not see a
step before me ; and that He should move your heart to help
me seems so wonderful, so good.   I am so glad I can thank
you now, but ah, so much *"over there,"* where words will express so much more in the beautiful atmosphere of heaven.
Your letter and kind gift was mailed *the very same day* that
I was praying in great distress and trial   I knew not but
that I should be without even a home.   My verse was Psalms
50 : 15.   O, how I had to pray that day   So day by day I
was comforted, and now to-day the answer has come."

Here, then, is a portion of the story of a sweet life who
trusted God, not as a God of the past, nor far off, but ever
living, ever present, ever faithful, and believed Him *able, willing,* and that He *would help* her in her daily life.   She tried
her Lord, to prove if his promises were indeed true, and she
clung to them to the very last.   No one knew her need.
No one knew what she was praying for.   The stranger did
not know anything of her.   She had asked money of no one
but the Lord.   Hesitant ever, she dared not name any
amount of the Lord, but that ever present Spirit of God
guided her heart, made her *fix the amount,* and then touched
the heart of the stranger and fixed the amount also in his
mind, and then, by his own guidance saved the letter from
being lost, and behold ! when opened the *prayer of the one
and the gift of the other was the same.*

What a comfort, what a privilege, then, it is for the true-
hearted Christian thus to feel, *" There is one who careth for
us."*

Why He Failed.

A prominent business man failed in the Spring of 1877. He had been for years a prominent and consistent member of a Christian church. He had even supported a church once almost entirely. Nothing was known against his character, *but he failed; he failed in business.* No one knew the reason why, but there it was, *failure.*

At last, in moments of bitter repentance before God, he unbosomed himself to his pastor, and said, "*Long ago I promised to give the Lord one-tenth of all the profits I gained from my business, and while I did so, I was immensely prosperous and successful; never did any one have any such splendid success,—but I forgot my promise, stopped giving, thought that I did not need to spend so much, and I began to invest my means in real estate. When I stopped giving I stopped getting. Now all is gone. I lost my all because I did not keep my promise to the Lord.*"

This incident is a practical one, telling how utter is the impossibility of true success, without the aid of the Lord, and how absolutely necessary it is to our own peace and comfort of mind to religiously observe one's promises made to God. The Bible only too truly tells of the end of those who forget Him.

"*But Jeshurun waxed fat, then he forsook God which made him; and when the Lord saw it, he abhorred them, and said, 'I will hide my face from them.'*"

"*Ye can not prosper; because ye have forsaken the Lord, He hath also forsaken you.*" "*There shall be desolation; because thou hast forgotten the God of thy salvation, and hast not been mindful of the rock of thy strength.*"

HOW THE LORD

Controls the Winds and the Waves.

―・・―

John Easter's Prayer.

In his "Memorials of Methodism in Virginia," Dr. W. W. Bennet relates the following incidents in the life of John Easter, one of the pioneer ministers who labored there nearly one hundred years ago: He is represented as being the most powerful exhortatory preacher of his day. His faith was transcendent, his appeals irresistible, his prayers like talking with God face to face. Perhaps no man has ever been more signally honored of God as an instrument in the conversion of souls. On one of his circuits eighteen hundred members were added to the church in a single year.

Many thrilling scenes under his preaching yet linger among the people in those counties where he principally labored. A most extraordinary display of his faith was witnessed in Brunswick. At Merritt's meeting-house a quarterly meeting was in progress, and so vast was the concourse of people from many miles around, that the services were conducted in a beautiful grove near the church. In the midst of the exercises, a heavy cloud arose, and swept rapidly towards the place of worship. From the skirts of the grove the rain could be seen coming on across the fields. The people were in consternation; no house could hold one-third of the multitude, and they were about to scatter in all directions. Easter rose in the midst of the confusion—"Brethren," cried he at the top of his voice, " be still while I call upon God to stay the clouds, till His word can be preached to perishing sinners." Arrested by his voice and manner, they stood between hope and fear. He kneeled down and offered a fervent prayer that God would then stay the rain, that the preaching of His word might go on, and afterwards send refreshing showers. *While he was praying, the angry cloud, as it swiftly rolled up to them, was seen to part asunder in the midst, pass on either side of them, and close again beyond, leaving a space several hundred yards in circumference perfectly dry. The next morning a copious rain fell again, and the fields that had been left dry were well watered*"

The Hushed Tempest.

The following circumstance is communicated to *The Christian* by a minister of the editor's acquaintance, as a memorial of God's care for the poor and needy who trust in him:

It was about the year 1853, and near the middle of a Canadian Winter we had a succession of snowfalls, followed by high winds and severe cold. I was getting ready to haul my Winter's stock of wood, for which I had to go two miles over a road running north and south, entirely unprotected from the keen cold west winds that prevail the most of the time in that part of Canada during the Winter months.

The procuring of my Winter's supply of wood was no small task for me, for I had very little to do with, and was unable to endure much fatigue, or bear the severe cold. I had, however, succeeded in securing the services of an excellent hand to chop, and help me load, and had also engaged a horse of one neighbor, and a horse and sled of another, and was ready on Monday morning to commence my job. Monday morning the roads were fair, the day promised well, and my man was off at daybreak to the woods to have a load ready for me. There had been quite a fall of snow during the night; not enough to do any harm if it only lay still, but should the wind rise, as it had after every snow-fall before, it would make it dreadful for me. Soon as possible I harnessed my team, and started. I had not gone a quarter of a mile before it became painfully evident that a repetition of our previous "blows" was impending. The sky was dark and stormy, the wind rose rapidly, and in every direction clouds of the newly fallen snow were beginning to ride on the "wings of the wind," pouring over the fences, and filling the road full! My heart sank within me. What could I do? At this rate, by next morning the roads would be impassable, and it was so cold! Besides, if I failed to go on now, it would be very difficult to get my borrowed team together again, and impossible to get my man again; and we could as well live without bread as without wood in a Canadian Winter.

Every moment the wind increased. In deep distress, I looked upon the threatening elements, exclaiming over and over, "What shall I do?" I felt then that there was but one thing that I could do, and that was just what poor sinking Peter did; and with feelings I imagine something like his, I looked up to God, and cried out, "O, my God, this is more than I am able to bear. Lord, help me! The elements are subject to thee; thou holdest the winds in thy fist. If thou wilt speak the word, there will be a great calm. O, for Jesus' sake, and for the sake of my little helpless family, let this snow lie still and give me an opportunity of accomplishing this necessary labor comfortably!" I do not think it was above fifteen minutes after I began to call upon the Lord before there was a visible change The wind began to subside, the sky grew calm, and in less than half an hour all was still, and a more pleasant time for wood-hauling than I had that day, I never saw nor desire to see. Many others beside me enjoyed the benefit of that "sudden change" of weather, but to them it was only a "nice spell of weather," a "lucky thing;" while to me it was full of sweet and encouraging tokens of the "loving-kindness of the Lord." And now, after so many years, I feel impelled to give this imperfect narrative, to encourage others in the day of trouble to call upon the Lord; and also, as a tribute of gratitude to Him who has " never said to the house of Jacob, seek ye my face in vain."

Praying in Fair Weather.

The ways in which God saves those whom he wishes to deliver from death, are sometimes too wonderful for our understanding. A certain ship was overtaken in a severe and prolonged storm at sea. She had a noble Christian man for a captain, and as good a sailor as ever trod the quarter-deck, and he had under him a good and obedient crew. But they could not save the ship; she was too badly strained, her leaks were too great for the pumps, she must go to the bottom. The captain committed them all to the care of the God in whom he put his trust, and made ready to take to their boats. Just then a sail was descried, and, by signals of distress, drawn to their relief. All on board were taken off safely and put on the ship, soon after which they saw their own ship go down.

Now comes the peculiar part. The ship was soon overtaken in a dreadful storm, was cast on her beam ends, and everything seemed to be lost. The passengers were praying, and many of the old seamen were calling on God to save them from the great deep. The captain of the ship had done his best, but could not right the vessel, and all was given up to go down. The captain, whose ship was lost, then asked if he might take his crew and try to right the vessel.

"Take them, and do what you can," was the reply. He called to his men and told them they must save that ship; he inspired them with confidence, for they knew he was a true man of God. They executed his orders with alacrity and care. They cut away the masts, and cleared away the rigging, and brought all the force they could to right the vessel. God prospered the effort—the ship righted; they got the pumps at work, rigged a sail, and were finally all saved. It seemed as if it was necessary to put the captain of the first ship and his crew on the second ship, that they might save it and those on board when the terrible storm came.

Now it was particularly noticed in connection with this deliverance, that the captain of the lost vessel did not make any ado in prayer, or in calling on God, while the storm was raging; and knowing that he was a Christian man, they asked him the reason of this. He answered them, *that he did his praying in fair weather;* " *and then,*" said he, "*when the storm comes, I work.*" He did not distrust God then, any more than in fair weather; but he knew that God requires man to do all he can to save himself, and praying might lose him his ship, when his own efforts must save it.

The Rescue from the Ville du Havre, and the Loch Earn.

A remarkable illustration of God's mysterious way is found in connection with the rescue of some of the passengers of the ill-fated French steam-ship, Ville du Havre, which was sunk by a collision with the Loch Earn, November 22, 1873, on her voyage from New York to France. After the sinking of the Ville du Havre, with some two hundred of her passengers, the rest were taken up by the Loch Earn, from which most of them were afterwards transferred to the Trimountain. Others remained on board the Loch Earn, where in consequence of its disabled condition they seemed again in imminent danger of being lost.

On the 11th of December, while Mr. D. L. Moody was conducting a noonday prayer-meeting in the city of Edinburgh, Rev. Dr. Andrew Thompson read a letter from a Christian lady, the mother of one of these imperiled passengers, which contained the following account:

"After the Trimountain left them, and they had examined their ship, many a heart failed, and they feared they would never see land again. They could not navigate the vessel, and were left to the mercy of the winds and waves, or rather to the care of Him who ruleth wind and waves. Vain was the help of man. The wind drove them out of the course of ships, northward. You are aware that two ministers were left on board the Loch Earn. One, Mr Cook, a truly godly man, did all he could to encourage their hearts. Every day, at noon, he gathered them together, and earnestly, by prayer, strove to lead them to the Savior; and this he continued to do till they reached England. The day before they were rescued they knew that very shortly the ship must go down. The wind had changed, bringing them nearer the track of ships, but they had little hope of being saved. Mr. Cook told them of his own hope, that death to him would be eternal life, and he urgently entreated them to put their trust in 'Him who was mighty to save.' At the same time he told them he had no doubt they would be rescued, that even then a vessel was speeding to save them, that God had answered their prayers, that next day as morning dawned they would see her. That night was one of great anxiety.

"As morning dawned every eye was strained to see the promised ship. There truly she was, and the British Queen bore down upon them. You may think that with thankful hearts they left the Loch Earn. One thing is remarkable— *the officer in charge on board the British Queen had a most unaccountable feeling that there was something for him to do,* and *three times during the night he changed the course of the vessel, bearing northward.* He told the watch to keep a sharp lookout for a ship, and immediately on sighting the Loch Earn bore down upon her. At first he thought she had been abandoned, as she lay helpless in the trough of the sea, but soon they saw her signal of distress. It seems to me a remarkable instance of faith on the one side and a guiding Providence on the other. After they were taken on board the pilot-boat that brought them into Plymouth, at noon, when they for the last time joined together in prayer, Mr.

Cook read to them the account of Paul's shipwreck, showing the similarity of their experience. '*What made that captain change his course against his will?*' but the ever present *Spirit of God.*"

The Storm Made Calm.

At a Sunday morning meeting at Repository Hall, January 25, 1874, a Christian brother, in illustration of the power and faithfulness of God, and his willingness to hear and answer prayer, related these facts in his own experience. An account of them was subsequently published in the *Christian*:

"In 1839 I was a sailor on board the brig Pandora, Captain G——, bound from Savannah to Boston, with a cargo of cotton. When off the coast of Virginia, some twenty-five miles distant from Chesapeake Bay, we encountered a heavy gale. Saturday evening, December 21st, the wind blew gently from the south. On sounding, we found ourselves in thirty fathoms of water. At midnight the wind veered to the eastward, gradually increasing until four o'clock Sunday morning, by which time the brig was under close-reefed topsails and foresail. The wind still increasing, every stitch of canvas was taken in, and now the vessel lay helpless and unmanageable in the trough of the sea, not minding her helm at all, while the wind blew a perfect hurricane. The vessel being very light, loaded with cotton, made much leeway, and though we had worn ship four times during the preceding night, hoping, if possible, to weather some shoals which the captain judged were near, and to make Chesapeake Bay, where we might have a clear beach before us in case the vessel should strand, yet at eight o'clock Sunday morning we were in but seventeen fathoms of water.

"The gale now increased with fearful violence, waves rising like mountains, and rain and sleet pouring from the dismal clouds. At ten, A. M., being then in fifteen fathoms of water, and drifting rapidly towards the shore, the captain summoned all hands into the cabin to consult about throwing our deck-load overboard, in order to leave us a better chance to secure ourselves to the rigging, and thus save our lives when the vessel should strike, which he judged would be in about half an hour. Not a gleam of hope appeared, and here our distress was increased by observing that the captain seemed under the influence of liquor, to which he had probably resorted in order to stifle his fears of approaching death.

"The order was given, and we went to work to throw the cotton over, while the captain, frightened and despairing, went into the cabin to drown his fears in drink. Seeing the state of things, and believing that shipwreck was imminent, I found two of my shipmates who were Christians, and who had prayed daily with me in the forecastle, and I asked them if they had any faith in God now, that he would hear our prayers and deliver us? They both said they had, and I told them to pray, then, that the Lord might rebuke the winds and calm the waves.

"With an unspeakable mingling of fear and hope we applied ourselves to the task of casting the cotton into the sea, at the same time lifting up earnest and united prayers to God for deliverance from the threatened destruction, occasionally gliding in close contact with each other, and speaking words of hope in each other's ears, and feeling, as we toiled, a blessed confidence that our prayers were not in vain.

"It did not seem more than five minutes from the time we commenced to throw the cotton overboard, for we had scarcely tumbled twenty bales into the sea, when we heard a shout from the quarter deck:

"'Avast heaving cotton overboard! *The wind is coming out from our lee!* Avast there!'

"It was the captain's voice, bidding us stay our hands; we obeyed, and looking up we saw him clinging to the rigging, apparently so drunk that he could hardly stand, *while away over our lee-bow we could see blue sky and fair weather*, and *it seemed that in less than ten minutes fom the time the hurricane was at its height, the wind had chopped around in shore, and was gently wafting us away from danger, and out into deep water again.*

"There were glad souls on board the Pandora that day, as she swung around in obedience to the helm, and we laid her course again for our destined port. And some who before had mocked at prayers and blasphemed the God we loved, admitted then that God had answered prayer, and that he had delivered us from death.

"And I love to repeat the story to the praise of the Lord, who yet lives to hear, and bless, and save his trusting children."

No Fear of Thunder.

Some years ago a camp-meeting was held in Southern Indiana It rained nearly all the time of the meeting. Father Haven, a man mighty in prayer, rose to preach. Just as he announced his text it thundered, and the congregation seemed to be restless and alarmed. The old hero instantly said, "Let us engage a moment in prayer." He prayed that God would allow the storm to pass by and not disturb them.

After having plead for a few moments he said, "Friends, keep your seats; it will not rain one drop here to-day." He commenced to preach, and it thundered again He repeated his assurance, and thus it continued until the storm-cloud was almost over the encampment. It divided north and south, and passed about a quarter of a mile on either side of them, reunited again and passed on, and not one solitary drop of rain fell on that encampment.

The Prayer of the Pilgrims for Rain Answered.

It is well known that many of the good men who were driven from England to America by persecution in the seventeenth century, had to endure great privations. In the Spring of 1623 they planted more corn than ever before; but by the time they had done planting, their food was spent. They daily prayed, "Give us this day our daily bread;" and in some way or other the prayer was always answered. With a single boat and a net they caught some fish, and when these failed, they dug in the sand for shell-fish. In the month of June their hopes of a harvest were nearly blasted by a drought which withered up their corn and made the grass look like hay. All expected to perish with hunger.

In their distress the pilgrims set apart a day of humiliation and prayer, and continued their worship for eight or nine hours. God heard their prayers, and answered them in a way which excited universal admiration. Although the morning of that day was clear, and the weather very hot and dry during the whole forenoon, yet before night it began to rain, and gentle showers continued to fall for many days, so that the ground became thoroughly soaked, and the drooping corn revived.

The Enemies of a God Fearing Nation.

"An answer to prayer," says Le Clerc, "may be seen by what happened on the coast of Holland in the year 1672. The Dutch expected an attack from their enemies by sea, and public prayers were ordered for their deliverance. It came to pass that when their enemies waited only for the tide, in order to land, *the tide was retarded, contrary to its usual course, for twelve hours,* so their enemies were obliged to defer the attempt to another opportunity; which they never found, *because a storm arose afterwards,* and drove them from the coast."

Changing the Course one Point.

Walking across Palace Square in Rio de Janeiro, Brazil, with an American ship-master, (says a correspondent of the *Watchman,*) he invited me to accompany him to his hotel.

While there he showed me a very large gold medal he had received from the British government for saving a ship's company at sea. The circumstances were these. One night at sea, when it was the captain's "mid-watch,"—the watch from twelve, midnight, till four o'clock in the morning—just before turning in, he gave the officer of the watch the ship's course; the direction in which she was to be steered. While undressing, it was impressed on his mind that he ought to change the course a point; but he could see no reason for the change, as the ship was on the right course for the port of her destination. He turned in and tried to fall asleep, as it was only four hours to his watch; but the impression that he ought to change the ship's course kept him awake. In vain he tried to throw off that impression; and yielding to it, he went on deck and gave the order for the change. On returning to his berth, he was asleep as soon as his head was on the pillow. The next day he sighted a ship in distress, and made sail for her. The ship was in a sinking condition, and he rescued the whole ship's company. Shortly after, a gale of wind arose and carried the sinking ship to complete destruction. Had not the American captain changed the course of his ship that evening, he would not have come in sight of the ship in distress, and all of the company would have perished.

Query—What made that Captain arise in the middle of the night and, contrary to all science, reason and his own will, change the course of his vessel, but a Supreme Being, whose power he could not resist, and what made him *exactly* reach that sinking *ship just in time.*

The Fulton St. Prayer Meeting.

ANSWERS TO PRAYER FROM ITS HISTORY, RECORDS AND CORRESPONDENCE.

———•♦•———

THE following Incidents of Prayer and the remarkable Answers, have been obtained from the records of the Fulton Street Prayer Meeting in New York City. They include both facts which have been related by speakers in their daily meetings, or furnished from the letters of those who have solicited Prayer and received the Answer to their Faith.

They are of the utmost diversity of subjects, literally including the "all things" of the Bible, and temporal as well as spiritual interests.

Numerous as the incidents are, which we here give, still they cover only *one-sixtieth* part of the whole Record of the Blessed Meeting.

History can never tell of the wonders done in Answer to the Prayers of these trusting ones; but Faith can rejoice, for here is fulfilled daily those cheerful Promises of the Lord: "*If ye abide in me and my words abide in you, ye shall ask what ye will, and it shall be done unto you.*" "*Ask and receive, that your joy may be full.*"

Saved from a Life of Degradation.

"Your prayers for my husband have been answered; *on the very day* I wished your prayers for him, and *before the hour of prayer had expired*, he came into the house, and said, 'I

am going to do better.'   He had not been home before for
several weeks.   He was a profane, hard-drinking man.   He
has since joined the church.   'All hail the power of Jesus'
name.' "

Recovery of an Invalid.

"One year ago, the prayers of this meeting were asked for
an invalid who had years of intense suffering before her,
unless soon relieved.   Prayers were offered for her.   Now we
would like to acknowledge the loving-kindness and tender
mercy of our God, for, since that time, she has slowly but
steadily improved, even under most trying and unfavorable
circumstances, and has now recovered comparative strength."

Relief in Business.

"*None of those who trust in Him shall be made desolate.*"

"Some three weeks ago, I wrote you, stating that *my business had been a failure,* and asked your prayers that God, in
His mercy, would point out a way for me to *provide for my
family.*   The clouds grew thicker and blacker, but the more
earnest were my prayers.   *Last Saturday the Lord came to
my rescue,* and provided me with the necessities of life, and
to-day I wish you to join with me in thanksgiving to Almighty
God for these favors—'For He is good; His mercy endureth
forever.' "

A Daughter Saved from Marriage with a Corrupt Man.

"I pray you give God praise and thanks for His merciful
deliverance of my dear daughter from the *evil influence* of the
man to whom she had given her love and promise of marriage.
THE LORD gave her strength and courage to break her engagement, in answer to our earnest prayers.   Oh, implore *Him* to
keep that man out of her path, for he is constantly lying in

wait to meet her when she goes out. He wanted her to read bad books, but told her that they were not wrong. He constantly laid temptation in alluring forms before her. To HIM alone be the thanks for this step she has taken."

A Skeptic Overpowered.

"More and more God is pouring out His Spirit, gloriously answering your prayers and ours. I have been constantly asking your prayers, and though, for a while, the vision tarried, *yet it has come. The young man,* from a neighborhood where there was *not one Christian,* and *he himself scarcely less than a skeptic, is now sitting, in his right mind, at Jesus' feet."*

Saved from Death.

"My brother, that lay apparently at the point of death, has been restored to comparative health."

An Intemperate Young Man Reclaimed.

"Rejoice with me, and thank God for his gracious answer to prayer. The intemperate young man for whom I requested prayer some months ago, has turned away from his cups, and is earnestly striving to overcome his appetite for strong drink. He is competent to be the means of doing so much good."

The Conversion of Intimate Friends.

"Some time since, I sent request for prayer for the conversion of friends. Since then *three* have united with the church."

Raised up from Death's Door.

"Our former pastor was raised up from death's door, in answer to your prayer. *The doctor gave him up.* He says the Lord alone saved him, in answer to prayer. Praise His name."

23

The Desire of the Heart Fulfilled.

"A few weeks since I sent a request for prayer in my behalf, asking you to pray God very earnestly that He would grant me the desire of my heart, for which I was praying almost unceasingly. *On the evening of the same day* on which I supposed you would receive my request, *the answer came,* lifting a great burden from my heart. I send this in acknowledgment of God's loving-kindness to me, and to encourage every burdened, praying one, to *trust Him more.*"

A Poor Old Sick Lady Restored.

"The poor, sick old lady for whom I requested your prayers some time since, wishes to return thanks to Almighty God, for *restoring her health,* and *sending friends.* It is wonderful how your and our requests are answered."

A New Birth.

"Give thanks with me. Since I wrote you last, our son has given himself to Jesus."

A Church Saved from Strife.

"It is with heartfelt gratitude to God that I write you of answer to your prayer. Last Spring, I asked your prayers in behalf of our church It was almost destroyed by a man trying to get into our Conference without proper papers, and could not. He then broke up a Presbyterian church, and formed another. He gathered a number of our members with him, and tried hard to take our parsonage, but did not succeed. Thank God! though we are few, and have had a hard struggle, we still hold our property, our circuit has doubled, God is reviving His work, and is now answering your prayers."

Reason Restored.

"Last March, I requested you to pray for a dear friend in Massachusetts, who was deprived of her reason through sickness and great trouble. *Give thanks unto God, she is fully restored.*"

"Arise and Walk."

"It will be just one year since Jesus came and took me by the hand, and *I arose from what was supposed to be my death-bed*, and *walked to the astonishment of all.* I have not claimed the fullness of the promise, but feel that I may. I prayed God not to heal my body wholly, until I was more patient under my cross."

The Appetite for Strong Drink Taken Away.

"Sometime ago I wrote to you for my husband. He was *a victim to strong drink* at that time, but *blessed be God, he has not drank one drop for five months.*"

Spiritual Strength.

"I feel your prayers; I think I know the day and the hour, for I felt strengthened with strength in my soul."

Healing of Soul and Body.

"I have reason to rejoice that I have been greatly blessed in answer to your prayers. Two young lady friends of mine have been enabled to claim the blessed promise of full salvation, not only to the healing of the soul, *but the body also*

My own experience helped them. On the 16th of January, last, in answer to constant prayer offered by myself and friends, I arose from what all thought to be my death-bed, and walked all over the house ; also many miles on the streets during the next few months. I did not claim the full extent of the promise as I craved only relief from such terrible pain, as was then my portion to bear. I think God in his goodness would have granted full restoration to health, as I was so anxious to work for Him, but I pleaded with Him *not to heal my body* until my mind had had the discipline I felt it needed."

An Intemperate Husband Saved by Prayer.

"Some three weeks since, I asked you for my intemperate husband, that you would pray that he might be *willing to be saved*. *He has been made willing to give up the intoxicating cup,* and says he has *not any desire* for it. To God be all the praise."

Religion Lost, Religion Regained.

"I wrote you two months since, asking an interest in your prayers for a young man that experienced religion a year ago, but failed to confess Christ by uniting with the church. Your prayers have been answered. Last night my heart was made to rejoice by seeing him confess Christ, before the world. He is now happy in the love of Jesus, and will be useful and active in the church."

Drunkards Reformed.

"Return thanks to God for two men signing the pledge, about one month ago, who have been enabled to keep it through great temptation *They were drunkards for over twenty years* Their reformation was in answer to a praying mother's prayers, and to the prayers for them at your meeting."

A Hopeless Case.

"A little less than a year ago, prayers were desired at the Fulton street prayer-meeting for a man whose case seemed wholly hopeless. Shortly after he gave up drink, and became a Christian; is now a happy man, and has a happy family.

"Please carry this thank offering to God, that he has given us such a Savior, and such a way to escape from temptation."

A Harvest of Conversions.

"Last Fall, I wrote you to pray for us. You did pray. The result was a wonderful increase of spiritual life—*fifty conversions.*"

A Family Made Happy.

"Two years ago, I wrote asking your prayers for a dear sister, brothers and nieces. Since then, one brother, about sixty, and my two nieces have been converted, and are now rejoicing in a Savior's love."

The Power of the Holy Spirit.

"About two years ago we requested your prayers for the Holy Spirit upon a revival work then in progress in our church." *The Lord answered us* by giving us *over four score souls.*"

Hearts Made Glad.

"We return most hearty thanks for the answer to prayer given. I wrote more than a year ago last August of our low state. Last Winter twenty young persons were converted, and continue to work faithfully"

Given Up by Man, but Rescued by the Great Physician.

"The writer was himself raised up by prayer, from the gates of death, offered by the heart and lips of one who is now a sufferer. *Two of the most skillful physicians in the land had given me up.*"

The Story of a Wayward Life, Saved by Prayer.

"In the last fourteen years I have stood beside the death-beds of eight who were near and dear to me, and the last words that each spoke to me as they were leaving the world were, "*Will you not meet me in Heaven?*" I have been a wayward child. Eight years ago I became addicted to strong drink. I became a drunkard, which brought my dear old father down to an untimely grave. I made a promise on his death-bed that I would not drink any more, and for six long years I kept that promise, but at last I broke it. I again became a drunkard, which began to tell on my wife. I promised her that I would not drink, but that promise was broken time after time. Within this year, in the week of prayer, I attended the prayer-meetings, asked prayers for me, and on the night following, I erected the family altar, which had for four years been neglected, and, thank God, it is there yet. I am now trusting in the promise that *He will not let his children be tempted beyond what they are able to endure.*"

A Wonderful Cure.

An earnest Christian woman who believed the Lord greater than any earthly physician, cries, " *O, praise the Lord. He hath delivered me in six troubles, and in the seventh he hath not forsaken me.*" "And the seventh was the worst. By the help of *eight physicians,* and in answer to prayer, partly of this meeting, a fearful tumor has been taken from me weighing twelve pounds, with three gallons of water in the sack. O, praise the Lord, for He is good, and his mercy endureth forever."

This case was one of extraordinary risk and apparently impossible achievement; but the Lord gave faith to try, and skill to win the victory. No earthly power could have dared the venture.

Given Up.

"Our pastor, after four months' sickness, preached to us last evening the most solemn sermon I ever heard, and says he was raised up in answer to prayer. The physicians gave him up several times, and say they have never known such an instance of recovery."

Chains Broken at Last.

"Long months, week by week, I have asked you to pray that my husband might be saved from the eternal doom of a drunkard. God has mercifully given him strength to break the fetters that bound him fast."

Better than We Expected.

"We asked your prayers; they have been answered. They were answered more and better than we had hoped or dreamed they could be."

Prayer Answered for Employment.

"A foreigner without means and friendless tried in vain for ten months to succeed in finding some employment He requested your prayers to God, and *God answered*. In less than eighteen hours a splendid position was offered to him. He and his wife give thanks, and pray that they may devote their lives usefully to the cause of God who has been so good to them."

Found Employment.

"God has answered our united prayers, and given employment to his child."

An Old Lady Saved from Little Annoyances.

"Your prayers have been heard and answered in mercy. The old lady has not been quite so much annoyed. Thank God for some peace for the aged one, not able to bear what younger people can, that go out into the world and can find relief. I thank my heavenly Father for his loving-kindness and tender mercy for those that cry to him in trouble."

Insanity Dispelled.

"I sent a petition months ago, for prayers for an insane husband Your prayers have been answered. He has rapidly recovered."

Reclaimed.

" I must ask you to return thanks with me that your prayers have been answered. An intemperate brother has been reclaimed."

Restored to Health.

"One month since, I requested prayer specially for my own family. My oldest son, who was then sick, has been restored to his usual health. *'The prayer of faith hath indeed saved the sick.'*"

Temptations Removed.

"Some months ago I asked your prayers for a son in college, amid great temptations. I desire to give thanks that those temptations have been removed."

The Heart of a Clergyman Turned from Thoughts of Ambition.

"I sent a request to you for a young man, who was called, and eminently fitted for the ministry, but was tempted, by ambition, not to listen to the divine call, and obstacles had hedged his way somewhat. After I requested your prayers in his behalf, this temptation was removed, and nearly one hundred persons were converted in the church which was under his care."

A Grateful Tribute.

"For a long time I have been the subject of personal affliction, caused by *two internal tumors* of the *worst type.* Speedy dea'h seemed inevitable; yet there was a little hope that a surgical operation might possibly remove the difficulty and prolong my day. To this hope I clung, submitted to the operation, and it was a success To the earnest prayers of Christian people is due this grateful acknowledgment."

Was a Perfect Slave to Liquor.

"Please return *thanks* to our kind Heavenly Father for this answer to prayer. All last Winter requests were sent in for a gentleman, a perfect slave to liquor. Those prayers were answered, and he is attending church regularly, striving to do what is right to please his Heavenly Master."

Always Answered.

"Several times in years past I have asked for the prayers of this meeting, and always found them answered."

Cured of Epilepsy.

"I wrote you to aid me by your prayers, that my afflicted son, who was troubled with epilepsy, might be cured. Thanks be to the Heavenly Father, he is better."

Almost Lost.

"Your prayers and mine for my son have been answered. He was almost lost, on the downward road of intemperance. He has now reformed."

A Situation Obtained by Prayer.

"Yesterday I sent a request that God would give me sustaining grace and abiding faith, and in his own good time give me a situation where I might be able to support my family. In that very afternoon, I made a contract of $1,200 a year. Praise the Lord."

A Bountiful Blessing.

"Some time ago I solicited your prayers for a blessing on my services, and *never, in all my life* before have I been blessed as since that time. 'Tis truly wonderful; it has seemed as if I must have become some one else, and that it could not longer be me speaking with such boldness, and apparent success. Bless the Lord, O my soul, and all that is within me, bless his holy name."

Saved from the Company of a Bad Lover.

"A week ago I begged you to pray for my daughter, who had given her heart to an unworthy man, praying that God might guide her to see him as he is, and turn her love from him. She is a child of God. In answer, God has caused a rupture between them."

Away from Home, but not away from God.

"Some weeks since I sent in a request for prayer for my sons who had fallen victims to intemperance and vice. My heart rejoices to-day in the hope that it has.

"Two who left home, and had gone to distant cities to seek employment, have written me to pray that they may be able to forsake sin in all its forms, and come to Christ and be Christians. One of them was skeptical when he left home. The one remaining at home has resolved to quit drinking."

God Always Answers Believing Prayer.

"Your prayers asked on several occasions have all been graciously answered. Return thanks unto the Lord that sendeth mercy."

The Hardest Heart Yields at Last.

"Several years since your prayers were solicited in behalf of one who seemed given over to hardness of heart and reprobacy of mind. Since that time there has been some reform in his life. God only knows how far those prayers have been answered in restraining grace. Last week he said to the friend who had solicited your prayers for him, 'I wish you would ask Fulton Street prayer-meeting to pray again for me. *I believe it did me good.*'"

Up from the Lowest Depths.

"One year ago I wrote you respecting prayer for my husband. He has since been reclaimed from the lowest depths of a drunkard's life, and is now a member of the Christian church. Thanks be to God, the giver of all good."

Saved and Honored.

"Almost three years ago I asked you to pray for a young man that was wandering from God. Thank God, your and my prayers were answered. He is now an active Christian, a superintendent of the Sabbath school, and a most zealous member of the Young Men's Christian Association of this place."

Almost Persuaded.

"Some weeks since I requested prayer for a member of this Institution who was 'almost persuaded' to be a Christian. Thanks to our Father, and to those who have offered prayer in her behalf, she has been *altogether persuaded*, and has united with the Lord's people."

Answered the Same Day.

"You received a letter yesterday. My husband rose for prayers the same night."

Oh, How Precious.

"I wrote five months since for prayers for myself, and I now write to say that I have found my Savior very precious to my soul."

Praying for a Pastor.

"Several months ago I wrote asking you to pray for a feeble church in need of a pastor. Since then I am happy to say that this church has been blessed and we now have a pastor."

A Telegram of Prayer.

An incident was related at one of the meetings by a clergyman who had written a telegram asking for prayers. God heard it before it was sent.

"When we were in Switzerland, my daughter was taken very ill, so that the doctor despaired of her life. I felt the need of sympathy and help and prayer, and I made up my mind that I would send a telegraphic dispatch to this meetıng, where I had so often united with you in prayer. I wrote the dispatch and was pıepared to send it, when all at once there was poured out such a joyful faıth and confidence in God on me as I never felt before ın all my life, and I fell on my knees ın devout thanksgıvıng for the assurance that God gave me that he had heard and answered our prayers, for we had prayed for that dear daughter's life. There lay the tele-gıam ıeady to be sent. There I was waiting and prayıng. In less than half an hour my wife came into the room and said, 'There is a change for the better in our daughter,' and the telegram was never sent, though I belıeve the writing of it was the prayer that God answered."

He Did not Keep His Promise, but God Did.

A remarkable instance of how God keeps his promıses and is faithful, and how man often forgets to keep his, and at last receives deserved punishment for hıs thanklessness to God, was recently related ın the Fulton Street prayer-meeting.

A very urgent case was presented by a friend. He said: "A friend of mıne is seeking Jesus. A lıttle while ago his only child lay near death. He prayed God to restore her to health, promising to serve the Lord for the rest of hıs life ıf the child's life was spared. Hıs daughter recovered, but *the man forgot the promise he had made and sought not after God.* In a very lıttle whıle the chıld was suddenly taken sick again, and almost as suddenly died. The father remem-bered hıs vows, and feels that this is God's solemn warnıng to him to seek the Savior."

A Double Prayer Answered.

At the Fulton Street prayer-meeting a number of remark-able cases were related of real answers to prayer for recovery to health, and obtaınıng of positions.

"I must tell you how God has been answering prayer, for his glory and for your encouragement. Your prayers were asked for a sick wife. She was thought by the doctors to be beyond recovery, but in response to prayer God spared her life, and she and her husband returned their heartfelt thanks to Him. But there was another trouble. The husband had long needed employment, and was in great pecuniary distress. He had been praying for help, beseeching the Lord to open up a way for him. But help did not come, and the cloud seemed darker, and the poor man got discouraged. Friends begged him to hope on, and not to give up his trust in that God who, in answer to prayer, had raised his sick wife to health. He continued to pray, and on the long, dark night, morning at last dawned. He is now in a good position, and sends a request to friends to thank God with him for this two-fold goodness of the Lord.

How the Lord Blessed an old Advertisement.

"I had another acquaintance who was also greatly distressed. With a wife and family to care for, and all his means gone, and no prospect of employment, he was in trouble indeed. We induced him to present his case for prayer here, as it would encourage him to have others pray for him. Then we inserted an advertisement in one of the daily papers, offering his services, hoping the Lord would bless the means used and answer prayer. Day by day passed, but no response came. Some two weeks after the advertisement was inserted, a merchant picked up *an old paper*, and noticing the advertisement, showed it to his partner, remarking, 'Why, this is just the man we need' Observing the *old date* on the paper, his partner said he thought it would be too late to respond; but the trial was made. The man was requested to call, and proved to be just what these merchants had been wishing for, and was very quickly engaged. He feels that the Heavenly Father who cares for the sparrows, undoubtedly met his need, and that all the circumstances connected with the case were providential."

Hating the Accursed Drink.

A brother rose in the meeting and said, "I believe it is God's will that I should tell you how He saved me, about two years since. I came into the meeting when it was held in the old church, and was at the time under the influence of liquor. The missionary took me into the gallery and talked with me, and prayed with me, and God heard prayer and saved me. I became a new man in Christ, and have lost all appetite for drink; I hate the accursed stuff."

A Drunkard for Thirty Years.

Another told a remarkable story of his life: "I was a drunkard for thirty years, and I tried all kinds of means to get free, but all failed. I pledged myself over and over again, and swore off many a time. At last, Jesus met me at the mission meeting, and he saved me. He took away the appetite for drink from me. I am a different man; I am tempted in various ways at times, but when tempted I think of Jesus and look to Him, and He saves me."

The Hopeless One Brought Home.

"A pastor related the incident of the conversion of a man who had disgraced his family, and all through drink. All the people in the village where he lived regarded him as a hopeless case. But he was prayed for, and one night in answer to an appeal to those desiring Christ to rise, he rose. He soon became a new man, and a steadfast soldier of the Cross, completely delivered from his hopeless situation, and all his appetites taken away."

"No Man can pluck them out of my Father's Hand."

A brother says, "Jesus says this, and I rest just there." "A year ago I was in Philadelphia. I had resolved not to drink any liquor that day, but my resolution was soon broken. In the evening as I wandered the streets, that voice of God, *'Turn ye, turn ye,'* gave me great uneasiness. Although I tried hard not to go, yet the Spirit was at work within me, and against my will led me to the meetings of the Young Men's Christian Association. When the call came for those desiring prayers, I felt that it was my last call, and I pushed forward and rose. Friends prayed with me, and that night, as I pleaded for mercy, the burden of my sin was lifted and I was free. Christ took the appetite for drink away, and He has kept me ever since, and will keep me to the end, for He says, *'Fear not, for I have redeemed thee; I have called thee by thy name; thou art mine.'* Oh! I know He won't let me go."

Answer to Prayer in Temporal Matters.

A speaker said at one meeting, "God answers prayer in temporal matters. In a Western college, at a time when the last morsels of food had been eaten, and some had to go away from the table empty, four of the number retired to pray, and before they had ceased praying relief came. Provisions in large quantities were received, thus verifying the old promise, 'Before they call I will answer.'"

The Lord proved True.

"The Lord reigns," another exclaimed, "I have proved that during my long life! It has looked dark very often, and I have been in difficult places, but again and again the Lord has brought me through triumphantly. I have found the promise true." "Trust in the Lord, and do good, so shalt thou dwell in the land, and verily thou shalt be fed."

A Little Boy's Question.

A brother related a touching incident which occured in Brooklyn. "A little boy asked his father at the dinner table, *'Papa, why don't you read the Bible?'* The father was a passionate man, and was about driving the boy out of his presence, but his anger made the little fellow weep. That brought tears to the mother's eyes, and then the father followed suit. The boy's tears moved him, and the question struck his heart; and father and mother, up to that hour unconverted, were soon on their way to the prayer-meeting, where they found Jesus."

A Little Girl's Question.

A touching little story, with eternal results in it, was told at one of the meetings, illustrating that word of God's book, "A little child shall lead them." "A dress-maker called on a very wealthy lady in a city not far from New York, and took with her her little girl, five years old. The lady took a fancy to the child, and showed her over the house. She expressed great admiration at all she saw, and, particularly attracted by the carpet, said to the lady: 'Why, I should think Jesus must come here very often, it is such a nice house, and such a beautiful carpet—He must come here very often He comes to our house, and we have no carpet; I am sure He must come here very often, doesn't He?' The lady not answering, the child repeated the question, when the reply came, with deep emotion, "I am afraid not" The child left, but God's message was delivered The lady related the incident to her husband in the evening, and both were led to seek the Savior.

24

God Cared for Me.

At a meeting a young man in broken English, said: "If any man ought to believe in prayer, I ought to. My friends turned me out of my home, because I was seeking for Christ. I was too much Christian my landlady said. I told her I wished I was all Christian. It was seven o'clock in the evening when she refused to let me come into the house. I went then to the prayer-meeting in Water Street; we had such a good meeting, that I quite forgot that I had no place to sleep. The services over, I found it was raining fast, and I had no place to which to go. I went back into the room, and kneeling at one of the benches, I begged God to give me a place to rest. I did not go home my usual way that night, but on the way I took I met an old friend, and walking with him to his house he begged me to stay the night, as he did not like to be alone. I staid there that night, though I had never told him of my condition. What was it but an answer to prayer. Many a time since has God thus provided for my wants. O friends, let your heart go out for Him, then He will never let you want."

The Blind Can See.

Said another, "I came here yesterday to ask you to pray for my sister. She has been sick some time, and then she lost her *sight*. I did not get an opportunity to present my request because so many took part; but I thought I would just take my sister's case to Jesus, remembering that 'the prayer of faith shall save the sick.' In the afternoon I found her in sad need of sleep. I told her just to look to Jesus, because it was written of Him, 'So He giveth His beloved sleep.' We prayed together, and I left her in a *profound slumber*. 'This morning when I called on her she could *see me*.' Friends, the Lord does answer prayer."

REFERENCE BOOKS
FOR
BIBLE STUDENTS.

JAMIESON, FAUSSET & BROWN'S Popular Portable Commentary. Critical, Practical, Explanatory. Four volumns in neat box, fine cloth, $8.00; half bound, $10 00.

A new edition, containing the complete unabridged notes in clear type on good paper, in four handsome 12 mo volumes of about 1 000 pages each, with copious index, numerous illustrations and maps, and a Bible Dictionary compiled from Dr Wm Smith's standard work

Bishop Vincent of Chautauqua fame says · " The *best* condensed commentary on the whole Bible is Jamieson, Fausset & Brown "

CRUDEN'S UNABRIDGED CONCORDANCE TO THE HOLY SCRIPTURES. With life of the author. 864 pp., 8vo , cloth (net), $1.00 ; half roan, sprinkled edges (net), 2.00 ; half roan, full gilt edges (net), $2 50.

SMITH'S BIBLE DICTIONARY, comprising its Antiquities, Biography, Geography and Natural History, with numerous maps and illustrations. Edited and condensed from his great work by WILLIAM SMITH, LL. D. 776 pages. 8vo, many illustrations, cloth, $1.50.

THE BIBLE TEXT CYCLOPEDIA. A complete classification of Scripture Texts in the form of an alphabetical list of subjects. By Rev. JAMES INGLIS. Large 8vo, 524 pages, cloth, $1.75.

The plan is much the same as the " Bible Text Book " with the valuable additional help in that the texts referred to are quoted in full Thus the student is saved the time and labor of turning to numerous passages, which, when found, may not be pertinent to the subject he has in hand.

THE TREASURY OF SCRIPTURE KNOWLEDGE; consisting of 500,000 scripture references and parallel passages, with numerous notes 8vo, 778 pages. cloth, $2 00.

A single examination of this remarkable compilation of references will convinc the reader of the fact that "the Bible is its own best interpreter."

THE WORKS OF FLAVIUS JOSEPHUS, translated by WILLIAM WHISTON, A. M., with Life, Portrait, Notes and Index. A new cheap edition in clear type. Large 8vo, 684 pages, cloth, $2.00.

100.000 SYNONYMS AND ANTONYMS. By Rt. Rev. SAMUEL FALLOWS, A. M., D. D. 512 pages, cloth, $1.00.

A complete Dictionary of synonyms *and words of opposite* meanings, with an appendix of Briticisms, Americanisms, Colloquialisms, Homonims, Homophonous words, Foreign Phrases, etc , etc.

" This is one of the best books of its kind we have seen, and probably there is nothing published in the country that is equal to it."—*Y. M. C. A. Watchman.*

CHICAGO
148-150 Madison Street
Fleming H. Revell Co.
NEW YORK:
30 Union Square East

SUGGESTIVE BOOKS --
-- FOR BIBLE READERS.

NEW NOTES FOR BIBLE READINGS. By the late S. R. BRIGGS, with brief Memoir of the author by Rev. JAS. H. BROOKES, D. D., Crown 8vo, cloth, $1.00 ; flexible, 75 cents.

"NEW NOTES" is not a reprint, and contains *Bible Readings* to be found in no other similar work, and, it is confidently believed, will be found more carefully prepared, and therefore more helpful and suggestive.

Everyone of the 60,000 readers of "Notes and Suggestions for Bible Readings" will welcome this entirely new collection containing selections from D. L. Moody, Major Whittle, J. H. Brookes, D. D., Prof. W. G. Moorehead, Rev. E. P. Marvin, Jno. Currie, Rev. W. J. Erdman, Rev. F. E. Marsh, Dr. L. W. Munhall, etc.

NOTES AND SUGGESTIONS FOR BIBLE READINGS. By S. R. BRIGGS and J. H. ELLIOTT.

Containing, in addition to twelve introductory chapters on plans and method of Bible study and Bible readings, over six hundred outlines of Bible readings, by many of the most eminent Bible students of the day. Crown 8vo, 262 pp. Cloth, library style, $1.00 ; flexible cloth, .75; paper covers, .50.

THE OPEN SECRET ; or, The Bible Explaining Itself. A series of intensely practical Bible readings. By HANNAH WHITALL SMITH. 320 pp. Fine cloth, $1.00.

That the author of this work has a faculty of presenting the "Secret Things" that are revealed in the Word of God is apparent to all who have read the exceedingly popular work, "The Christian's Secret of a Happy Life."

BIBLE BRIEFS ; or, Outline Themes for Scripture Students. By G. C. & E. A. NEEDHAM. 16mo., 224 pages, cloth, $1.00.

"Here are sermons in miniature, which any preacher will find it profitable to expand into sermons in full measure. The book gives both the hint and the help, for the best kind of pulpit discourse."—*Watchword.*

"Not a word redundant. Here you have meat without bones, and land without stones."—*Rev. C. H. Spurgeon.*

BIBLE HELPS FOR BUSY MEN. By A. C. P. COOTE.

Contains over 200 Scripture subjects, clearly worked out and printed in good legible type, with an alphabetical index. 140 pages, 16mo.; paper, 30c.; cloth flex., 60c.

"Likely to be of use to overworked brethren."—C. H. SPURGEON.
"Given in a clear and remarkably telling form."—*Christian Leader.*

RUTH, THE MOABITESS ; or Gleaning in the Book of Ruth. By HENRY MOORHOUSE. 16mo., paper covers, 20c.; cloth, 40c.

A characteristic series of Bible readings, full of suggestion and instruction.

BIBLE READINGS. By HENRY MOORHOUSE. 16mo., paper covers, 30 cents ; cloth, 60 cents.

A series by one pre-eminently the man of one book, an incessant, intense, prayerful student of the Bible.

SYMBOLS AND SYSTEMS IN BIBLE READINGS. Rev. W. F. CRAFTS. 64 pages and cover, 25 cents.

Giving a plan of Bible reading, with fifty verses definitely assigned for each day, the Bible being arranged in the order of its events. The entire symbolism of the Bible explained concisely and clearly.

NEW YORK: 12 Bible House, Astor Pl. Fleming H. Revell CHICAGO: 148 & 150 Madison St.

⋈HAND BOOKS FOR BIBLE STUDENTS⋈

THE LIFE OF CHRIST. Rev. JAS. STALKER, M. A, A new edition, with introduction by Rev. GEO. C. LORIMER, D. D. 12mo. cloth, 166 pages, 60 cents.

This work is in truth "*Multum in Parvo*," containing within small compass a vast amount of most helpful teaching, so admirably arranged that the reader gathers with remarkable definiteness the whole revealed record of the life work of our Lord in a nutshel' of space and with a minimum of study.

THE LIFE OF ST. PAUL. By Rev. JAS. STALKER, M. A. 12m cloth, 184 pages, 60 cents.

As admirable a work as the exceedingly popular volume by this author on "The life of Christ"

"An exceedingly compact life of the Apostle to the Gentiles It is bristling with information, and is brief, yet clear. As an outline of Paul's life it cannot be surpassed "— *N Y. Christian Inquirer.*

THE BIBLE STUDENTS' HANDBOOK. 12mo cloth, 288 pages 50 cents.

One of those helpful works, worth its price, multiplied by several scores It contains an introduction to the study of the Scriptures, with a brief account of the books of the Bible, their writers, etc , also a synopsis of the life and work of our Lord, and complete history of the manners and customs of the times, etc.

THE TOPICAL TEXT BOOK. 16mo cloth, 292 pages, 60 cents.

A remarkably complete and helpful Scripture text book for the topical study of the Bible. Useful in preparing Bible readings, addresses, etc

THE BIBLE REMEMBRANCER. 24mo. cloth, 198 pages, 50 cts.

A complete analyses of the Bible is here given, in small compass, in addition to a large amount of valuable Biblical information, and twelve colored maps.

BIBLE LESSONS ON JOSHUA AND JUDGES. By Rev. J. GURNEY HOARE, M. A. 16mo cloth, 124 pages, 50 cents.

FIFTY-TWO LESSONS ON (1) The Works of Our Lord ; (2) Claims of Our Lord Forming a year's course of instruction for Bible classes, Sunday schools and lectures. By FLAVEL S. COOK, M. A , D. D. 16mo. cloth, 104 pages, 50 cents.

FIFTY-TWO LESSONS ON (1) The Names and Titles of Our Lord; (2) Prophesies Concerning Our Lord and their Fulfillment. By FLAVEL S. COOK, M. A , D. D. 16mo. cloth, 104 pages, 50 cents.

Extremely full in the matter of reference and explanation, and likely to make the user "search the Scriptures"

OUTLINE OF THE BOOKS OF THE BIBLE. By Rev. J. H BROOKES, D. D. Invaluable to the young student of the Bible as a "First Lesson" in the study of the Book. 180 pages. Cloth, 50 cents, paper covers, 25 cents.

CHRIST AND THE SCRIPTURES. By Rev. ADOLPH SAPHER 16mo. cloth, 160 pages, 75 cents.

To all disciples of Christ this work commends itself at once by its grasp of truth, its insight, the life in it, and its spiritual force —*Christian Work.*

NEW YORK: 12 Bible House, Astor Pl.   Fleming H. Revell   CHICAGO: 148 & 150 Madison St.

New Books for ·-·
·- Thinking Minds.

WHAT ARE WE TO BELIEVE? or, The Testimony of Fulfilled Prophecy   By Rev. JOHN URQUHART.   16mo., 230 pages, cloth, 75 cents.

" This book, so small in bulk but so large in thought, sets forth a great mass of such testimony in lines so clear and powerful that we pity the man who could read it without amazement and awe.   It is the very book to put into the hands of an intelligent Agnostic." — *The Christian*, London.

MANY INFALLIBLE PROOFS.   By Rev. ARTHUR T. PIERSON, D. D.   317 pp 12mo   Cloth, $1.00, paper, 35 cents.

" It is not an exercise in mental gymnastics, but an earnest inquiry after the truth."— *Daily Telegram*, Troy, N Y.
" He does not believe that the primary end of the Bible is to teach science ; but he argues with force and full conviction that nothing in the Bible has been shaken by scientific research "—*Independent*

HOW I REACHED THE MASSES; Together with twenty-two lectures delivered in the Birmingham Town Hall on Sunday afternoons   By Rev CHARLES LEACH, F. G. S   16mo , cloth, $1 00.

There is much of very welcome good sense and practical illustration in these addresses. Pithy and pointed in admonishment, and wholesome in their didactic tone, they ought to exercise a good influence.

ENDLESS BEING; or, Man Made for Eternity.   By Rev. J. L. BARLOW.   Introduction by the Rev. P. S. HENSON, D. D.   Cloth, 16mo., 165 pages, 75 cents.

An unanswerable work , meeting the so-called annihilation and kindred theories most satisfactorily   The author held for years these errors, and writes as one fully conversant with the ground he covers.   It is a work which should be widely circulated.

PAPERS ON PREACHING.   By the Right Rev Bishop BALDWIN, Rev Principal RAINY, D D , Rev. J. R. VERNON, M. A., and others. Crown, 8vo, cloth, 75 cents.

" Preachers of all denominations will do well to read these practical and instructive disquisitions   The essay on " Expression in Preaching " is especially good —*Christian*.

THE SABBATH; its Permanence, Promise, and Defence. By Rev. W. W. EVERTS, D. D.   12mo., 278 pages, cloth, $1.00.

No phase of the Sabbath question is left undiscussed, while every topic is treated in the briefest manner, and every touch of light shows the hand of a master.
" An incisive and effective discussion of the subject "—*N. Y. Observer*.
" A thoughtful Christian defence of that divine institution."—*Christian Advocate*.

QUESTIONS OF THE AGES.   By Rev. MOSES SMITH.
Cloth 12mo, 132 pages, 75 cents.

What is the Almighty?	*Is there Common Sense in Religion?*
What is man ?	*What is Faith ?*
What is the Trinity ?	*Is there a Larger Hope ?*
Which is the Great Commandment .	*Is Life Worth Living?*
	What Mean these Stones?

" Discusses certain of the deep things of the Gospel in such a wise and suggestive fashion that they are helpful   One, answers negatively and conclusively the question, Is there a larger hope? '—*The Congregationalist*.

NEW YORK
12 Bible House, Astor Pl   **Fleming H. Revell**   CHICAGO
148 & 150 Madison St

TEXT BOOKS

Theological and other Bible Students,

TRAINING CLASSES, &c., &c.

Published by FLEMING H. REVELL COMPANY.

WORKS OF PROF. REVERE FRANKLIN WEIDNER, D. D.

Biblical Theology of the Old Testament. Based on Oehler.. $1.25.

"The author has done well in his effort to recast Oehler's work, and put it into a form more apprehensible to American students . . . We congratulate Prof. Weidner on its accomplishment We shall hope to hear from him again."—*The Advance.*

"Oehler's famous work is bulky, as the products of German scholarship are apt to be. This reproduction of it gives its distilled essence in a form well adapted alike to the needs of the class-room in the theological seminary, and to the wants of the pastor actively engaged. Nor would it be amiss for teachers of Bible classes to give the work careful study."—*The Moravian.*

Biblical Theology of New Testament.—Vols. 1 and 2, each $1.50.

"The great merit of his work is the method of original and independent investigation conducted without reference to any previously formed system of theology. When united to Prof Weidner's laborious investigation and devout spirit, this method produces results that are exceedingly suggestive."—*Advance.*

"All in all, this is a book that Theologians, Bible Students, and Sunday School Teachers will want and cannot do without."—*Religious Telescope.*

Exegetical Theology. Based on Hagenbach and Krauth ...... $1.25.

" Prof. Weidner's method is the sound and the fruitful one pursued by all the best writers on the subject, but it is in no sense a translation. . . . His statements of a subject and of a line of argument are made with neatness, precision, and in that suggestive manner which is a prime merit in work of this sort."—*The Independent.*

"In his selection of literature Prof Weidner has shown great care and skill Only that which is of practical value is mentioned. The book is just what it purports to be, a textbook, it is arranged for the wants of the student. But its use is not confined to the theological class room. Ministers *who study* (alas that the number of those who do not *study* is so great!) will find in it valuable and helpful material."—*Prof. Harper.*

Historical and Systematic Theology..................... $1.50.

The science of Theological Encyclopædia is one of the most important branches taught in a Theological Seminary. Its aim is to present a summary view of what is embraced in theological knowledge. It explains the inner organization of Theology, maps out its divisions, and shows them in their relation to one another. Methodology is the practical application of Theological Encyclopædia It shows the order in which the various topics are best taken up, indicates the best methods, and points out the most useful books. In this work a full and clear presentation of the various disciplines be longing to each department is given, together with valuable lists of books The sciences of Symbolics and Dogmatics are treated with special fulness, and the literature under Dogmatics is given according to the various denominations and according to subjects. This second volume is as compact and thorough in its treatment as the first on *Exegetical* Theology. The latter part of the work contains an Appendix on the "History of Dogmatics," covering 120 pages, reprinted from the author's *Introduction to Dogmatic Theology.*

An Introduction to Dogmatic Theology. Based on Luthardt. $2.00.

"The German method of study, as outlined in this book, is what our divines sometimes lack. In this brief volume we have a treasury of information, we have a succinct account of the dogmatic teachers of the Ancient Church, of the Middle Ages, of the Reformation age and so on—with terse biographies. We are thus enabled to glance over the whole field. . . . The book is well worth the reading of our clergy."—*The Churchman* (Episcopal).

"The work is made one of great practical value for the student, presenting within moderate compass what one would be obliged to seek for otherwise through whole

libraries. It is clear, comprehensive, condensed, with admirable analysis of the subject, yet with enough of the synthetical element to secure unity in the result."—*From
The Standard.*

Practical Theology—$1.00.

Studies in the Book. For training classes.

> Vol. I. Studies on the historical books of the New Testament, Seven
> General Epistles and Revelation. 16mo, cloth interleaved for notes... **$1.00**
> Vol. II.—Studies on I Thes , II Thes., Gal., I Cor., II Cor and Romans.. 1.00
> Vol. III.—Studies on Col., Eph., Philemon, Phil , Heb., I Tim., II Tim.,
> and Titus.. 1.00

"Prof. Weidner has here given us the fruit of years of study and instruction. His
notes are just shrewd and discriminating and no one can faithfully peruse them without gaining an enlarged and moving conception of the contents of the Bible."—*Standard.*

"We have for these books only commendation."—*Bible Teacher.*

Treasury of Scripture Knowledge. (Bagsters.)

> Consisting of five hundred thousand Scripture references and parallel pas-
> sages, numerous illustrative notes, 8vo., cloth, 700 pages **$2 00**

"You have conferred a favor on the Bible students of America by issuing your
edition of Treasury of Scripture Knowledge. Bible students who desire to compare
Scripture with Scripture will find the ' Treasury' to be of better help than any other
book of which I have any knowledge."—*R. R. McBurney, Gen. Sec. Y M. C. A., New
York.*

"These works will be a valuable aid to the pastor, to students in theological
seminaries and to those who may be prosecuting the study of Theology without the
living teacher."—*National Baptist.*

Inglis' Bible Text Cyclopedia.

> By Rev. JAS. INGLIS. A complete classification of Scripture Texts in the
> form of an alphabetical list of subjects. Large 8vo., 524 pages, cloth. **$1.75**

"We know of no other work comparable with it in this department of study."—
Sunday School Times.

"The aim of this volume is to place every text of Scripture under its appropriate
topic and names and subjects are taken up which do not appear in any other Cyclopedia."—*Standard.*

Notes on the Parables and Miracles.

> By TRENCH. Two volumes in one, 868 pages, large 8vo., cloth......... **$2 00**

Trench remains as popular to-day as ever, the greatest work on the Parables or
Miracles extant.

A Brief Introduction to the Study of Theology.

> By Prof. R. V. FOSTER, D. D , 16mo., cloth............................. **$1.00**

"It aims to deepen the impression, in the minds of both ministers and laymen, of
the 'breadth and depth and dignity of Christian theology.' A notably interesting and
practical part of the book is that which discusses personal requisites to the study of
theology."—*The Interior.*

Biblical Studies. An outline of Old Testament Theology.

> By Prof. R. V. FOSTER, D. D., 12mo., 365 pages, cloth................. **$1.50**

A New Catechism; or, Manuel of Instruction for Students and other
Thoughtful Inquirers.

> By Rev. J. T. HYDE, D. D , 12mo., 176 pages, cloth.................... **$1.00**

CHICAGO: *148-150 Madison Street.* **Fleming H. Revell Co.** **NEW YORK:** *30 Union Square East.*

Matthew Henry's Commentary.

A new large type edition. The best type and best edition issued, 6 vols. in box, fine cloth...$15.00

Same in half Morocco... .... $18.00

"Biblical students who are most familiar with the very best commentaries of this generation are most able to appreciate the unfading freshness, the clear analysis, the spiritual force, the quaint humor, and the evangelical richness of MATTHEW HENRY'S EXPOSITION OF THE OLD AND NEW TESTAMENTS."—*New York Observer.*

"First among the mighty for general usefulness we are bound to mention the man whose name is a household word —MATTHEW HENRY. He is the most pious and pithy, sound and sensible, suggestive and sober, terse and trustworthy."—*Rev. C. H. Spurgeon.*

Jamieson, Faussett, and Brown's Popular Commentary.

Critical, practicable, explanatory. A new edition, containing the complete unabridged notes in clean type, on good paper, in four handsome vols., with copious index, numerous illus. and maps, and dictionary compiled from Dr. Smith's standard works. Four vols., in neat box, fine cloth... $8.00

Half morocco. 10 00

"The best condensed Commentary on the whole Bible is the Commentary on the Old and New Testaments by Jamieson, Faussett and Brown It contains notes of the choicest and richest character on all parts of the Holy Bible. It is the cream of the Commentaries carefully collected by three eminent scholars. Its critical introduction to each book of Scripture, its eminently practical notes, its numerous pictorial illustrations, commend it strongly to the Sunday school worker and to the clergyman. Then it is such a marvel of cheapness."—Rt. Rev. J. H. VINCENT, D. D., in *"Aids to Bible Study."*

The leading clergymen and college professors of the country unite with Bishop Vincent in placing this Commentary in the first rank of all Biblical aids.

Stalker's Life of St. Paul.

12mo., cloth.. .60

Bristling with information. As an outline of Paul's life, it cannot be surpassed.— *New York Christian Enquirer.*

Stalker's Life of Christ.

12mo., cloth.................... .... .60

Multum in Parvo is the apt description of these life studies. Especially valuable as text-books for reading circles.

"It is a remarkably lucid, accurate and suggestive analysis of the Christ Life which is presented in this book. We value it as a rare manual for the study of the divine man."—*Illustrated Christian Weekly.*

Robinson's Harmony of the Four Gospels in the Words of the Authorized Version.

Edited by Dr. B. DAVIES. 16mo.. .60

Handbook to Grammar of the Greek Testament.

By Rev. S. G. GREEN, D. D. Together with a complete vocabulary, and an examination of the chief New Testament Synonyms. Illustrated by Examples and Comments. New and Revised Edition. 8vo.. .... $2.00

Constant reference is made to the revised New Testament of 1881, and more especially to the Greek text of Drs. Westcott and Hort. The Vocabulary has been entirely remodeled, and the work in its new form is offered to tutors, classes and private students, in the confidence that it will be found more than ever adapted to their needs

A Syllabus of the Outlines and Literature of Old Testament History

By Prof IRA M. PRICE, Ph. D., Leipsic $1 50

This work is a systematic and chronological analysis of the history found in the Old Testament, with copious references to the latest and best literature on each topic, especially such as are corroborated by the newest discoveries in the East. The work is for the use of students, pastors and other christian workers.

CHICAGO:
148-150 Madison Street. Fleming H. Revell Co. NEW YORK: 30 Union Square East

By-Paths of Bible Knowledge.

"The volumes issuing under the above general title fully deserve success. They have been entrusted to scholars who have a special acquaintance with the subjects about which they severally treat."—*Athenæum.*

15. Early Bible Songs.
With introduction on the Nature and Spirit of Hebrew Song, by A. H. Drysdale M. A.. $1 00

14. Modern Discoveries on the Site of Ancient Ephesus.
By J. T. Wood, F. S. A. Illustrated.................................. $1 00

13. The Times of Isaiah.
As illustrated from Contemporary Monuments. By A. H. Sayce, LL. D. .80

12. The Hittites; or the Story of a Forgotten Empire.
By A. H. Sayce, LL. D. Illustrated. Crown, 8vo..................... $1 20

11. Animals of the Bible.
By H. Chichester Hart, Naturalist to Sir G. Nares' Arctic Expedition and Professor Hull's Palestine Expedition. Illustrated, Crown, 8vo $1 20

10. The Trees and Plants Mentioned in the Bible.
By W. H. Groser, B. Sc. Illustrated.................................. $1 00

9. The Diseases of the Bible.
By Sir J. Risdon Bennett... $1 00

8. The Dwellers on the Nile.
Chapters on the Life, Literature. History and Customs of Ancient Egypt. By E. A. Wallis Budge, M. A., Assistant in Department of Oriental Antiquities, British Museum. Illustrated................. $1 20

7. Assyria; Its Princes, Priests and People.
By A. H. Sayce, M. A., LL. D., author of "Fresh Light from Ancient Monuments," "Introduction to Ezra, Nehemiah and Esther," etc. Illustrated $1 20

6. Egypt and Syria.
Their Physical Features in Relation to Bible History. By Sir J. W. Dawson, Principal of McGill College, Montreal, F. G. S., F. R. S., author of "The Chain of Life in Geological Time," etc. Second edition, revised and enlarged. With many illustrations........... $1 20

5. Galilee in the time of Christ.
By Selah Merrill, D. D., author of "East of the Jordan," etc. With Map $1 00

4. Babylonian Life and History.
By E. A. Willis Budge, M. A., Cambridge, Assistant in the Department of Oriental Antiquities, British Museum, illustrated........ $1 20

3. Recent Discoveries on the Temple Hill at Jerusalem.
By the Rev. J. King, M. A., Authorized Lecturer for the Palestine Exploration Fund. With Maps, Plans and Illustrations............ $1 00

2. Fresh Lights From the Ancient Monuments.
A Sketch of the most striking Confirmations of the Bible from recent discoveries in Egypt, Assyria, Babylonia, Palestine and Asia Minor. By A. H. Sayce, LL. D., Deputy Professor of Comparative Philology, Oxford, etc. With fac-similes from photographs................. $1 20

1. Cleopatra's Needle.
History of the London Obelisk, with an Exposition of the Hieroglyphics. By the Rev. J. King, Lecturer for the Palestine Exploration Fund. With Illustrations.................................... $1 00

CHICAGO:
148-150 *Madison Street.* Fleming H. Revell Co. NEW YORK:
30 *Union Square East.*

The "Northfield Books."

Writings of Rev. F. B. MEYER, B. A.

Mr. Meyer always writes to edification.—C. H. SPURGEON.

Joseph. Beloved—Hated—Exalted. *Cloth, 16 mo.,* $1.00.

In the present volume Mr. Meyer retells with skill and pathos the old-world story of the Israelitish youth who rose through pit and prison to the post of Premier of Egypt; a story of undying interest and worth, not only as a true tale of Eastern romance, but as a unique example of the value of piety, purity of life and fidelity in service.

10TH THOUSAND.

Abraham: or, The Obedience of Faith. *Cloth, 16 mo.,* $1.00.

A book we would very heartily commend to those who desire to make progress in Christian life and experience; each will find it helpful and suggestive, sending new light upon many a well-known narrative.—*Christian Progress.*

The contents of the book before us are such that no one can rise from its perusal without feeling consciously strengthened in God and inspired afresh for the Godly life.—*Sunday-School Chronicle.*

Really a very beautiful work, which will be read with delight by many a fireside. After all, this home-like treatment of Scripture biography, with the object of bringing out the spiritual lessons, is amongst the highest and most profitable studies.—*The Freeman.*

13TH THOUSAND.

Israel: A Prince with God. *Cloth, 16 mo.,* $1.00.

Mr. Meyer has great descriptive power. He can tell a narrative well. This subject in his hand glows with life, and the scenes and events in the history of his hero pass vividly before you, and are ever being used to force home some important principle.—*British Messenger.*

With a keen moral insight, and a deep spiritual sympathy, he describes the piety and weakness of the best beloved of the Patriarchs.—*Christian Leader.*

Exceedingly good, not only spiritual, but also thoughtful, fresh, suggestive and thoroughly practical.—*C. H. Spurgeon, in Sword and Trowel.*

From first to last the book is richly suggestive and spiritually fruitful.—*Word and Work.*

15TH THOUSAND.

Elijah: and the Secret of his Power. *Cloth, 16 mo.,* $1.00.

The leading object of this volume is to show that Elijah's God is our God; and how a like dependence may be ours if our dependence is in the living God. It is encouraging and stimulating; yet full of solemn warnings. Some parts are grandly written and of thrilling interest.—*Footsteps of Truth.*

Good, exceedingly good! Mr. Meyer is a great gain to the armies of Evangelical truth; for his tone, spirit and aspirations are all of a fine Gospel sort.—*Sword and Trowel.*

NEW YORK :: Fleming H. Revell Co. :: CHICAGO.

WRITINGS OF REV. F. W. MEYER, B. A.

"Tried by Fire:" Expositions of the First Epistle of Peter. *Cloth, 16 mo., $1.00.*

We doubt whether any work has appeared since the time of Leighton, on the same subject, which equals the one before us. These expositions of one of the richest of the Epistles are brightly and beautifully written, and infused by a lofty and evangelical Christian spirit—*Primitive Methodist.*

21ST THOUSAND.

The Present Tenses of the Blessed Life. *Cloth, 32 mo., 50c.*

We commend the book as one that cannot fail to be read with profit. —*Evangelical Christendom.*

A gem and brimful of spiritual life.—*Methodist New Connexion Magazine.*

20TH THOUSAND.

Christian Living. *Cloth, 32 mo., 50c.*

Full of sweetness and light. No Christian can read it and fail to receive stimulus in the direction whither the true-hearted would go.—*Congregational Magazine.*

Special stress is made in this little volume on the practical side of the Christian life. Thoughts calculated to strengthen and inspire in the performance of every-day duties, are put in clear and simple form.—*Advance.*

They prove most refreshing reading; and for the culture of the religious life we can recommend nothing better.—*Standard.*

19TH THOUSAND.

The Shepherd Psalm. Meditations on the 23d Psalm. *Cloth, 32 mo., 50c.*

We have never read anything so charming on the Twenty-third Psalm. It is full of beauty and poetry. Anything that this gifted and spiritual author writes requires no recommendation, as he is well known to the Christian public.—*Irish Congregational Magazine.*

Mr. Meyer has given us a devotional work on this inspired Psalm which every Christian man and woman should not only read but carry about in his pocket in order to snatch even amid the busy employment of life an uplifting and elevating thought. This little book is worth its weight in gold.—*Central Baptist.*

CPSIA information can be obtained at www.ICGtesting.com
Printed in the USA
LVOW120736201111

255768LV00003B/112/P